The Independent Hostel Guide 2000

Britain and Europe

Edited
by
Sam Dalley

One of a series of
guides for outdoor
enthusiasts and budget
travellers

The Backpackers Press

ISBN 0 9523381 9 x

2

The Independent Hostel Guide 2000: Britain and Europe

9th Edition

Edited by: Sam Dalley

British Library Cataloguing in Publication Data
A Catalogue record for this book is available from the British Library
ISBN 0 9523381 9 x

Published by: The Backpackers Press, 2 Rockview Cottages, Matlock Bath, Derbyshire, DE4 3PG, Tel/Fax: +44 (0) 1629 580427

© The Backpackers Press, 2000

Printed by: Centerprint, Nottingham
Cover Artwork : Box Room Designs

Distributed in the UK by:-
         Cordee Books and Maps, 3a De Montfort Street
         Leicester, LE1 7HD, Tel: (0116) 2543579

Distributed overseas by:-
         Penguin Books NZ, NZ, Tel: 09 415 4700
         Faradawn, South Africa, Tel: 11 885 1847
         Wilderness Press, USA, Tel: 510 558 1696
         Peribo PTY Ltd, NZ and Australia, Tel:
         Australia 029457 0011

CONTENTS

INDEPENDENT HOSTELS

The independent hostels included in this book cater for travellers and outdoor enthusiasts who require comfortable, friendly places to stay at budget prices.

They vary to an amazing degree in many aspects – some are tiny while others sleep hundreds, some are in city centres while others are hidden away in remote wildernesses, some provide the latest in comfort and amenities while others provide the bare essentials for a comfortable stay. The hostels are all privately run and this ensures that each has it's own particular character. No membership is required for a stay at any of these hostels.

Many of the City Backpackers specialise in access to the surrounding nightlife and provide all you need to sleep and cook. Camping barns are often little more than a stone tent with a sleeping platform to lay your bed roll on and a stone bench for food preparation. Between these two extremes is a wealth of charming and individual accommodation in family hostels and bunkhouses. Most provide bunk accommodation in dorms, often requiring the use of a sleeping bag, and some have private rooms. Self-catering kitchens are generally available and at some hostels home-cooked meals are a speciality.

All the hostels in this book can provide accommodation to individuals and groups on a nightly basis, although it is usually advisable to check beforehand that there is a bed available.

THE NEW 2000 EDITION

The 2000 edition for the first time includes backpackers' hostels situated in major cities and tourist centres of mainland Europe.

It includes 9 new maps with hostel positions shown on them (the numbers on the maps correspond to the hostels' page entries.)

The maps can be found on the pages given below:-

Map of Europe   pages 10 – 11
Map of England   pages 44 – 47
Map of Wales   pages 128 – 131
Map of Scotland pages 164 - 167
Map of Ireland   pages 246 - 249

To find out which hostels are in a particular area, either refer to the relevant map and find which pages to consult, or look at the index of hostels-by-county/country at the back of the book.

To find the entry of a particular hostel consult the alphabetical index of hostels at the back of the book.

To find out more about hostels and other associations in Britain, Europe and Worldwide consult the Contacts pages on pages 320 to 322 or take a look at www.hostel.com on the web.

SYMBOLS

🕅	Mixed dormitories
🕅	Single sex dormitories
P	Private rooms
▭	Blankets or duvets provided
▯	Sheets required
H	Sheets required - can be hired
◆	Sleeping bags required
H	Sleeping bags required - can be hired
▦	Hostel fully heated (including common room)
▭	Common room heated
▥	Drying room available
⚲	Hot water available
◣	Showers available
⦂⦂	Cooking facilities available
▢	Shop at hostel
��	Meals provided at hostel (with notice)
⅊ᴬᴹ	Breakfast only at hostel (with notice)
⅊➡	Meals available locally
▣	Clothes washing facilities available

《🚲》 1m	Within 1 mile of a Sustrans cycle route
《🚲》 3m	Within 3 miles of a Sustrans cycle route
《🚲》 5m	Within 5 miles of a Sustrans cycle route

ABBREVIATIONS

pp	per person
GR	Ordnance Survey grid reference
IR£	Irish pounds
£	pounds Sterling
Euro	Euros
FF	French Francs
BEF	Belgium Francs
CHF	Swiss Francs
DM	Deutschmarks
NOK	Norwegian Krone
ITL	Italian Lire
ATS	Austrian Schilling
HUF	Hungarian Florint

TELEPHONE CODES

Mainland Europe hostel numbers are given complete with international codes. The English, Welsh, Scottish and Irish numbers are given with national area codes. Instructions on converting to international codes are given at the beginning of each of these sections.

PUBLIC TRANSPORT, UK / IRELAND

Tourist Information Centres often provide information on public transport in their area. To obtain the TIC phone number call directory enquiries (192) and ask for the TIC in a town near to your visit.

If you can gather a group of 3/4 together hiring a car is often a cheaper alternative to public transport. Ask the hostel owners if they know of any good car hire deals in their area.

Trains UK (0345) 484950
National Express Coaches UK (0990) 808080
Scottish Citylink Coaches (0990) 505050
Bus Eireann (Ireland) +353 1 836 6111

LOCAL BUS SERVICES

England
Midlands (01952) 223766
Norfolk (0500) 626116
Derbyshire (01298) 23098,
(01246)   250450,   (01332)
292200
Yorkshire (01132) 457676
Lake District (01946) 632222,
(01434) 381200
Northumberland   (01434)
602217, 01670 533128
Wales
Powys   (01982)   552597,
(01591) 851226
Ceredigion (01267) 231817
Pembrokeshire   (01239)
613756
Dolgellau (01341) 422614

Llanberis (01286) 870484
Conwy (01492) 575412
Scotland
Galloway (0345) 090510
Fort William (01397) 702373
Mallaig (01967) 431272
Aviemore (01479) 811566
Scottish Highlands (01463)
222244, Skye (01599) 534862,
(01478) 612622
Ross-shire (01445) 712255
Western Isles (01859) 502011
Ireland
Northern Ireland (01265)
43334
Donegal +353 77 82619, +353
74 22863
Co Offaly +353 509 20124

FERRIES

From Oban to the Scottish Isles (01631) 562285
To the Isle of Mull (01680) 812343
Caledonian Macbrayne, operate to the Scottish Isles (01687) 462403
To the Isle of Muck (01687) 450224
John O'Groats Ferries to the Orkneys (01955) 611353

MAINLAND EUROPE

All phone numbers are given with the international code. As a general rule, to phone from within the same country as the hostel, simply remove the digits directly following the + and add a 0

Reykjavik ICELAND

UK and Ireland maps are
on the following pages.
44–47 England
128–131 Wales
164–167 Scotland
246–249 Ireland

SWEDEN

NORWAY

Oslo
34

Stockholm

IRELAND
Dublin

UK

DENMARK

Copenhagen

London

26 NETH.
Amsterdam

30

31,32
Berlin

POLAND

23

24 *25*

Bruxelles
BELG.

GERMANY

LUX.

12-20
Paris

Prague

Bratislava CZECH
Vienna REP.

33

Bern *29*

27 *28*

40

41

42

FRANCE

SWITZ.

AUSTRIA

Budapest
HUN.

Ljubijana

SLO.

Zagreb

PORT.

ITALY

CRO.

BOS.

SPAIN

21 *22*
MONACO

Sarajevo

Lisbon

Madrid

35,39
Rome

Tirane
ALB.

MOROCCO

Algiers

Tunis

ALGERIA

TUNISIA

Choose a place of interest and then refer to page number/s shown in italics (*12–19*) for hostels in that area

Europe

BLUE PLANET
05 rue Hector Malot
75012 Paris
FRANCE

Blue Planet is in the heart of Paris ten minutes' walk from the Bastille and fifteen from the Marais. Visit the Viadue des Arts, with craftsmen's workshops. There are great shops, restaurants and cinemas or go for a wander down the Seine and experience the great views of the city.

The Hostel is a family operated business, ensuring personal attention twenty-four hours a day. Being newly renovated it has a colourful personality with many rooms having showers and toilets for no extra charge. One block away is the subway servicing Paris' main metro lines and it is in walking distance from two of Paris' train stations.

www.hostelblueplanet.com

TELEPHONE CONTACT Celue, Tel: +33 1 43 42 06 18
Fax: +33 1 43 42 09 89, Email general@hostelblueplanet.com
OPENING SEASON All year
OPENING HOURS All day
NUMBER OF BEDS 100
BOOKING REQUIREMENTS Please book before 1pm - by fax, phone or Internet
PRICE PER NIGHT 100FF (15.30 Euro)

PUBLIC TRANSPORT
It is 20 metres from the hostel to station Gare de Lyon. Take line underground No1 to Gare de Lyon. From Gare du Nord take RER D, platform 44 (2 levels down) or Bus 65 in the direction of Gare Austerlitz, alight at Gare du Lyon.

DIRECTIONS
From Gare du Lyon the hostel is 20m on the right.

BED & BREAKFAST
42 rue Possonnière
75002 Paris
FRANCE

In the heart of Paris lies our cheerful getaway. From its convenient position between les Halles, le Mazais, the upscale opera district and the Picasso Museum it is an ideal location to experience the unique atmosphere of Paris and visit its beautiful sites. In the evening enjoy the cuisine in its many restaurants and the nightlife or relax at the biggest cinema in Europe 'Theatre Rex' just across the street - we have no curfew.

Bed & Breakfast is comfortable and respectable and the owner Michael who is fluent in English, Spanish, Hebrew and Arabic will welcome all ages, groups and families. The hostel offers four, six, or eight bedded rooms, all with satellite TV, stereo and heater. Hot showers are available if you need to refresh after a busy day sightseeing, as well as toilets. Sheets, blankets, towels and an ample breakfast are all included in the price.

TELEPHONE CONTACT Tel, + 33 14 02 68 308
Fax: + 33 14 02 68 791
OPENING SEASON All year
OPENING HOURS All day
NUMBER OF BEDS 50
BOOKING REQUIREMENTS Recommended by phone or fax - best to phone in advance to arrange arrival time.
PRICE PER NIGHT 100FF (16 Euro) per person - no credit cards.

PUBLIC TRANSPORT
The nearest train stations, Gare du Nord and Gare de l'est, are 10 minutes from the hostel. From Airport or Rail stations take the Metro line 8 or 9 to Bonne Nouvelle stop.

DIRECTIONS
From Bonne Nouvelle Metro station, walk 100 feet around the corner to the hostel.

WOODSTOCK HOSTEL
48 Rue Rodier
75009 Paris
FRANCE

Your home away from home! Woodstock is known for its cosiness as well as its party atmosphere, and is the ideal place to meet other backpackers and make life long friends. Watch out though, once you're here, you might never want to leave! Located in one of the most exiting neighbourhoods in Paris, Montmartre, full of cafes, clubs, bars and artists and musician hangouts. A neighbourhood which was home to van Gogh and picasso, and if it was cool enough for them it's cool enough for you!

Woodstock Hostel is just seconds away from supermarkets and baking shops to stock up if you want to prepare dinner in our kitchen and then enjoy it in the outdoor courtyard. Afterwards relax and enjoy the multinational and warm atmosphere in our own bar. We have Internet and Email access for guests. The showers, luggage store and breakfast are all included in the price and there is also table football.
www.woodstock.fr

TELEPHONE/FAX CONTACT Eric, Tel: +33 1 48 78 87 76, Fax: +33 1 48 78 01 63, Email: flowers@woodstock.fr
OPENING SEASON All year
OPENING HOURS 7.30am to 2.00am
NUMBER OF BEDS 35
BOOKING REQUIREMENTS Please telephone, fax or Email with a visa or mastercard number
PRICE PER NIGHT Summer: 97F(pp dorm) 107F(pp double) Winter: 87F(pp dorm) 95F(pp double)

PUBLIC TRANSPORT
Just 10 minutes walk from Gare du Nord, 20 minutes from Gare De L'est.

DIRECTIONS
2 minutes walk from Metro Station Anvers (line 2). Depart Anvers Metro and on your left there is a park, walk through the park - on the other side there are 2 streets one of them is rue Rodier where the hostel is located.

YOUNG & HAPPY HOSTEL
80 rue Mouffetard
75005 Paris
FRANCE

The Young and Happy hostel is in the heart of the Latin and student quarter just ten minutes walk from Notre-Dame and La Sorbonne University. The street is lively with restaurants, bars, cafe and supermarkets and the oldest French market.

Our clean and cheerful hostel welcomes all and offers cooking facilities, safe deposit box, free maps and large information stand. We have Internet and Email access for guests.

www.youngandhappy.fr

TELEPHONE/FAX CONTACT Tel: + 33 1 45 35 09 53
Fax: +33 1 47 07 22 24, Email: smile@youngandhappy.fr
OPENING SEASON All year
OPENING HOURS 8.00 am to 2.00 am
NUMBER OF BEDS 65
BOOKING REQUIREMENTS Please telephone, fax or email
PRICE PER NIGHT 97FF to 137FF per person

PUBLIC TRANSPORT
Look for Metro Stop: Place Mone, on line 7, or take Bus No47 and stop at Place Monge.

DIRECTIONS
In the Latin Quarter take Monge Street up to Place Monge. Turn on Ortolan Street and the second street is Mouffetard, you will see the hostel.

ALOHA HOSTEL
1 rue Borromee
75015 Paris
FRANCE

Centrally located, Aloha Hostel is within walking distance of Paris' most famous sights; The Eiffel Tower, The Arc De Triomphe, The Champs-Elysees, The Musee Rodin, The Musee des Armes and the lively boulevard Montparnasse. With the Metro station only a stone's throw away from the door the rest of this fascinating city is yours to discover. Cheap accommodation no longer means staying in cramped dormitories, in large impersonal 'institutions'. At Aloha we offer discount accommodation in charming, newly renovated rooms with traditional Parisian decor and no more than 4 people per room, private double rooms are also available. We know what travelling on a budget demands, in fact Aloha's founders were once backpackers themselves. A free breakfast is served each morning and to prepare other meals we provide our guests with a fully equipped kitchen. A variety of supermarkets and grocery stores are all close by; as is a laundromat. We have Internet and Email access for guests. Our friendly English speaking staff will make you totally relaxed and at home during your stay, and at night the fun begins at Aloha, with cheap drinks, music and special events (like film nights) in a cool, cosmopolitan atmosphere. Fun that's the point isn't it! **www.aloha.fr**

TELEPHONE/FAX CONTACT Corinne, Tel: +33 1 42 73 03 03, Fax: +33 1 42 73 14 14, Email friends@aloha.fr
OPENING SEASON All year
OPENING HOURS 8.00 am to 2.00 am
NUMBER OF BEDS 60
BOOKING REQUIREMENTS Please telephone, fax or Email
PRICE PER NIGHT From 97FF (winter) to 117FF (summer)

PUBLIC TRANSPORT
There is a train station just 2 stops from the hostel called Montparnasse Bienvenue.

DIRECTIONS
Depart subway at Volontaires Station on the U2 line. Take first right, then first left, then second left and you will see the hostel.

LA MAISON HOSTEL
67 bis rue Dutot
75015 Paris
FRANCE

La Maison Hostel's location will enable you to enjoy the many famous sights of Paris: the Eiffel Tower is only a 15 minute walk away and it is very easy to get around with the Metropolitan. Just ask the friendly helpful English-spoken staff for tips!

You will feel just like you are at home at the hostel which offers all the amenities backpackers require: small size dormitories/private rooms with en-suite bathrooms at a bottom of the range price. We have Internet and Email access for guests. There is also a common area to socialise with your fellow backpackers from all walks of life.

www.mamaison.fr

TELEPHONE/FAX CONTACT Eric/Laurence, Tel: +33 1 42 73 10 10, Fax: +33 1 42 73 08 08, Email: cafe@mamaison.fr
OPENING SEASON All year
OPENING HOURS 8.00am to 2.00am - curfew at 2.00am
NUMBER OF BEDS 70
BOOKING REQUIREMENTS Please telephone, fax or Email with a credit card number
PRICE PER NIGHT Summer: 117FF(pp dorm) 137FF(pp double) Winter: 87FF(pp dorm) 127FF(pp double)

PUBLIC TRANSPORT
The nearest railway station is Montparnasse (3 Metro stops away).

DIRECTIONS
From Volontaires Metro Station (line 12), turn left onto Volontaires Street, then right onto Rue Dutot (2 blocks). The hostel is on the left hand side.

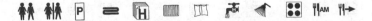

LE VILLAGE HOSTEL

20 rue D'Orsel
75018 Paris
FRANCE

Le Village Hostel is in a lively merchant street right in the middle of Montmartre, one of Paris' most picturesque districts, which for many years attracted poets and artists to its village-like neighbourhood. Right next to the hostel is the Saint-Pierre neighbourhood, with its famous material market which makes an unusual Parisian visit. Art lovers will enjoy the Museum of Primitive Art. In the evening you can walk to the Pigalle neighbourhood, where you will find the famous Moulin Rouge cabaret, rock-music bars, nightclubs and the most popular concert halls in Paris. The hostel is newly renovated with beautiful furniture, beams and cosy rooms all with private bathroom and telephone. In addition most rooms and the terrace offer a unique view (that many Parisians would envy) of the famous Sacre-Coeur Basilica. The common room and Cafe, provide a friendly atmosphere where you can simply relax or meet other guests and exchange tourist tips. We have Internet and Email access for guests. Once you are surrounded by the decor of Le Village Hostel, you will still feel Montmartre's past artistic glory. Find more information on:

www.cheaphostel.com

TELEPHONE/FAX CONTACT Philippe +33 1 42 64 2202
Fax: +33 1 42 64 1432, Email: bonjour@villagehostel.fr
OPENING SEASON All year
OPENING HOURS 7.30 am - 2am
NUMBER OF BEDS 60
BOOKING REQUIREMENTS Please call, fax or Email with a visa or mastercard number.
PRICE PER NIGHT Summer per person : 127FF Dorms, 147FF Doubles. Winter per person : 97FF Dorms, 117FF Double

PUBLIC TRANSPORT
The hostel is 10 mins walk from Gare du Nord and 20 mins walk from Gare de L'Est. Near to Metro route.

DIRECTIONS
From Anvers Metro Stop (line 2) - turn right out of the station, walk up rue Steinkerque and right onto rue d'Orsel. Hostel is on the left.

3 DUCKS HOSTEL
6 Place Etienne Pernet
75015 Paris
FRANCE

The city of lights and romance has more to offer than Lady Di's crash and the Eiffel Tower. In their shadow you will find Paris' most notorious hangout, the one and only 3 Ducks Hostel - one of the famous five hostels in Europe. Located just ten minutes' walking distance to the Eiffel Tower, in a building which used to be one of the stables linking Paris to the Royal Palace of Versailles, the 3 Ducks Hostel with its large interior courtyard and its pub is a meeting place where people can hangout, have a beer (one of the less expensive in the city) and share tips.

The very friendly bilingual staff welcome everybody (no children under 10 please) and share their knowledge of the city. They will do their very best to make your stay in Paris unforgettable. There is also a large information stand giving details of other hostels in Europe and free maps of the city. We have internet and Email access for guestsBlankets and breakfast are included in the price of your stay.
www.3ducks.fr

TELEPHONE/FAX CONTACT Yaelle, Tel: +33 1 48 42 04 05, Fax: +33 1 48 42 99 99, Email backpack@3ducks.fr
OPENING SEASON All year
OPENING HOURS 7.00am to 2.00 am
NUMBER OF BEDS 70
BOOKING REQUIREMENTS Please fax your booking requirement with credit card details.
PRICE PER NIGHT 97FF - 127FF per person

PUBLIC TRANSPORT
From Gard Du Nord take line No 4 in the direction of Porte d'Orleans then change to line No 8 toward Balard and stop at Commerce.

DIRECTIONS
From Metro Station Commerce take right on Commerce Street towards the church. The 3 Ducks hostel is on the right side of the church.

AUBERGE INTERNATIONALE DES JEUNES

10 rue Trousseau
74011 Paris
FRANCE

The youth hostel is situated conveniently in the city centre of Paris, next to the Place Bastille and its New Opera. This location is said to be excellent as it allows our guests to get a real taste of Paris life. Not only does it provide access to many monuments and museums, it is also surrounded by charming pubs, restaurants and cafes.

The hostel has been entirely refurbished and offers a high level of comfort and cleanliness. By striving to continuously improve the service, the hostel has been able to acquire a sound reputation amongst many tourist operations such as the Paris Tourist Office. The Auberge Internationale des Jeunes is particularly noted for combining an excellent location in the city centre, comfortable rooms and helpful staff. Above all the hostel offers the most favourable price/quality combination amongst the youth hostels in Paris. Overnight price includes breakfast, safe, luggage storage, sheets, blanket & pillow. Internet access available. Find more on: **www.aijparis.com**

TELEPHONE/FAX CONTACT + 33 1 47 00 6200
FAX: +33 1 47 00 3316, Email: aij@aijparis.com
OPENING SEASON All year
OPENING HOURS All day - no curfew
NUMBER OF BEDS 190
BOOKING REQUIREMENTS Please send credit card number, expiry date and booking details by mail, fax or Email.
PRICE PER NIGHT 91FF Mar to Oct. 81FF Nov to Feb.

PUBLIC TRANSPORT
Near Ledru-Rollin Metro Station on Line 8.

DIRECTIONS
Car: Follow "Bastille" then turn on rue Du Faubourg Saint Antoine. Drive up to number 126 and turn left on rue Trousseau. Metro: walk on rue Du Faubourg Saint Antonine to number 126, left rue Trousseau.

YOUTH CENTRE INTERNATIONAL-CANNES

35 au de Vallauris
06400, Cannes
FRANCE

The International Youth Centre is situated in a peaceful location in the centre of Cannes. Come and enjoy the beautiful French Riviera resort with its beach and many sports.

The hostel has a 'home from home' atmosphere. Facilities include three fully equipped kitchens, laundry facilities, living room, telephone, safe and parking. Breakfast is included on your first night's stay which can be enjoyed on the garden terrace - where you can meet the other guests and swap stories. During the summer, April - September, the hostel is open until 2am so you can experience the nightlife of this exciting resort - for the rest of the year the hostel is open until midnight. Brigitte, Annick and Nathalee look forward to welcoming you to Cannes.

http:/psso.wanadso.fr/hostelling.cannes/

TELEPHONE AND FAX CONTACT Tel/Fax: +33 4 93 99 26 79, Email: www.centre-sejous-youth-hostel.cannes@wanadoo.com
OPENING SEASON All year except for Christmas
OPENING HOURS 8am to 12.30 pm and 3pm to Midnight (2am summer months)
NUMBER OF BEDS 64
BOOKING REQUIREMENTS By Email, phone, writing or fax please.
PRICE PER NIGHT 50FF to 80FF depending on season.

PUBLIC TRANSPORT
5 minutes from the centre and 10 minutes from Cannes train station. Bus Vallauris stop at Sandoux. From Bus Station take the No6 which stops in front of the Hostel.

DIRECTIONS
A detailed map will be sent with confirmation of booking. There is a bus but if you would like to walk it would take approximately 15 minutes from the bus station.

CENTRE DE LA JEUNESSE PRINCESSE STEPHANIE

24, Avenue Prince Pierre
MC 98000
MONACO

This accommodation is located in the heart of Monaco, ideally placed to discover the Principality and explore the French Côte d'Azur and the Italian Riviera. It is an easy walk to Monaco ville, Monte Carlo and Fontvieille. Monaco ville is the old city, where you can visit the Prince Rainier's Palace, the cathedral and the Oceanographic Museum. Monte Carlo is famous for casinos and "boutiques" and Fontvieille is the commercial centre and Stadium. On the harbour you can imagine the formula 1 Grand Prix taking place. There is also free access to Larvotto's public beach via a 10 minute bus ride. The accommodation is provided in clean bunk-bedded rooms with washstands. In Summer, there are dormitories in the annex Belle Epoque villa. Facilities include: hot showers, common room with TV, nice garden for picnics, dishes to prepare your own cold meals, lots of local information (maps, lists of restaurants or museums etc), payphone, Internet rental and laundry facilities. There are no cooking facilities and no alcohol permitted. We have a friendly atmosphere for young travellers (16 to 31). Groups of 10+ aged between 11-31 are also welcome.

TELEPHONE CONTACT Tel: +377 93 50 83 20, Fax +377 93 25 29 82, E-mail : info@youthhostel.asso.mc
OPENING SEASON All year except mid-Nov to mid-Dec.
OPENING HOURS 7am to 12am (Curfew), July-Aug open till 1am.
NUMBER OF BEDS 32 increasing to 72 in July and August.
BOOKING REQUIREMENTS Advance booking is advised (by phone, letter, fax or Email)
PRICE PER NIGHT 80 FF with light breakfast and all bedding.

PUBLIC TRANSPORT
By train : Monaco-Monte-Carlo train station, take Galerie Prince Pierre (direction Fontvieille) 100 metres up (follow the signs). By bus : stop at Place d'Armes. Walk up Avenue Prince Pierre, 2 minute walk.

DIRECTIONS
By car : leave your car in La Colle public parking and walk 100 metres up Avenue Prince Pierre (on right pavement).

SNUFFEL SLEEP IN
Ezelstraat 47-49
8000 Brugge/Bruges
BELGIUM

Looking for a home away from home in Begium's most charming town Bruges? 'Snuffel Sleep In' is a character budget hotel without budgeting on friendliness, hospitality and great atmosphere, centrally located in the old part of town.

Facilities include fully equipped kitchen, hot showers, open minded vibes, no curfew or lockout, library, bicycle store, laundry and groceries next door and patio. There is a large information stand and our helpful and informative staff will be able to provide any tips you may need during your stay. The laid back bar has 19 different kinds of infamous Belgian beers for you to try and a happy hour every night, as well as Internet access and a varied music collection. There are art exhibitions, all kinds of games and during the summer period special activities for you to join in with.

TELEPHONE/FAX CONTACT Tel: + 32 5033 3133, Fax: +32 5033 3250, Email: snuffel@flanderscoast.be
OPENING SEASON All year
OPENING HOURS 8.00am - midnight
NUMBER OF BEDS 52
BOOKING REQUIREMENTS Please telephone, fax or Email
PRICE PER NIGHT 350BEF (8.68 Euro)

PUBLIC TRANSPORT
Regular bus service 3 or 13 from the station. Disembark at first stop after Market-Place

DIRECTIONS
From the market place take Vlamingstraat, turn 1st left onto Pottenmakerstraat then right onto Ezelstraat. Snuffel Sleep In is on the left hand side of the road.

PASSAGE
Dweersstraat 26
8000 Brugge / Bruges
BELGIUM

Passage, an 18th-Century house situated in the heart of medieval Bruges, offers accommodation in 2 x 7-bedded rooms, 2 x 6-bedded rooms, and 6 x 4-bedded rooms. For more privacy family rooms and double rooms are also available in the small luxury house next door.

With it's hardwood floors and high ceilings, a stay at Passage will give you the impression of travelling through time. The cosy bar has a great art-deco style and the restaurant offers a wide variety of world-famous Belgian beers and traditional Belgian cuisine. There's even a section for vegetarians.

Recommended by Let's Go, Rough Guide, Lonely Planet, Berkeley Guide, Frommers, and Guide de Routarde, Passage is the place to be... for its character, personality, wonderful cosmopolitan atmosphere and typical Belgian cuisine. We are also Bruges' most central hostel.

TELEPHONE/FAX CONTACT (Vandendorpe Sabine),
Tel: +32 50 340232, Fax: +32 50 340140
OPENING SEASON All year
OPENING HOURS Reception open 8.30am till approximately midnight. Night access is available by using a code.
NUMBER OF BEDS 50 + 24 in building next door.
BOOKING REQUIREMENTS Booking is recommended. Please fax or telephone.
PRICE PER NIGHT From 380 BEF (9.42 Euro) per person. Doubles 1400 BEF (34.73 Euro) for two persons, breakfast included.

PUBLIC TRANSPORT
Bruges is well connected by train and coach services.

DIRECTIONS
The hostel is downtown just 10 minutes' walk from the train station. From the station follow Mainstreet and take the first street on the left. We are just opposite Parking Zilverpand.

CENTRE VINCENT VAN GOGH-CHAB

Rue Traversiere, 8
1210 Brussels
BELGIUM

For more than twenty years we have been accommodating backpackers from all over the world in one of the grooviest and cheapest hostels in town. We are located in the city centre just fifteen minutes walk from the Old Town. The famous Dutch painter, Vincent van Gogh had his workshop here, and you can still feel the vibes!

The Hostel offers accommodation for people aged between 17 and 35. It is friendly, safe and clean with no curfew. Other facilities include garden, fully equipped kitchen, great bar to relax and enjoy Belgian beers, free locker-room, Internet access and guided tours in the summer. Check out our website or Email at the address given below.

www.ping.be/CHAB

TELEPHONE/FAX CONTACT Jean-Yves Hulet,
Tel: +32 2 217 0158, Fax: +32 2 219 7995, Email: chab@ping.be
OPENING SEASON All year
OPENING HOURS All day
NUMBER OF BEDS 220
BOOKING REQUIREMENTS By telephone, fax or Email please
PRICE PER NIGHT 340BEF(Dorm), 410BEF(6 Bed), 480(4 Bed), 560BEF(twin), 700BEF(single) per person, breakfast & shower included.

PUBLIC TRANSPORT
Close to all railway stations serving the city. Near to Metro Line 2 'Botanique' Station and buses.

DIRECTIONS
Close to the Botanical Garden, corner of Royal Street. Easy to reach from Midi Train Station, take Metro line 2 'Botanique Station'. From North Station, take Bus 61 stop at 'Traversiere'. From Central Station take Bus 65 and stop at 'Botanique Station', or walk 15 minutes.

BACKPACKERS VILLA SONNENHOF

Alpenstrasse 16
3800 Interlaken
SWITZERLAND

Backpackers Villa Sonnenhof was the first backpacker accommodation in Switzerland and has a quality certificate. The accommodation is centrally located in a villa with a park, just ten minutes walk from either the West or Ost train stations in the town. Our staff have plenty to experience and adventure activities can be arranged like river rafting, canyoning, bungee jumping, paragliding, skiing and snowboarding.

The hostel has a friendly atmosphere. All rooms are clean and most come with Jungfrau-view balconies. There is no curfew or lockout and membership is not required. Facilities include free hot showers on every floor - just what you need after all those activities, fully equipped kitchen, laundry service, table soccer, billiards, Internet access or you can get away from it and refresh in the meditation room.

www.villa.ch

TELEPHONE/FAX CONTACT Tel: +41 33 826 71 71
Fax: +41 33 826 71 72, Email: backpackers@villa.ch
OPENING SEASON Mid December - end of October
OPENING HOURS Reception 7.30-11.00am and 4.00-9.00pm
NUMBER OF BEDS 70
BOOKING REQUIREMENTS Please book by telephone, web page or Email.
PRICE PER NIGHT CHF29-32 (18-20 Euro) dorm, CHF75-80 (40-50 Euro) double.

PUBLIC TRANSPORT
Walking distance from West or Ost train stations.

DIRECTIONS
In the centre of Interlaken at Höhematte (large greenfield). Follow the brown signs from the stations - just 10 minutes' walk.

BACKPACKERS LUCERNE

Alpenquai 42
6005 Lucerne
SWITZERLAND

Backpackers Lucerne is centrally located in the heart of Switzerland. It is in a peaceful neighbourhood next to Lake Lucerne and the city centre.

Have fun, feel at home and meet travellers from all over the world. Facilities include a cosy common area with free kitchen facilities, a bar, games, books, bikes, rollerblades, table football, and table tennis. Sheets can be rented and a laundry service is available. Bookings for outdoor activities can be made here and advice for mountain trips can be obtained.

Enjoy your stay here in a homely atmosphere. Accomodation is in double rooms and in 4 bed rooms. Children are welcome (with family discount). All rooms have a balcony.

TELEPHONE/FAX CONTACT Regula or Mark, Tel: +41 41 360 04 20, Fax: +41 41 360 04 42
OPENING SEASON March to December
OPENING HOURS Reception open 7.30 - 10.00 am ; 4 - 11 pm. No lockout, no curfew.
NUMBER OF BEDS 78
BOOKING REQUIREMENTS Bookings can be made by phone or fax.
PRICE PER NIGHT CHF 22 (13.90 Euro) per person (room with 4 beds), CHF 28 (17.70 Euro) per person (double room).

PUBLIC TRANSPORT
The hostel is 0.6 miles from the nearest rail station.

DIRECTIONS
From the station pass by the Congress Centre (next to the station) and follow Inseliquai to Alpenquai. The lake is on your left.

CITY BACKPACKER
HOTEL BIBER
Niederdorfstrasse 5
8001 Zurich
SWITZERLAND

The City Backpacker is a friendly hostel situated in the heart of Zurich's picturesque Old Town. Most of the tourist sites and many places of interest are within walking distance including a lake, museum, bars, disco, nightlife and parks.

All the things that a backpacker needs are available at the hostel. We have a self-catering kitchen, showers and washing machine. There is also a nice terrace and common room with Internet station and a book-exchange. We have a luggage store and offer discounts on local facilities and products including swiss army knives.

For information and reservations just phone, fax, write or send an Email. Check it out and see you soon..

TELEPHONE/FAX CONTACT receptionist, Tel: +41 1 251 9015, Fax: +41 1 251 9024, Email: backpacker@access.ch
OPENING SEASON All year
OPENING HOURS Check in 0800 - 1200 and 1500 - 2200 hrs. No curfew once you have checked in.
NUMBER OF BEDS 64
BOOKING REQUIREMENTS Booking by phone, fax or Email is advisable in summer months.
PRICE PER NIGHT CHF 29.

PUBLIC TRANSPORT
Zurich is well connected to mainland Europe by rail and coach services. The hostel is in the Old Town and only 10 minutes' walk from the main railway station.

DIRECTIONS
From the main railway station cross the river Limmat and take a right into the old town. Follow Niederdorfstrasse until No. 5. (Niederdorfstrasse is the main walking street in the Old Town).

RUCKSACK HOTEL FOR BACKPACKERS
Kanal Street 70, 23552 Lubeck
GERMANY

The Lubeck Rucksack Hotel was the first backpacker-hostel opened in Germany in 1991. The town looks back on a history of more than 850 years and there are many old and famous churches and buildings including the Holsten Gate or the Buddenbrooks House. The MUK (music and congress hall) offers a programme ranging from classical to contemporary music. Take a relaxing boat trip along one of the two rivers that surround the town or take in the atmosphere in the cafes or pubs. The surrounding area is beautiful and worth a trip - Travemunde is where the ferries leave for Scandinavia - take a stroll along the shore of the Baltic Sea. Hamburg with its famous nightlife and sights is only 45 minutes' train journey. The hostel has 30 beds, divided into 2, 4, 6 and 10 bedded rooms each with hand basins - the bathrooms are on the first floor. On the ground floor there are two rooms with bathrooms suitable for disabled visitors. A fully equipped kitchen offers you the facility to cook your own meals or breakfast can be provided by arrangement. Each guest has their own key to come and go - so there's no curfew.

TELEPHONE/FAX CONTACT Tel: +49 451 706892,
Fax: +49 451 7073429
OPENING SEASON All year
OPENING HOURS 24 hours
NUMBER OF BEDS 30
BOOKING REQUIREMENTS Preferably fax or telephone booking.
PRICE PER NIGHT 24DM (13 Euro) - 34DM (18 Euro) in dorms, double/twin rooms 40DM (21 Euro per person).

PUBLIC TRANSPORT
The train station, Lubeck-Hauptbahnhof (1km), is 15 mins walk or take bus No (1,11,13,21 or 31) to Pfaffenstrasse and walk for 2 minutes down Glockengiesserstrasse. Ferries from Hamburg (65km) to the UK, and from Travemunde(17km)/Puttgarden (80km) to Scandinavia.

DIRECTIONS
BAB to Lubeck Zentrume. There is a map at the central station or telephone for directions.

LETTE'M SLEEP 7
Hostel for Backpackers
Lettestrabe 7
10437 Berlin
GERMANY

The Lette'm Sleep hostel is located in the very heart of the German capital. The hostel is in the middle of the number one district Prenzlauerberg, which is famous for nice cafes, trendy pubs and wild clublife. It is quick and easy to reach the main station; Berlin-Zoo, within 20 to 40 minutes, any other stations in Berlin, as well as the airports in and around the city. The most important underground line U2 stops nearby and will take you to all of Berlin's major highlights and attractions.

The hostel has a mixture of double and shared rooms, all with hand basins and lockers. The multilingual staff offers 24 hour service. You can relax in the backyard which has a beer garden atmosphere. Other facilities include nice showers, ticket service, Internet access, TV, snacks, beverages and good cooking facilities. There is no curfew or lockout and the hostel is wheelchair friendly.

www.backpackers.de

TELEPHONE CONTACT +49 30 44733623
Fax: +49 30 44733625 Email: info@backpackers.de
OPENING SEASON All year
OPENING HOURS All day
NUMBER OF BEDS 44
BOOKING REQUIREMENTS Please telephone, fax or Email
PRICE PER NIGHT 26DM (13 Euro)

PUBLIC TRANSPORT
Near Underground line number 2 (U2), station Eberswalder Strasse.
From Airport take Bus X9 to Zoologischer Garten then onto U2.

DIRECTIONS
Car: From City Centre head towards Prenzlauer Berg (on Prenzlauer Allee), at the crossing with Danziger St turn left then second right (Duncker St), then second left (Lette St). By foot: From underground Eberswalder St turn left onto Pappelalle then first right (Raumer St), next left into Lychener St, then right onto Lette st.

FREDERIK'S HOSTEL

Str.der Pariser
Kommune 35
10243 Berlin
GERMANY

Frederik's is five minutes' walk from the East Side Gallery, it is in a neighbourhood with modern illegal bars (tell no one!), close to Mitte - the traditional city centre and near to all the artistic bars of Prenzlauerberg. Crossing the river you are in Kreuzberg where you can experience other bars, punks, artists, markets and good cheap food.

Frederik's has everything a fun hostel should - a great relaxing reception with helpful and happy staff that will take care of you and give you information, maps, coffee, tips for the never ending parties and suggestions for walking tours. Clean, safe and comfortable rooms with feather duvets, heating in the winter, magic showers with hot water 24 hours a day, Internet access, Berlin history books and a courtyard with benches and trees. We welcome new ideas, to help to make this place even more special. When you stay you will get the feeling of staying in a hippy commune. The cosy bar beneath the hostel keeps people dancing, having fun and even falling in love. Actually, with so many things happening Frederick's is becoming the most important centre in Berlin! **http://www.frederiks.de**

TELEPHONE/FAX CONTACT Sarah, Tel: +49 30 2966 9450, Fax: +49 30 2966 94.52, Email hostel@frederiks.de
OPENING SEASON All year
OPENING HOURS All day
NUMBER OF BEDS 80
BOOKING REQUIREMENTS By phone, fax, Email, or post.
PRICE PER NIGHT From 22DM (dorm) up to 49DM (single)

PUBLIC TRANSPORT
7 minutes' walk from S-Bahnhof Ostbahnhof (central train station) and 3 minutes' walk from U-Bahnhof Weberwiese underground.

DIRECTIONS
Car: from the centre east Alexanderplatz, turn right into Kare-Marx-Alle. After 5 mins turn right, the third house on the righthand side is the hostel. From the stations just walk down the street!

4 YOU MUNICH HOSTEL

Hirtenstr 18
80335 Muchen/Munich
GERMANY

4 You Munich hostel/youth hotel is 200m from the central train station, in the heart of this beautiful city and near to all the sights and places of interest. The hostel has been ecologically renovated and the building has 200 beds in single, double, 4, 6, 8 or 12 bed rooms and facilities for the disabled. You can rent bed linen from us, or use your own linen or sleeping bag. So that our guests can make the most of their stay and experience all the atmosphere there is no lockout or curfew and we have a reception area which is open 24 hours a day to provide you with all the information you need. If you wish to relax after a hard day's sightseeing you can stay within the hostel which has table soccer, pool, Internet facilities, or enjoy a meal in our own restaurant. The hostel is famous for our superb breakfast buffet.

Our house also features two floors of single and double rooms. All these rooms are equipped with a private bath or shower, toilet, desk, radio/alarm clock and telephone.

TELEPHONE/FAX CONTACT Christine, Tel: + 49 89 55 21 660 Fax: + 49 89 55 21 6666, Email:info@the4you.de
OPENING SEASON All Year
OPENING HOURS All day
NUMBER OF BEDS 200
BOOKING REQUIREMENTS Please phone, fax or Email
PRICE PER NIGHT From 26DM (13.29 Euro) to 64.50DM (32.98 Euro)

PUBLIC TRANSPORT
The main train station (Hauptbahnhof) is just 200m from the hostel. This is also the base for a lot of Metros, S-Bahns and Travis Busse.

DIRECTIONS
By car please ask for the City Centre. By foot we are three minutes from main station. At the end of the platform turn left and take the exit Arnulfstr. Across the road you will see a yellow hotel called Eden Holiday Wolf. We are in the street behind, 100m on your left.

ALBERTINE
HOSTEL

Storgata 55
Sofienberg
0506 Oslo
NORWAY

The Albertine Hostel is a unique starting point for an adventurous visit to Oslo. You can find Grunerlokka, Norway's 'Greenwich Village' with numerous exotic restaurants and shops close by and Karl Johan, Oslo's steaming main street just a 10-15 minute stroll away.

The hostel offers a relaxed and international atmosphere with 106 rooms all with showers and toilet and is suitable for all age groups. The 4 and 6 bedded rooms provide single gender accommodation on a shared basis. If you prefer your own room there are single and twin rooms available. Duvet and pillow is included and you can hire bed linen and towels at reception or alternatively you can bring your own - sorry no sleeping bags are allowed. Cooking facilities are available - please bring your own utensils. There are a limited number of parking spaces, but the bus and tram stop close by.

www.anker.oslo.no

TELEPHONE/FAX CONTACT Tel: +47 22 99 72 10
Fax: +47 22 99 72 20, Email: albertine@anker.oslo.no
OPENING SEASON From 8th June to 25th August
OPENING HOURS All day - no curfew
NUMBER OF BEDS 366
BOOKING REQUIREMENTS Booking all year by telephone, fax or Email. Advance booking advisable during June and August.
PRICE PER NIGHT NOK120 (6 bed), NOK145 (4 bed), NOK360(twin)

PUBLIC TRANSPORT
From Railway Station take Tram 11,12 and 15 or bus 30, 31 and 32. Ask for Hausmannsgate stop.

DIRECTIONS
We are in walking distance from the railway station please see our web site.

FREEDOM TRAVELLER
Via Gaeta, 25
00185, Roma
ITALY

Located in the heart of bella Roma, Freedom Traveller aims to provide every need for the weary backpacker. The hostel is a five-minute walk from the Termini Train and Metro Stations, and a short distance from the Coliseum, Roman Forum, Pantheon, Spanish Steps and other major sites. Vatican City and Saint Peter's Basilica are easily accessed by nearby bus or metro stops. There is an Internet Cafe next door and walking tours of ancient Rome run on a daily basis.

The hostel has dormitory style rooms for 4-6 people; private accommodation is also available. Two full kitchens with unlimited access, fresh sheets and blankets, hot showers and a huge terrace are all available to our guests, as well as information, tips and maps. The friendly staff speak English, French and of course Italian. There is no curfew and baggage storage is available for the day of departure.

Check out our web page at www.freedom-traveller.it

TELEPHONE CONTACT +39 06 478 23 862
OPENING SEASON All year
OPENING HOURS 9am to midnight (no curfew for guests)
NUMBER OF BEDS 38
BOOKING REQUIREMENTS You can call, Email or show up in person.
PRICE PER NIGHT 30,000ITL (15.50 Euro) high season 25,000ITL (13 Euro) low season (for dormitory accommodation).

PUBLIC TRANSPORT
Five minutes' walking distance from the Termini Train and Metro Station which are the central hub for trains, metro and local buses.

DIRECTIONS
From Termini Station exit from Platform 1. Head left on via Marsala. After the traffic lights via Gaeta will be the first street on the right. (via Marsala changes into via Volturno at the traffic lights).

PENSIONE ALESSANDRO
Via Vicenza,42
00185 Roma
ITALY

Ideally situated close to the train station and everything you need, Pensione Alessandro will provide you with the best possible stay in Rome. Here is a place you can meet backpackers from all over the world. Our friendly, young, international staff will gladly help you get the most out of the city by giving you information about anything you may want to know. We are within walking distance of all the major attractions, or if you prefer, there is plenty of public transport very close by.

Our clean and friendly hostel is for backpackers only and has dormitory style accommodation with rooms of four to eight beds. There is no curfew, and the reception is open 24 hours. Feel free to use the hot showers at any time, as well as the full kitchen at no extra charge. There are lockers in the rooms, or if you like, the staff will be happy to lock valuables in our safe facilities. Pensione Alessandro also arranges day and night tours of the city for those of you who are pressed for time, but still want to see the best of Rome.

TELEPHONE/FAX CONTACT Tel: +39 06 446 1958,
Fax: +39 06 493 80534
OPENING SEASON All year
OPENING HOURS All day
NUMBER OF BEDS 100
BOOKING REQUIREMENTS Please telephone ahead of stay
PRICE PER NIGHT 30,000ITL (15 Euro) per person

PUBLIC TRANSPORT
The hostel is a 3 minute walk from Termini train station. There are also Metro and Bus stations located at Termini.

DIRECTIONS
By car exit off Highway Roma Nord Salaria in the direction of Termini train station.

NAVIGATOR
Via Buonarotti 39
Roma
ITALY

Located in the heart of Rome, Hostel Navigator is only a short walk from the main train station (Termini) and all the sights and attractions that Rome has to offer.

Hostel Navigator is a safe and modern hostel which provides a fresh and funky vibe that so many hostels lack these days, while managing to retain a warm and cosy atmosphere.

The hostel offers clean dormitory style accommodation with TV, video, air conditioning and a fully equipped kitchen. There is cheap internet service as well as the facility to receive telephone calls and faxes.

TELEPHONE CONTACT Mr Mario +39 06 44 70 26 86
OPENING SEASON All year
OPENING HOURS Lock out between 11am and 2pm
NUMBER OF BEDS 32
BOOKING REQUIREMENTS Via Email or telephone.
PRICE PER NIGHT 25,000 ITL - 40,000 ITL depending on room

PUBLIC TRANSPORT
Near Main Train Station (Termini). Located near sub-way station Piazza Victoria Emanevele.

DIRECTIONS
In the centre of Rome easily found on foot from subway station or train station.

M & J PLACE HOSTEL

Via Solferino 9
00185 Roma
ITALY

Greetings from Roma! The staff from 'M&J Place Hostel' would like to introduce you to our hostel. It is located by Rome's main train station 'Termini' and near to all attractions (Colosseum, Trevi Fountain and others) in the heart of Rome.

The hostel has 150 beds with rooms ranging from 2 to 8 people (no bunk beds), most of the rooms have private bathrooms. We have a fully-equipped kitchen, common room with TV, VCR and satellite. Our services include a 24 hour reception, linen and bedding, daily cleaning, no curfew, luggage storage, Internet access and free information and maps. The hostel has many connections (discounts) with local restaurants, pubs, gelaterias, discos, scooter rentals, laundry and money exchange. We also can arrange walking, bike and Pompei tours.

www.mejplacehostel.com

TELEPHONE CONTACT Gallo, Mario and Luigi +39 06446 2802
Email: mejplace@micanet.it
OPENING SEASON All year
OPENING HOURS All day
NUMBER OF BEDS 150
BOOKING REQUIREMENTS Booking advised by telephone or Email
PRICE PER NIGHT From ITL 25,000 (12.50 Euro)

PUBLIC TRANSPORT
The main train station, bus station and metro station are just 2 minutes' walk away.

DIRECTIONS
Exit near platform 1 from Termini (main) train station. Turn left on Via Marsala, walk for 150m. At the traffic lights turn right on Via Solferino. Look for the No9 (first door on the street!) We are on the first floor.

MARIO & LUIGI HOSTEL
Via Solferino 9
00185 Roma
ITALY

Situated in the heart of Roma, the newly opened 'Mario & Luigi hostel' is located only two minutes' walking distance from termini (main) train station.

We offer our guests 60 beds in spacious rooms and a friendly atmosphere. We have a fully equipped kitchen, common room with TV, VCR and satellite, and we provide free linen and bedding. There is no curfew and reception is open 24 hours. We offer luggage storage, Internet access and free information and maps.

Of course when visiting Roma you will need to explore and so we can arrange walking or bike tours. Discounts are also available for our guests to many amenities in Roma.

www.mejplacehostel.com

TELEPHONE CONTACT Mario +39 06 446 2802
Email: mejplace@micanet.it
OPENING SEASON All year
OPENING HOURS All day
NUMBER OF BEDS 60
BOOKING REQUIREMENTS Booking is advisable by telephone or Email.
PRICE PER NIGHT From ITL 20,000 (10 Euro)

PUBLIC TRANSPORT
The main train, bus and metro stations are all within 2 minutes' walk from the hostel.

DIRECTIONS
From the Termini train station, exit near Platform No1 and turn left on Via Marsala. Walk for 150m. At the traffic lights turn right onto Via Solferino. Look for Number 9 (the first door on the street!) the hostel is on the 2nd floor.

YOHO INTERNATIONAL YOUTH HOTEL

A-5020 Salzburg
Paracelsusstrasse 9
AUSTRIA

The Yoho Salzburg is one of the best and most traditional youth hostels in Austria, maybe in Europe. It is one of the most popular meeting points for travellers of all countries of the world. Coming here makes you feel like coming home.

The hostel offers an excellent breakfast and the swinging bar provides excellent food, a happy hour everyday and the best music to take care of our hungry and thirsty guests. There are daily films, CNN, Internet cafe and fax machine and the friendly staff are always willing to assist. The Busabout stops directly at the Yoho and the best tour operators for sightseeing, adventure and skiing tours pick up directly from the front door.

YOHO-Salzburg is a must - easy to find - hard to leave

TELEPHONE/FAX CONTACT Renate or Gottfied,
Tel: +43 662 879 649, Fax: +43 662 878 810
OPENING SEASON All year
OPENING HOURS All day
NUMBER OF BEDS 130
BOOKING REQUIREMENTS Please ring the same day or day before your stay.
PRICE PER NIGHT 150ATS (12 Euro) dorm to 200ATS (16 Euro) twin room.

PUBLIC TRANSPORT
Near to the train station.

DIRECTIONS
Car: Go down from the highway at 'Salzburg Mitte' straight ahead, under the train underpass, then turn second right. Another 100 metres and you will see the hostel. Train Station: 200m to the city, at train underpass turn left (Gablesberger Strasse), then as above.

WOMBATS CITY HOSTEL
Grangasse 6
A-1150 Wien/Vienna
AUSTRIA

This newly constructed hostel has a design based on a colour concept from the University of Modern Arts. Centrally located the hostel is very convenient to all parts of the city and all public transport is within easy walking distance.

The Hostel has no curfew and you will not be locked out. It has all the facilities you would expect from a backpackers' hostel, including internet corner and laundry. Accommodation is available in 4 and 6 bed dormitories and there are double rooms all with shower and toilet. The International and friendly staff are one of the best points of Wombats City Hostel. Staff from France, Ireland and Germany will help you with all aspects of your stay. You can relax and enjoy the hospitality of the Wombat's pub where you can drink beers from all over the world and get some snacks until 2.00 am. Enjoy your stay.

www.wombats.at

TELEPHONE/FAX CONTACT Tel: +43 1 897 2336, Fax: +43 1 897 2577, Email:wombats@chello.at
OPENING SEASON All year
OPENING HOURS 24 hours
NUMBER OF BEDS 164
BOOKING REQUIREMENTS Please phone, fax or Email
PRICE PER NIGHT ATS175 (12.72 Euro) 6 bed room, ATS190 (13.81 Euro) 4 bed room, ATS 245 (17.80 Euro) 2 bed room. All prices per person per night.

PUBLIC TRANSPORT
The major subways (U3,U6) are within easy walking distance, only 3 stops on the U3 to downtown. Take the airport shuttlebus to Westbahnhof, or from Sudbahnhof take tram 18 to Westbahnhof.

DIRECTIONS
From Westbahnhof take main exit and turn right onto Marlahilfer Strasse, follow until No 152. Turn right into of Rosinagrasse and go straight on till Grangasse.

TRAVELLERS HOSTEL DIÁKSPORT
Budapest 1134
Dózsa György Út 152
HUNGARY

Travellers Hostel Diáksport is a large recently renovated hostel open to all and especially popular with younger guests. It lies just 2 subway stops from downtown and incorporates the best known backpackers' bar in the city.

Accomodation is provided in comfortable 1,2,3 and 4 bed rooms and also in larger dormitories. Reception with tourist information is available 24 hours a day. Access is possible all day with no curfew or lock-out. The wide range of facilities includes satellite TV, Internet access, 24 hour bar with pool table and buffet, public telephone with international calls, private lockers, washers and driers, well-equipped kitchen and conference centre if pre-arranged. Activities such as caving, canoeing and city tours can also be arranged.

TELEPHONE CONTACT Tel: +36 1 340 8585, Fax: +36 1 320 8425, Email: travellers@matavnet.hu
OPENING SEASON All year
OPENING HOURS 24 hrs
NUMBER OF BEDS 140
BOOKING REQUIREMENTS Booking is possible by telephone, Email or fax.
PRICE PER NIGHT 2500-3500 HUF per person per night

PUBLIC TRANSPORT
From Keleti pu. (train station) take metro 2 to Deák tér (3 stops) then metro 3 to Dósza György út (4 stops). Alternatively take electric bus no.79 from Garay Utca to Dósza György út stop. The Dósza György bus and metro stops are just 50m from hostel.

DIRECTIONS
By car follow the M7 as far as Dósza Gyorgy Ut. By subway take the M3 blue line to the Dósza György stop.

ENGLAND

All phone numbers are given with the national code required to phone from anywhere in the UK. To phone from overseas remove the first 0 and add 44.

S C O T L A N D

123

122

Carlisle

121

120

Penrith

Workington

Keswick

Shap

118

116

117

Windermere

114

Kendal

115 *112*

109,110

113

Ulverston

Douglas

Preston

Liverpool *98*

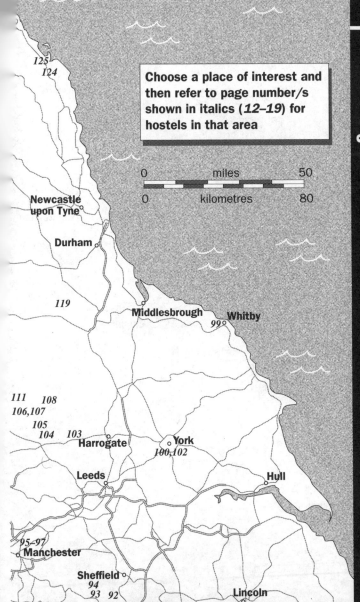

Choose a place of interest and then refer to page number/s shown in italics (*12–19*) for hostels in that area

0   miles   50

0   kilometres   80

125
124

Newcastle
upon Tyne

Durham

119

Middlesbrough   *99*   Whitby

111   *108*
106,107
105
104   *103*   Harrogate   York
               100,102

Leeds   Hull

95–97
Manchester

Sheffield
94
93   *92*   Lincoln

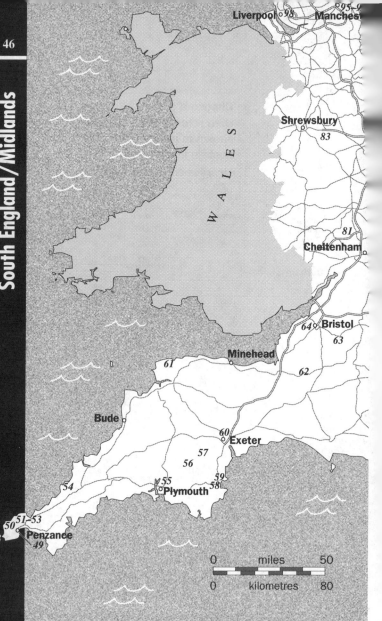

Liverpool 98 Manchester 95

Shrewsbury
83

Cheltenham
81

W A L E S

64 Bristol
63

Minehead
61 62

Bude

60 Exeter
57
56
59
55 58
54 Plymouth

51-53
50
48 Penzance
49

0   miles   50

0   kilometres   80

Sheffield
94
93 92
91
Derby
Nottingham
88
Lincoln
87
86
Norwich
Leicester
84, 85
Peterborough
Birmingham
Coventry
82
Northampton
Cambridge
Colchester
Luton
Oxford
80
London
73–79
Reading
Canterbury
71 72
Dover
Salisbury
Southampton
68
70
69
Brighton
65
66, 67
Bournemouth

Choose a place of interest and
then refer to page number/s
shown in italics (*12–19*) for
hostels in that area

South England/Midlands

WHITESAND'S LODGE

Land's End Backpackers
Sennen, Cornwall
TR19 7AR

Whitesand's Lodge, a converted granite farmhouse, is situated in Cornwall's natural rugged beauty, surrounded by sea, cliffs, hills, walkways and wildlife. There are two types of accommodation, the dormitories with self-catering kitchen for groups and backpackers, and the guest house, with more comfort, for couples and families. The general facilities are used by everyone. These include a cosy TV/video lounge with log fire, library, drying room, board store, summer barbecues and our funky rainbow bar and restaurant providing delicious good value wholesome food all day. There is a studio space for workshops and tent space is also available.

Whitesand's Lodge, 5 minutes from the coastal path and white sandy beach, provides a very exciting location for outdoor activities: from surfing, rock climbing, mountain biking and hiking the coastal paths to bird watching and retracing the area's ancient history. This is a great place for young and adventurous people from all over the world to have fun, to be challenged and to relax in one of Britain's most enchanting areas. Email: Whitesan@globalnet.co.uk

TELEPHONE/FAX CONTACT Toby or Greg, Tel: (01736) 871776,
OPENING SEASON All year
OPENING HOURS Open all day, no curfews.
NUMBER OF BEDS 26 in backpackers, 11 in guest house.
BOOKING REQUIREMENTS Groups should book.
PRICE PER NIGHT £10 (backpackers dorms), £14.50 (guest house). Group packages discussed. Full breakfast from £4.

PUBLIC TRANSPORT
Train station and National Express coaches at Penzance (9 miles). From Penzance take a local bus to Land's End. Ask for first stop in Sennen village (before Land's End). Phone Whitesand's for pick up availability or call a Taxi on 810751 (Marcus).

DIRECTIONS The hostel is first left as you enter Sennen Village on the A30, 9 miles from Penzance. 1½ miles from Land's End.

PENZANCE BACKPACKERS

The Blue Dolphin
Alexandra Road
Penzance, TR18 4LZ

Penzance, with its mild climate, its wonderful location looking across to spectacular St Michael's Mount, with all the coach and rail services terminating here, is the ideal base for exploring the far SW of England and the Scilly Isles. Whether you are looking for sandy beaches and sheltered coves; the storm lashed cliffs of Land's End; sub-tropical gardens; internationally acclaimed artists; the remains of ancient cultures; or simply somewhere to relax and take time out, Penzance Backpackers is for you.

We are situated in a lovely tree-lined road close to the sea front, with the town centre, bus station and railway station only a short walk away. Accommodation is mostly in small bunk-bedded rooms with bed-linen, a fully equipped self-catering kitchen, hot showers, comfortable lounge, lots of local information and a warm welcome all included in the price.

TELEPHONE CONTACT (01736) 363836
OPENING SEASON All year
OPENING HOURS 24 hours
NUMBER OF BEDS 30
BOOKING REQUIREMENTS It's best to phone.
PRICE PER NIGHT 1st night from £9 per person, 2nd night onwards from £8 per person, discount for long stays.

PUBLIC TRANSPORT

Penzance has a train station and is served by National Express. Fifteen mins' walk from train/bus station to hostel or alternatively catch buses 1, 1a, 5a or 6a from Tourist Information/bus/train station. Ask for top of Alexandra Road bus stop.

DIRECTIONS

From Tourist Information/bus/train station either follow Quay and Promenade to mini-roundabout, turn right up Alexandra Rd, we are a short way up on the left; or follow main road through town centre until second mini-roundabout, turn left down Alexandra Rd; we are on right.

1m

KELYNACK BUNKBARN

Kelynack Camping Park
Kelynack
St Just
Penzance
Cornwall
TR19 7RE

Kelynack Bunkbarn nestles in the secluded Cot Valley, one mile from the Atlantic Coast in the heart of the Land's End Peninsula Area of Outstanding Natural Beauty. The Barn has one twin room, one two-bedded and one four-bedded bunkroom. Blankets and pillows are provided. There is a toilet/shower room and communal kitchen with full cooking facilities. Adjacent is the bike store and a laundry/drying room shared with the campers on site. A small shop on site opens between April and September.

St Just, a mile away has plenty of food shops, some banks and a selection of pubs and eating houses. Kelynack is ideal for coast and moorland walking, spending time on the beaches, birdwatching, rock climbing and exploring the ancient villages, standing stones and tin mining heritage of unspoilt West Penwith.

TELEPHONE CONTACT Steve Edwards (01736) 787633
OPENING SEASON All year
OPENING HOURS Arrive after 2pm and vacate by 10am. All day access during stay.
NUMBER OF BEDS 8
BOOKING REQUIREMENTS Booking is advised (25% deposit).
PRICE PER NIGHT £6 adult, £4 child (under 12). No meters.

PUBLIC TRANSPORT
There is a frequent bus from Penzance Rail Station to St Just. Hostel is one mile south of St Just

DIRECTIONS
GR 373 301. The hostel is 200 yards east of the B3306, 1 mile south of St Just, 5 miles north of Land's End and 20 mins' walk from the coastal path.

3m

THE OLD CHAPEL BACKPACKERS

Zennor
St. Ives
Cornwall
TR26 3BY

Zennor is a small picturesque village situated between St Ives and Land's End and is a haven for walkers, bird watchers and anyone who wants a taste of the rural way of life or just simply to relax! The hostel is located very close to the pub and St Ives is nearby for shopping, clubbing, cinemas, restaurants and some of the finest beaches in Cornwall.

The Old Chapel Backpackers has been converted to a very high standard and is perfectly situated for clear views over the sea and moorland. We have four rooms that sleep six people, one room that sleeps four and a family room with double bed. There are washbasins in every room and the hostel is centrally heated throughout. We cannot offer self-catering but we can provide breakfast, packed lunches and evening meals if required. There is also a café on the premises serving delicious soup, rolls and cakes.

TELEPHONE CONTACT (01736) 798307 Paul or Hetty
OPENING SEASON All year, winter by prior arrangement.
OPENING HOURS All day
NUMBER OF BEDS 32
BOOKING REQUIREMENTS Booking is advisable with a deposit of 20% of balance.
PRICE PER NIGHT £10 per person Summer, Easter, Whit Week and Christmas. £9 per person all other times.

PUBLIC TRANSPORT
There are train stations at St Ives (4 miles) and Penzance (10 miles). Local buses run to/from St Ives every few hours. The taxi fare from St Ives is approximately £5.

DIRECTIONS
Approximately 4 miles from St Ives on Coastal Road heading towards Land's End.

5m

ST. IVES BACKPACKERS
"THE GALLERY"
Town Centre, St. Ives
Cornwall
TR26 1SG

At last! Some budget accommodation in St. Ives! This recently opened backpackers' hostel is situated in a charismatic 1845 former Wesleyan school in the centre of town, handy for all local amenities. Accommodation is in mixed dormitories with private rooms also available.

St. Ives offers plenty of interest and beauty to a wide range of visitors. The town itself has an abundance of charm with old buildings and alleys, the harbour is busy with small boats, the beaches are golden and inviting, and the art galleries, including the Tate, provide further stimulation. There are loads of things to do here - walking the coast path, climbing, PADI scuba diving courses, sailing, fishing, surfing, sunbathing and relaxing. Cycle hire available.

www. backpackers.co.uk

TELEPHONE CONTACT The manager, Tel: (01736) 799444, Email: St-ivesbackpackers@dial.pipex.com
OPENING SEASON All year
OPENING HOURS 24 hours (within reason).
NUMBER OF BEDS 70+
BOOKING REQUIREMENTS Booking in advance is advisable and is essential for groups. A deposit is required to secure a booking.
PRICE PER NIGHT £8 in winter up to £12 in August.

PUBLIC TRANSPORT
St. Ives is easy to reach by public transport with National Express coach and rail services. There is a FREE shuttle between Newquay Backpackers and St. Ives Backpackers.

DIRECTIONS
The hostel is 3 minutes' walk from the bus or train station - turn left into Gabriel Street and the hostel is opposite the cinema and Job Centre. By car take the A30 from Exeter and follow signposts to St. Ives from the end of the A30.

5m

HEATHERBELL INN
Longstone Hill
Carbis Bay
St. Ives
Cornwall
TR26 2LJ

Heatherbell Inn is within two miles from the centre of St. Ives with beaches, scenic views, busy harbour and plenty of art galleries. Enjoy the lovely beach on your doorstep at Carbis Bay or venture to St. Ives by train - which takes you a ride along the cliffs, walking or public transport which is located nearby. There are some great walks in the area and you can easily pick up a cliff walk to Land's End.

The Inn has 20 rooms providing mixed or single sex dormitories and private rooms. Come and enjoy the three bars, snooker table and during the summer months the entertainment - Irish bands, etc.

TELEPHONE CONTACT (01736) 298604
OPENING SEASON All year
OPENING HOURS 8am to midnight
NUMBER OF BEDS 20
BOOKING REQUIREMENTS None
PRICE PER NIGHT £8.00 to £10.00 per person

PUBLIC TRANSPORT
Carbis Station is situated 400 yards from the Inn, Sterth Station 2 miles and Penzance Station 7 miles. The nearest National Express Coach stop is 100 yards.

DIRECTIONS
Take the A30 through Cornwall bypassing all the towns until Hayle. Depart the Hayle bypass. At St.Ives roundabout take the St.Ives Road passing through the village of Lelant. One mile down the road is Heatherbell at 30 mph sign.

 3m

NEWQUAY INTERNATIONAL
B·A·C·K·P·A·C·K·E·R·S

69-73 Tower Road
Newquay, Cornwall
TR7 1LX

This hostel is for surfers and international travellers with the emphasis on meeting people and making new friends. This is what makes us so popular. We offer comfortable surroundings and a friendly informal atmosphere. We have a fully equipped kitchen, vending machines, central heating, satellite TV, video lounge, Internet facilities, hot showers and h&c in each room. We also have facilities for storing surfboards and wetsuits and we provide a clothes wash/dry service. There are barbecues at the hostel and we provide a free service to coach/train stations and the airport. The hostel is in the best area to enjoy Newquay's beaches and night life and there's no Curfew !!! You are provided with a discount card which gives 10% off cafés, 20% off surf hire, 50% off discos and 10% off surf shops. Brochure available. *www.backpackers.co.uk*

TELEPHONE CONTACT Ray, Tel: (01637) 879366,
Email: backpackers@dial.pipex.com
OPENING SEASON All year
OPENING HOURS 24 hours
NUMBER OF BEDS 40 +
BOOKING REQUIREMENTS Booking is essential for groups and advisable for individuals, deposit required.
PRICE PER NIGHT From £12 (August) to £8 (Sept to May).

PUBLIC TRANSPORT
Newquay has a train station and is served by National Express. Hostel is 10 mins' walk from bus/train station.

DIRECTIONS
10 mins' walk or free pickup from Bus/Train station. Walk through town centre, turn left after Sailors pub, go to the top of the road, the hostel is opposite on the left. By car take the A30 from Exeter, then A392 to Newquay, follow town centre then Fistral beach signs to Tower Road. The Hostel is on the left.

3m

PLYMOUTH BACKPACKERS INTERNATIONAL HOSTEL

172 Citadel Road
The Hoe
Plymouth
PL1 3BD

Plymouth Backpackers is located just five minutes' walk from the ferry port, where boats leave for Roscoff and Santander on most days. The hostel is close to all amenities, being a few minutes' walk from the famous Barbican, Mayflower Steps and city centre. Also near to the bus and railway stations. Excursions to Dartmoor, canoeing on the Tamar River, local boat trips, sailing and walking the coastal paths can be arranged from Plymouth. There is also a sports/leisure centre and skating rink within 5 mins' walk of the hostel.

We have 2,4 and 8 bedded dorms, plus some single and double rooms, linen is included in the price. There is a fully equipped kitchen, TV lounge and a residents' bar sited in a comfortable, relaxing lounge.

TELEPHONE/FAX CONTACT Tel; (01752) 225158 Fax; (01752) 207847
OPENING SEASON All year
OPENING HOURS No curfew, all day access.
NUMBER OF BEDS 48
BOOKING REQUIREMENTS Not essential but is preferred.
PRICE PER NIGHT From £8.50 per person

PUBLIC TRANSPORT
Plymouth has a train station and is served by National Express coaches. Bus and train stations are near to the hostel. Phone for a courtesy car.

DIRECTIONS
From train station walk up Salt Ash Road to North Croft roundabout. Turn right along Western Approach to Pavilions. From bus station walk up Exeter Street, across roundabout to Royal Parade. Cross road to Union Street, Pavilions on your left. From Plymouth Pavilions walk towards the Hoe, turn left up Citadel Road, the hostel is in 100yds on the right hand side. Phone for a courtesy car.

THE PLUME OF FEATHERS INN BUNKHOUSE
Princetown
Yelverton
Devon
PL20 6QG

The Plume of Feathers Inn is situated in the moorland village of Princetown which is the main village in Dartmoor National Park. The park covers 368 square miles and is famous for its rugged beauty, quaint villages, prehistoric remains, and its many peaks, such as High Willhays (2039ft) and Yes Tor (2030ft). The Plume is a traditional, family-run Inn dating from 1785, it has log fires, real ale and plenty of atmosphere. The Alpine bunkhouse and New bunkhouse provide comfortable low cost accommodation and the Inn also has B&B accommodation and a 75 tent camping area with toilets and showers. There is a wide range of activities available in the Dartmoor area including: - sailing, fishing, riding, abseiling, white water canoeing, climbing, pony trekking and walking.

TELEPHONE/FAX CONTACT tel: (01822) 890240, fax: (01822) 890780
OPENING SEASON All year
OPENING HOURS All Day
NUMBER OF BEDS 42
BOOKING REQUIREMENTS To secure beds, book in advance with 50% deposit. Booking three to four months in advance may be required for weekends.
PRICE PER NIGHT From £2.50 to £5.50 per person.

PUBLIC TRANSPORT
Nearest train and National Express services are in Plymouth (17 miles) and Exeter (26 miles). The Transmoor Link bus service between Plymouth and Exeter stops at Princetown, bus fare is £4 - £5. Taxi fare from Plymouth approx £15, from Exeter approx £25.

DIRECTIONS
The Plume of Feathers Inn is in Princetown village square, next to the Dartmoor National Park, High Moorland Centre.

5m

DARTMOOR EXPEDITION CENTRE
Rowden
Widecombe-in-the-Moor
Newton Abbot
Devon
TQ13 7TX

Great for walking, climbing, canoeing, caving, archaeology, painting or visiting places of interest nearby. Stay at the Dartmoor Expedition Centre in two 300 year-old barn bunkhouses with their cobbled floors and thick granite walls. Simple but comfortable accommodation with bunk beds and a wood burning stove. Convector heaters (one in each area) and night storage heating (one in each barn). Kitchen area equipped with fridge, gas water heater and electric stoves and kettles. All crockery and pans provided, and there is freezer space available. Electric appliances are coin operated (£1 coins).

The House Barn has the living area downstairs and upstairs sleeps 9 plus 5 in an inner cubicle. The Gate Barn sleeps 11 downstairs and 9 upstairs. There are two upgraded rooms (1 double, 1 twin). Beds are provided with fitted sheet, pillow and pillowcase.

TELEPHONE CONTACT John Earle (01364) 621249.
OPENING SEASON All year
OPENING HOURS 7.30am to 10.30pm
NUMBER OF BEDS 32
BOOKING REQUIREMENTS Book as far in advance as possible with 25% deposit.
PRICE PER NIGHT £7 per person (£9 per person in private room).

PUBLIC TRANSPORT
Newton Abbot is the nearest train station. In summer there are buses to Widecombe (1½ miles from hostel). Taxi fare from station £20.

DIRECTIONS
GR 700 764. Come down Widecombe Hill into the village. Turn right 200yds after school and travel up a steep hill past Southcombe onto the open moor. Continue for one mile until you reach crossroads. Turn right and take first left after 400yds. Hostel is 200yds on left.

RIVIERA BACKPACKERS

6 Manor Road
Preston Sands
Paignton
Devon

The Riviera Backpackers, which is situated 60 metres from a great sandy beach, is a fun lodge where you can chill out or rave and boil in the cauldron of pubs that surround us. Or, if you fancy an evening in, we have a TV lounge with games and books.

We have a fully fitted kitchen and also an outside barbecue and patio area. Our bunks, with their duvets and linen included in the overnight price, play second fiddle to none as do our excellent showers. During the day you can walk, swim, cycle, fish or dive. We have fishing equipment for use free of charge. Free pick up and drop off from bus/train stations on request from individuals and small groups.

Tea and Coffee are free

TELEPHONE/FAX CONTACT Allan, Tel/Fax; (01803) 550160
OPENING SEASON All year
OPENING HOURS 24 hours
NUMBER OF BEDS 33
BOOKING REQUIREMENTS Groups should give two weeks' notice and send a deposit of £5 per person.
PRICE PER NIGHT £7.50 to £8.50. Seven nights for the price of six. Discount also available for groups.

PUBLIC TRANSPORT
Paignton has a train station and is served by National Express. The bus to/from Torquay passes Manor Road. Free pick up and drop off at train and bus stations on request from individuals and small groups.

DIRECTIONS From Paignton train or bus stations, head for the beach, turn left until you reach Preston Sands. Manor Road is just off the beach.

TORQUAY BACKPACKERS INTERNATIONAL HOSTEL

119 Abbey Road, Torquay,
Devon, TQ2 5NP

Torquay is on the English Riviera, famous for warm weather and mediterranean atmosphere. Turquoise sea, red cliffs, long sandy beaches and secret shingle coves combine to create one of the UK's most beautiful coastlines. Torquay is renowned as a watersport mecca with sailing, water-skiing, windsurfing, diving etc and for its nightlife with pubs, clubs and restaurants a mere stagger from the hostel which is in the heart of Torquay.

Hostel activities include beach barbecues, live music nights, international food nights and video evenings. There are also trips to Dartmoor exploring emerald river valleys where pixies dwell and the open tor-dotted moors. Night trips, at full moon can be a ghostly experience! The hostel offers travellers a friendly, almost family atmosphere. Those who find it hard to leave can easily find work.

TELEPHONE CONTACT (01803) 299924 Jane
OPENING SEASON All year
OPENING HOURS 24 hrs. Check in 9-11am and 5-9pm, late arrivals should phone. No curfew.
BOOKING REQUIREMENTS Not required for individuals. Groups are advised to book.
PRICE PER NIGHT 1st night £8; 2nd night onwards £7; long term weekly rate £39.

PUBLIC TRANSPORT
Torquay can be reached by coach or train from all major towns. From London take a train from Paddington Station, or a coach from Victoria. Travel from Heathrow by coach. Free pickup on arrival.

DIRECTIONS
Drivers: follow signs for town centre to Union St (one way) and up Abbey Road. Hostel is at top of Abbey Road on right (just before lights and casino).

GLOBE BACKPACKERS

71 Holloway Street
Exeter
EX2 4JD

Globe Backpackers is situated in a mid-18th-Century town house, centrally located, only minutes from the main high street, Cathedral and historic quayside. We offer dorm-style accommodation only, a kitchen (free tea and coffee), social/dining area and tv/video room. Other facilities include bicycle hire and Internet access. Exeter is a University and Cathedral city with a fun, relaxed atmosphere. One of the oldest cities in Britain, Exeter was founded by the Romans almost 2000 years ago. It is also the only city in Britain to open its 13th-Century underground waterways to the public. Exeter has an excellent mix of pubs, clubs, live music venues, restaurants and cafes. Just 20 minutes' drive away from either the sandy beach at Exmouth, a great place for all sail sports or to the edge of Dartmoor for activities such as walking, rock climbing, cycling and horse-riding.

www.globebackpackers.freeserve.co.uk

TELEPHONE/FAX CONTACT Caroline or David, (01392) 215521, Fax:(01392) 215531, Email:caroline@globebackpackers.freeserve.co.uk
OPENING SEASON All year
OPENING HOURS 8.00am-11.00pm (outside hours by arrangement)
NUMBER OF BEDS 60
BOOKING REQUIREMENTS Not essential, but recommend calling ahead to check availability.
PRICE PER NIGHT £10.00 all year round

PUBLIC TRANSPORT
Exeter is serviced by National Express, local bus companies and the various rail networks.

DIRECTIONS
Bus Station exit near Paris Cafe, cross road, take side turning Southernhay East. Stay on LH side until Southgate Hotel. We are diagonally opposite on other side of junction. Central rail station down Queen St to High St, turn right and at 1st set of lights, turn left South St, continue to junction at bottom of hill. Cross at lights and you will find us on right. St. David's the direct route is down St.David's Hill, over Iron Bridge, onto North St, then South St to the junction.

👫 👫 ⚌ 🗄 🗒 🚰 🧹 🎲 🍴 ⬜ 🚲 1m

OCEAN BACKPACKERS

29 St. James Place
Ilfracombe
Devon
EX34 9BJ

Ocean Backpackers is situated in an area known as Little Switzerland with cliffs, forests, hills and valleys, fishing harbour, postcard villages, coves and long sandy beaches to explore. Ilfracombe is an old fishing port with traditional pubs, fun bars, a nightclub, theatre, cinema and cafes to chill out in, overlooking the harbour. Special events include an arts festival and Victorian week. The town is on the edge of Exmoor National Park and with Woolacombe and Croyd beaches just up the road it is a mecca for surfers. A highlight is camping on Lundy island where there are puffins and flying fish. Seals, dolphins, sharks or whales are spotted most days.

The hostel is a refurbished ex-hotel so all rooms are ensuite and comprise of small dorms, twins, doubles or family rooms. There is a theme cafe serving food from five continents (inc organic) a late bar, communal kitchen, garden terrace, laundry, videos, parking, Email, storage for sports equipment and a safe. Bikes and tents can be hired or lessons on scuba-diving, abseiling and surfing can be arranged.

TELEPHONE CONTACT Pete or Kinga (01271) 867835
OPENING SEASON 1st February - 20th October
OPENING HOURS Reception 8.30 am - 10.00 pm. Access 24 hours
NUMBER OF BEDS 30
BOOKING REQUIREMENTS Booking advised but not essential.
PRICE PER NIGHT £8.00 including tea toast & fruit, £9.00 including duvet, £18.00 B&B, Group discounts. No DSS.

PUBLIC TRANSPORT
Direct coaches from London, Heathrow, Plymouth and Exeter. By train take the Tarka line to Barnstaple then bus to Ilfracombe.

DIRECTIONS
From M5 take A361. From Cornwall take A39 to Barnstaple then follow the signs to Ilfracombe. Ocean Backpackers is opposite the coach station in the centre of the town.

GLASTONBURY BACKPACKERS

Crown Hotel
Market Place
Glastonbury
Somerset
BA6 9HD

Glastonbury Backpackers is a vibrant lively hostel set at the very heart of Glastonbury. The town is shrouded in legend and myth; according to Arthurian legend, Glastonbury, or the Isle of Avalon as it is formally known, is the burial place of King Arthur and Queen Guinevere. More recently the town has become famous for its many religious and cultural festivals and events.

The hostel is situated in the Crown Hotel, a 16th-century coaching inn which has recently been renovated to provide a unique and lively place to stay. Accommodation comprises of backpackers' dorms and twin and double rooms, most with ensuite. There is a backpackers' kitchen and lounge area with TV. Enjoy the café and juice bar which is open all day and our own bar with live music, DJs and competition nights. The perfect complement to your Glastonbury experience!

TELEPHONE CONTACT (01458) 833353 Ben
OPENING SEASON All year
OPENING HOURS 8.00 am-11.30 pm - 24hrs by arrangement.
NUMBER OF BEDS 42
BOOKING REQUIREMENTS Not essential but recommended, call for more information.
PRICE PER NIGHT £9 to £15

PUBLIC TRANSPORT
National Express and the cheaper Bakers Dolphin coaches both do daily return runs to London (Victoria) dropping outside the hostel. By train go to Bristol Temple Meads Station then catch 376 bus from end of Station Drive. This bus goes direct to Glastonbury every hour from 5.30am until 10pm. The bus costs £2.50 and stops outside hostel.

DIRECTIONS At the bottom of the High Street, there is a paved area and a large stone tower known as the market cross. The Backpackers is the Crown Hotel adjacent to the cross.

CITY OF BATH YMCA

International House
Broad Street Place
Bath
BA1 5LN

The City of Bath YMCA offers a warm welcome and the best value accommodation. From its central location all the sights of this World Heritage City are easily reached on foot. Bath is also an ideal base for the explorer. Staying longer brings Stonehenge, Wookey Hole Caves, Cheddar Gorge, the southern reaches of the Cotswolds, and more exciting destinations all within reach.

With a total of 220 beds, we have a great deal of experience in making all our guests feel comfortable. We have a fully air conditioned lounge area, colour satellite TV and restaurant which offers a cosmopolitan à-la-carte menu at special YMCA subsidised prices. The Health and Fitness suite provides state-of-the-art-equipment and a qualified staff team who have worked hard to create a club atmosphere. 'Fitness with Fun' is our motto.

Couples, Families, Groups and Backpackers are all welcome - you don't have to be young or male. All these facilities and the YMCA's traditional sense of community will make your stay a truly memorable one.

TELEPHONE CONTACT (01225) 325900
OPENING SEASON All year
OPENING HOURS All day
NUMBER OF BEDS 220
BOOKING REQUIREMENTS None - advanced credit card booking guarantees reservation.
PRICE PER NIGHT from £11.00 bed and continental breakfast

PUBLIC TRANSPORT
Bath has a train station and is served by National Express.

DIRECTIONS
Located approximately 0.5 miles from rail and bus station. Broad Street is located near the Podium Shopping centre off Walcott Street.

1m

www.**BRISTOLbackpackers**.co.uk

17 Saint Stephens Street – Bristol – BS1

Opening May 2000

Martin, Katie and Jacqui, who between them have spent years backpacking around the world, are setting up an independent hostel in Bristol's historic city centre. The unusual English Heritage Grade II listed, Dickensian building on Saint Stephens St will provide the independent traveller with all the important informal "creature comforts" they are looking for. Spacious and clean dorms of 2 to 10 beds will accommodate up to 46 guests.

Bristol in a nutshell

The City - Set on a historic inland Floating Harbour, Bristol is a prosperous and vibrant cosmopolitan city rich in history. Georgian and Victorian architecture dominate most areas in particular the Old Centre, Harbour Side and Clifton. Although it is the largest city in Southwest England with high profile communication, computing, aerospace and finance industries, the spectacular Avon Gorge and countryside beyond is only a 25 minute walk from the centre. Overseas visitors often stay longer than planned especially if they hold UK work visas. **Entertainment** – Bristol's diverse and extensive all-year entertainment, nightlife and music scene more than caters for the 2 large universities and high number of young professionals. Walking between venues is easy, as they are primarily concentrated in the West End and City Centre. **Transport** – Bristol's coach and rail networks make it the Gateway City to the West Country and South Wales. In addition its extensive local bus and cycle networks make it easy and affordable to visit its many beautiful surrounding villages, towns, cities and countryside.

From April 2000 please call Directory Enquires (192) for our telephone number or access our web site for loads more information and useful links.

BOURNEMOUTH BACKPACKERS (SUNNYSIDE)

3 Frances Road
Bournemouth BH1 3RY

Welcome to Bournemouth on the sunny coast of England, one of the UK's leading beach resorts. We have it all: excellent clean beaches, one of the world's largest natural harbours - offering a wide variety of watersports, two piers, good shopping, top english language schools, renowned nightlife and a host of local activities. Bournemouth is an excellent base for exploring the beautiful Dorset scenery including some of the most spectacular coastline in the world. An area rich in history and legends: Thomas Hardy, Lawrence of Arabia, Dorset smugglers, Tolpuddle Martyrs, etc.

Bournemouth Backpackers is a clean, cosy hostel only 2-3 minutes' walk from the train/bus station. The town centre and nightlife are also accessible on foot. http://homepage.virgin.net/dr.lawha/backpack.html

TELEPHONE CONTACT Lawrence, Tel: (01202) 299491, Email: bournemouth.backpackers@virgin.net
OPENING SEASON All year
OPENING HOURS Summer 8.30-10.30 a.m. and 5.00-8.00 p.m. Late and winter check in by arrangement. No curfew
NUMBER OF BEDS 20
BOOKING REQUIREMENTS Essential during winter, recommended for summer weekends.
PRICE PER NIGHT £8 - £17 depending on season and room.

PUBLIC TRANSPORT
2-3 minutes' walk from main Bournemouth Rail/Bus station. Ferry terminal at Poole (approx 10km), International Airport (approx 8km). Direct Rail/Bus services to London, South Coast and North.

DIRECTIONS
Follow A338 to Bournemouth. Turn left at roundabout by train station. Turn left at next roundabout. Do a U turn at next roundabout. Take first left after B&Q superstore. Then second left into Frances Rd.

PORTSMOUTH FOYER

22 Edinburgh Road
Portsmouth
PO1 1DH

Portsmouth Foyer is in the heart of town, less than 5 minutes' walk from Portsmouth and Southsea railway station, just yards from the shopping centre, and with excellent road, rail and ferry links. Portsmouth is steeped in Naval history, has a great night life aimed at students and young people (over the age of 16) and is ideal for people travelling to and from Continental Europe.

The Foyer offers high quality, comfortable accommodation, with friendly staff available 24 hours. We provide single rooms, either en-suite with use of a shared kitchen, or with their own kitchenette and shared shower rooms/toilets. Some twin rooms may also be available from Summer 2000. Soap is provided and Towels are available. Groups of up to 45 guests can be accommodated. Portsmouth Foyer has an on-site cafeteria offering nutritious low cost meals (main meals from £1.50). *Portsmouth Foyer is a registered charity.*

TELEPHONE CONTACT Room sales administrator (023) 9236 0001
Email: sales@portsmouthfoyer.org
OPENING SEASON All year, including Christmas and New Year
OPENING HOURS 24 hours
NUMBER OF BEDS 106
BOOKING REQUIREMENTS Booking advisable but not essential. Deposit of £10 to secure booking, per person.
PRICE PER NIGHT £18 per person (1 free place for every 20 booked), £95 per person per week.

PUBLIC TRANSPORT
Portsmouth and Southsea Railway station is less than 5 minutes walk away. National Express coaches stop at Portsmouth.

DIRECTIONS
Taking the M275 into Portsmouth city centre, follow signs to Roman Catholic Cathedral, and you will pass Foyer on left. Foyer is 200 yards from Commercial Road, Portsmouth's main shopping centre. Street parking in Edinburgh Road by meter. Multi storey nearby. Phone Foyer for directions.

GUMBER BOTHY

Gumber Farm
Slindon
Near Arundel
West Sussex
BN18 ORN

Gumber Bothy is a converted traditional Sussex barn on the National Trust's Slindon Estate in the heart of the South Downs. It provides simple overnight accommodation or camping for walkers, riders and cyclists, just off the South Downs Way. The bothy forms part of Gumber Farm and is 5 minutes' walk from Stane Street, the Roman Road that crosses the South Downs Way at Bignor Hill. Facilities include 30 sleeping platforms in 3 dorms, good hot showers and basins, kitchen/diner with gas hob and washing up facilities, a few pots and pans provided, and breakfast foodstuffs available to order in advance. Paddock for friendly horses and racks for bikes. Wheelchair accessible (please phone for details). Sorry, but as we're a sheep farm we have to say no dogs and most definitely **NO CARS**. Under 16s accompanied by adults please. No under fives.

TELEPHONE CONTACT Mark or Juliet (01243) 814484.
OPENING SEASON Easter to the end of October.
OPENING HOURS Flexible.
NUMBER OF BEDS 30.
BOOKING REQUIREMENTS Booking by telephone. Booking required for groups of six or more, with 50% deposit.
PRICE PER NIGHT £6.00 per person.

PUBLIC TRANSPORT
Train stations, Arundel (urban) 5 miles, Amberley (rural) 5 miles, Chichester (8 miles). National Express stop at Chichester. Bus service 702 from Chichester bus station (opposite train station) stops at Royal Oak pub on A27 every ½ hour Monday to Friday. The Royal Oak is a 3 mile walk from the hostel. Taxi fare from Arundel to Northwood Farm is £10, followed by a 2 mile walk across country.

DIRECTIONS
OS Sheet 197 GR 961 119 (Bothy), GR 973 129 (Nearest car park). No vehicular access. One mile off South Downs Way on Stane Street bridleway (a straight Roman Road).

LITTLEHAMPTON BUNKHOUSE

14 Pier Road
Littlehampton
Sussex
BN17 5BA

Littlehampton on the mouth of the river Arun is a commercial and pleasure port, a centre for all water sports. It is the headquarters for many sea angling championships and a popular centre for divers with more than 100 wrecks to explore. West of the river is a large expanse of unspoilt beach. About 3 miles away is Arundel with its castle, wildfowl and wetland area. The South Downs Way, a favourite route for walkers and cyclists, passes through Arundel. Nearby is Chichester with its cathedral and festival. There are also country homes to view at Goodwood, Petworth and Parkham and at Bignor and Fishbourne there are Roman remains.

The bunkhouse, a converted boat house, is 50 yards from the river and public slipway and a few minutes walk from the town centre and beach. There are self-catering facilities and a snack bar just around the corner. Clean sheets are provided and there are 2 rooms with 12 and 4 bunks respectively. Electricity is metered.

TELEPHONE CONTACT Mrs Henry (01903) 715766
OPENING SEASON March to November (Inclusive)
OPENING HOURS Flexible
NUMBER OF BEDS 16
BOOKING REQUIREMENTS Booking (one month in advance with 25% deposit) is recommended during summer.
PRICE PER NIGHT £8 per person

PUBLIC TRANSPORT
Littlehampton has a train station.

DIRECTIONS
From **Train Station** turn left at cross roads and walk 4 mins to the right to Pier Road. By **car** follow signs to beach, turn right, follow right bend into Pier Road. Parking just before white house (No 14).

BRIGHTON BACKPACKERS INDEPENDENT HOSTEL

75/76 Middle Street
Brighton
BN1 1AL

Brighton Backpackers is an independently owned and run hostel founded in 1991 by Tim and Roger to offer the kind of open and stimulating atmosphere they found on their travels abroad. A laid back alternative for travellers from all over the world, there's no curfew here, no chores, and the common room is open all night. There are two kitchens, a free pool table, showers, central heating, good hi-fi, satellite TV, a well stocked fridge and a relaxed and friendly atmosphere. There is a computer for guests so you can check your Emails, browse the web or update your cv! We are on the seafront, in the centre of town where all the good social/shopping areas are, including the historic lanes and the bohemian North Lanes. The hostel is in two buildings: the main part is on Middle Street, about 50 yards from the sea. This is where the reception is located. On the seafront (around the corner) is the Brighton Beach Hotel annex, where we have rooms for 2-4 people (en-suite), with spectacular views of the beach and piers. Web site / Email: Stay@brightonbackpackers.com

TELEPHONE/FAX CONTACT Tel;(01273) 777717, Fax; 887778
OPENING SEASON All year
OPENING HOURS 9am to very late.
NUMBER OF BEDS 80
BOOKING REQUIREMENTS Advised to confirm beds.
PRICE PER NIGHT £9.00 per person. Special weekly rate.

PUBLIC TRANSPORT
Brighton has a train station and intercity coaches operate from Poole Valley coach station.

DIRECTIONS
From train station (10 mins), walk straight to the seafront, turn left and then first left. **From coach station** (3 mins), walk west along the sea front, Middle Street comes off the seafront between the two piers.

1m

THE OLD STABLES BUNKBARN

Brenley Farm
Brenley
Boughton
Faversham
Kent
ME13 9LY

The Old Stables Bunkbarn is a carefully converted 17th-century stable. It is in a quiet situation on an East Kent fruit and hop farm between the Pilgrims Way and the Saxon Shore Way.

The Old Stables has accommodation for 24 in two hostel style rooms with 16 and 8 bunks. Facilities include four hot showers and WC. There is a large warm common room and dining room/kitchen with hot water, and there are also laundry facilities. Meals are available locally. Sorry the bunkbarn is not suitable for disabled people and under 16s must be accompanied by an adult.

TELEPHONE CONTACT (01227) 751203 Mrs Berry
OPENING SEASON April to July & October to March, Groups only in winter months.
OPENING HOURS Service available between 7.30am - 10pm
NUMBER OF BEDS 24
BOOKING REQUIREMENTS Booking is required during winter. £2 deposit per person.
PRICE PER NIGHT £6.50 (self-catering).

PUBLIC TRANSPORT
Faversham is the nearest train station and National Express stop. On local buses ask for Brenley Corner. Taxi fare from Faversham is £5.

DIRECTIONS
At J7 on M2 leave roundabout to the south on Brenley Lane. After 400yds turn right at T junction. After another 400yds take left fork signed Brenley Farm. At the top of the drive the bunkbarn is the first large building on the farm.

KiPPS

40 Nunnery Fields
Canterbury
Kent
CT1 3JT

KiPPS is a 5-10 minute walk from the city centre of historic Canterbury with its renowned cathedral and top quality shops - a destination for pilgrims ancient and modern! Canterbury also makes an ideal stopover to start and finish a continental tour with easy access to the channel tunnel and the port of Dover.

Everyone is welcome to enjoy the friendly relaxed atmosphere, whether travelling as an individual, family or group. Accommodation varies from 6-bedded dormitories to twin and single rooms. Also available are family rooms where cots can be provided. The small hostel shop offers breakfast and snack items and can also provide the ingredients for a simple but filling meal. For pre-booked groups of 10 or more please enquire about our catering packages which include cooked breakfasts, packed lunches and evening meals. Smoking is prohibited within the house but not the garden. *www.amush.cx/kipps*

TELEPHONE CONTACT David Harman, Tel: (01227) 786121, Email kipps@FSBdial.co.uk
OPENING SEASON All year
OPENING HOURS No Curfew, reception 7.30am to 11.30pm
NUMBER OF BEDS 33
BOOKING REQUIREMENTS Advance booking recommended.
PRICE PER NIGHT £10.30 to £15. Discounts available for longer stays and groups. Credit cards accepted.

PUBLIC TRANSPORT
Canterbury East train station, on London Victoria to Dover line, is ½mile by footpath (phone hostel for directions). National Express coaches stop ½mile from hostel. The local C4 bus stops by the door of the hostel. Taxi fare from coach/rail stations is £3.

DIRECTIONS
Take B2068 to Hythe from City Ring Road (A28). Turn right at first traffic lights by church. KiPPS is 200-300 yds on left.

ASHLEE HOUSE
261-265 Gray's Inn Road
King's Cross
London, WC1X 8QT

Ashlee House is a little bit of Dublin in the heart of London! This backpackers is run by two Irish sisters and is situated 300m from King's Cross station. The station is unique in that it is the only station to be served by six different tube lines, the Thameslink and several overground lines. All these connections make Ashlee House highly accessible both to the West End, Covent Garden and all major tourist attractions, as well as the rest of Great Britain.

This backpackers offers clean, comfortable accommodation in a friendly and vibrant atmosphere. Prices start from £13.00 per night per person and include continental breakfast, linen and bedding. Other facilities include Internet access, satellite TV, laundry room and free luggage/valuable storage. Reception is open 24 hours and the staff are always willing to assist guests in any way they can.

TELEPHONE CONTACT Tel: (020) 7 8339400, Email: info@ashleehouse.co.uk, Web: www.ashleehouse.co.uk
OPENING SEASON All Year
OPENING HOURS 24 hours - no curfew
NUMBER OF BEDS 180
BOOKING REQUIREMENTS Booking is advisable but not essential
PRICE PER NIGHT From £13.00 per person

PUBLIC TRANSPORT
All the facilities you would expect from a major city. Links to Heathrow, Gatwick, Luton and Stanstead. Regular buses and underground connection from Victoria Station direct to Kings's Cross.

DIRECTIONS
King's Cross station is 2 mins away by foot. From the station take the exit for Grays Inn Road, departing the exit McDonald's will be on right. Keep McDonald's right, walk straight ahead, passing an exchange bureau, the police station and KFC. The road naturally turns to the right-this is Grays Inn Road - the hostel is 200 metres up the road on the right, opposite The Royal Throat Nose and Ear hospital.

3m

TENT CITY - HACKNEY
Millfields Road
Hackney, London
E5 0AR

Tent City Hackney is a lovely canal-side camp site and tented hostel in the heart of the Lea Valley nature reserve. Amazingly Tent City is also close to the City of London. The accommodation is in bunk beds in large marquee tents. The main building has free hot showers, toilets, and cooking facilities. There is an on-site shop and snack bar and laundry and ironing facilities.

We are open all summer, 24 hours a day with no curfew. We also provide free baggage and valuables storage, helpful volunteer staff and a relaxed and friendly environment. There is a children's play area, on-site entertainment and local canal-side pubs. There is plenty of room for travellers with their own tents. We believe that we are the cheapest accommodation in London. Please check our website for up to date information:-

www.tentcity.co.uk

TELEPHONE CONTACT Reception (020) 8 985 7656
OPENING SEASON June 1st to Aug 31st inclusive
OPENING HOURS 24 hours
NUMBER OF BEDS 100
BOOKING REQUIREMENTS Reservations are only taken for groups, everyone else is dealt with first come first served.
PRICE PER NIGHT £5.00 per person, £4.50 for groups of 10+

PUBLIC TRANSPORT
British Rail from Liverpool Street to Hackney Central, then bus 242 to Mandeville Street. Or tube to Liverpool Street and bus 242 to Mandeville Street. Or bus 38 from Victoria or Picadilly to Clapton pond, walk down Millfields Road, over bridge to Hackney Marshes.

DIRECTIONS
By car from central London:- aim for lower Clapton (part of Hackney on north east side of London). Drive down Millfields Rd and over bridge at the end. **By car from Dover**:- A2, Blackwall Tunnel, A102 (Clapton and Hackney direction), Kenworthy Rd, Daubenay Rd, Mandeville St and over the bridge.

3m

THE MUSEUM INN HOSTEL

27 Montague Street
London, WC1B 5BH

Right in the heart of London, the Museum Inn has an extremely relaxed, cosmopolitan atmosphere. It's in a quiet road opposite the British Museum - but within just a few minutes' walk of the West End and Covent Garden with theatres, clubs, restaurants, cinemas and shops in abundance.

Prices range from £13 to £17 per person per night, with a discounted weekly rate available in low season. The accommodation is multi-share in rooms of three to ten people, with a limited number of twins. The price includes continental breakfast, unlimited hot water, clean bed linen, all tax, cooking facilities, satellite TV, communal lounge and a valuables lock-up. Other facilities include a fax service, internet facilities and a job board. There's no curfew and staff are available 24 hours a day.

18-30 year old backpackers only. No DSS

TELEPHONE/FAX CONTACT Receptionist (020) 7 580 5360, Fax: (020) 7 636 7948
OPENING SEASON All year
OPENING HOURS 24 hours, no curfew
NUMBER OF BEDS 50
BOOKING REQUIREMENTS Booking is essential in summer. Credit card number secures reservation.
PRICE PER NIGHT £14 to £17 per person

PUBLIC TRANSPORT
Take London underground to Russell Square tube station.

DIRECTIONS
From Russell Square tube station : turn left along Bernard Street and in Russell Square walk diagonally across the gardens. At opposite corner you will find Montague Street. The Museum Inn is on the left at the bottom of the street (about 50 yards).

LEINSTER INN
7-12 Leinster Square
London
W2 4PR

The Leinster Inn is in a quiet square overlooking gardens yet close to Portobello Market, Hyde Park, Kensington Palace and Notting Hill (home to Europe's legendary Notting Hill carnival). Nearby Queensway offers bustling shops and restaurants as well as the combined shopping complex and cinemas at Whitlley's. The Leinster Inn is great for weeklies, with regular parties, great music and very lively atmosphere!

Prices range from £12.50 to £15 per night in multi-share rooms of four to eight people. Singles start from £25 and Twins and Doubles from £18 per person. Discounted weekly rates may be available in low season. The price includes continental breakfast, unlimited hot water, clean bed linen, all tax, cooking facilities, satellite TV, communal lounge and a valuables lock-up. Other facilities include a late night licensed bar, pool table, video games, Internet lounge, fax service and a job board. There's no curfew and staff are available 24 hours.

18-30 year old backpackers only. No DSS

TELEPHONE/FAX CONTACT Receptionist, Tel: (020) 7 229 9641, Fax: (020) 7 221 5255
OPENING SEASON All year
OPENING HOURS 24 hours, no curfew
NUMBER OF BEDS 200
BOOKING REQUIREMENTS Booking is essential in summer. Credit card or sterling cheque for first night secures reservation.
PRICE PER NIGHT From £12.50 to £15 per person.

PUBLIC TRANSPORT
Take London underground to Bayswater or Queensway tube station.

DIRECTIONS From Bayswater or Queensway tube stations: turn left and walk down to Porchester Gardens and turn left, then walk to end and turn right, then second left, hostel is on the right.

THE QUEST HOTEL
45 Queensborough Terrace
London
W2 3SY

The Quest is in a great location opposite Hyde Park and within a few minutes' walk of bustling shops, The Whiteleys complex, cafés, cinemas - not to mention Portobello Market and Notting Hill (home to Europe's legendary street carnival!). The hostel offers a warm and friendly atmosphere for all and is ideal for sightseeing.

Prices range from £13 to £15 per person per night, with a discounted weekly rate available in low season. The accommodation is multi-share in rooms of four to eight people, with a limited number of twins. The price includes continental breakfast, unlimited hot water, clean bed linen, all tax, cooking facilities, satellite TV, communal lounge and a valuables lock-up. Other facilities include a pool table, fax service, job board and internet facilities. There's no curfew and staff are available 24 hours a day.

18-30 year old (student) backpackers only. No DSS

TELEPHONE/FAX CONTACT Receptionist (020) 7 229 7782, Fax: (020) 7 727 8106
OPENING SEASON All year
OPENING HOURS 24 hours, no curfew
NUMBER OF BEDS 60
BOOKING REQUIREMENTS Booking is essential in summer. Credit card number secures the reservation.
PRICE PER NIGHT £13 - £15 per person

PUBLIC TRANSPORT
Take London underground to Queensway or Bayswater tube station.

DIRECTIONS
From Queensway or Bayswater tube stations: turn right and go onto Bayswater Road. Turn left and then second left (50 yards) to Queensborough Terrace. Quest is on the left.

 3m

THE VICTORIA HOTEL
71 Belgrave Road
London
SW1 2BG

The Vic is a lively hostel, full of characters and in an excellent location for sightseeing. It's right next to the River Thames for boat cruises and within a few minutes' walk of Buckingham Palace, Big Ben, The Tate Gallery, The Houses of Parliament and Victoria Station.

Prices range from £13 to £15 per person per night, with a discounted weekly rate available in low season. The accommodation is in multi-share rooms of four to eight people, with a limited number of twins. The price includes continental breakfast, unlimited hot water, clean bed linen, all tax, cooking facilities, satellite TV, communal lounge and a valuables lock-up. Other facilities include a pool table, fax service, job board and internet facilities. There's no curfew and staff are available 24 hours a day.

18-30 year old backpackers only. No DSS

TELEPHONE/FAX CONTACT Receptionist Tel: (020) 7 834 3077, Fax: (020) 7 932 0693
OPENING SEASON All year
OPENING HOURS 24 hours, no curfew
NUMBER OF BEDS 55
BOOKING REQUIREMENTS Booking is essential in summer. Credit card number secures the reservation.
PRICE PER NIGHT £13 - £15 per person

PUBLIC TRANSPORT
Take London underground to Pimlico tube station.

DIRECTIONS From Pimlico tube station: turn right, then second right (about 50 yards) onto Belgrave Road. The Vic is on the right.

1m

THE HYDE PARK HOSTEL

2-6 Inverness Terrace
London W2 3HY

The Hyde Park Hostel is in a beautiful location, opposite Hyde Park and Kensington Palace and within only a few minutes' walk of bustling Queensway, Notting Hill (home to Europe's legendary Notting Hill carnival) and Portobello Market. The nearby Whiteley's Shopping centre offers cafés, shops and a large cinema complex.

Prices range from £12.50 to £15 per person per night, with a discounted weekly rate available in low season. The accommodation is in multi-share rooms of four to eight people, with a limited number of twins. The price includes continental breakfast, unlimited hot water, clean bed linen, all tax, cooking facilities, satellite TV, communal lounge and a valuables lock-up. Other facilities include a pool table, fax service, Internet access, laundry facilities, job board, video games and on site travel agent. A brand new licensed bar will be opening in 2000. There's no curfew and staff are available 24 hours a day.

18-30 year old backpackers only. No DSS

TELEPHONE/FAX CONTACT Receptionist Tel: (020) 7 229 5101, Fax: (020) 7 229 3170
OPENING SEASON All year
OPENING HOURS 24 hours, no curfew
NUMBER OF BEDS 160
BOOKING REQUIREMENTS Booking is essential in summer. Credit card number secures the reservation.
PRICE PER NIGHT £12.50 - £15 per person

PUBLIC TRANSPORT
Take London underground to Queensway tube station.

DIRECTIONS From Queensway tube station turn left onto Bayswater Road. Take the first left, Inverness Terrace, and the building is on your right hand side at the beginning of the street.

3m

OXFORD BACKPACKERS

9a Hythe Bridge Street
Oxford
OX1 2EW

Oxford Backpackers is a purpose built hostel, in the heart of Oxford the leading university town of England. The hostel is two minutes' walk from the train and bus stations and close to the Tourist Information Centre and all the City's attractions. It is safe, clean and friendly. Small friendly dorms and two private rooms. Fully equipped kitchen, well supplied bar, laundry, games room, Internet access and organised activities add to the experience.

Oxford City is steeped in history and culture, you can explore Christ Church, Magdalen and New College of the University, Bodleian Library, the Oxford Story and Britain's oldest museum the Ashmolean Museum. Alternatively explore the canals and quiet villages of the Cotswolds. Oxford is only an hour away from Shakespeare's Stratford.

Web page: www.hostels.co.uk

TELEPHONE/FAX CONTACT Manager, Tel: (01865) 721761, Fax: (01865) 315038, Email: oxford@hostels.demon.co.uk
OPENING SEASON All year
OPENING HOURS Reception open from 8am to 12 midnight.
NUMBER OF BEDS 120
BOOKING REQUIREMENTS Booking is advised in Summer (April to Sept), 7 days in advance with deposit by credit card.
PRICE PER NIGHT From £11 per person. Discounts available for longer stays, groups and those booking ahead to Stratford-Upon-Avon Backpackers. Breakfasts available.

PUBLIC TRANSPORT
Oxford has train and National Express services. Hostel is 100yds from train station and easy walking distance from the coach station.

DIRECTIONS
From train station turn left, at fork bear left and hostel is on your right. From Oxford coach station turn right, hostel is over the bridge 100 yards on your left. By road follow signs to the train station.

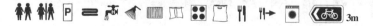

3m

BERROW HOUSE ACTIVITY AND CAMP CENTRE

Hollybush
Ledbury
Herefordshire
HR8 16T

Berrow House is situated in Hollybush between Rugged Stone Hill and Midsummer Hill of the Malvern Hills range. It is ideally suited for both families, groups and individuals (including those with special needs) to enjoy the countryside and the many attractions that the Malvern area has to offer. It is near the Forest of Dean and the Welsh border, at the start of the Worcestershire Way Walk, with the towns of Malvern, Ledbury, Tewkesbury, Worcester, and Gloucester, all within a half hour drive.

The Bunkhouse is a converted workshop, which made furniture for the Eastnor Estate. It includes sleeping accommodation for 5 in the main room, with sleeping accommodation for 3 on the upper floor. The main room has heating and easy chairs. The adjacent kitchen/dining room has hot water, cooker, cutlery, crockery and cooking utensils. Toilets, dryer and shower are adjacent. The annex, which was formally used as lambing sheds, has sleeping accommodation for 4 in two rooms. There is a kitchen equipped as in main bunkhouse. Heating, toilet, shower and cloakroom provided. Camping also available

TELEPHONE/FAX CONTACT Bill or Mary Cole, (01531) 635845
OPENING SEASON All year
OPENING HOURS 24 hours
NUMBER OF BEDS 8 (bunkhouse), 4 (annex) and 8 tents.
BOOKING REQUIREMENTS Not required for individuals.
PRICE PER NIGHT £6 per person

PUBLIC TRANSPORT
Nearest train station and National Express service are in Ledbury. this is 3 miles from the hostel and would cost approximately £3 in a taxi.

DIRECTIONS
Take A449 from Ledbury towards Malvern. Turn right on to A438 through Eastnor up hill. Berrow House is behind the next phone box on right in Hollybush. Look for camp sign.

STRATFORD-UPON-AVON BACKPACKERS

33 Greenhill Street
Stratford-Upon-Avon
Warwickshire
CV37 6LE

Stratford-Upon-Avon Backpackers is in the heart of Stratford-Upon-Avon, William Shakespeare's birthplace, and one of the most beautiful little towns in England. The hostel is five minutes' walk from the train and bus stations and all the town's attractions, including Shakespeare's birthplace, Royal Shakespeare Theatre, Nash's House, Anne Hathaway's Cottage and picturesque canals.

The hostel has cosy en-suite dorms with comfortable pine bunks and duvets. We have a sun lounge and rooftop garden with barbecue, Internet facilities and a great kitchen and dining area. To stay you will need some ID with a photo (ie passport or student card).

Web page: www.hostels.co.uk

TELEPHONE/FAX CONTACT Manager, Tel: (01789) 263838, Fax: (01865) 315038, Email: stratford@hostels.demon.co.uk
OPENING SEASON All year
OPENING HOURS Reception open 8am to 10pm. No Curfew.
NUMBER OF BEDS 50
BOOKING REQUIREMENTS Booking advised in Summer (April to Sept) and all weekends, 7 days in advance, deposit by credit card.
PRICE PER NIGHT From £11 per person. Discounts available for longer stays, groups and those booking with Oxford Backpackers.

PUBLIC TRANSPORT
Stratford has a train station and is served by National Express. Hostel is only 5 minutes' walk from train and coach stations.

DIRECTIONS
From train station:- Follow path out of station and walk towards town. We are 4 minutes' walk on RH side. **From main Coach/Bus stop in Bridge Street**:- Walk up Bridge Street and cross over two intersections. We are 5 minutes' walk on LH side. If travelling by road follow the signs for the train station.

STOKES BARN
BUNKHOUSE
Newtown House Farm Office
Much Wenlock
Shropshire
TF13 6DB

Stokes Barn is located on top of the limestone escarpment of Wenlock Edge, an area of outstanding natural beauty and in the heart of Shropshire's countryside. Set within open fields on our working farm, the barn offers comfortable, fully heated, dormitory accommodation in the tastefully converted 19th-Century threshing barn and granary with the old dairy converted to a kitchen. The is also a separate cottage which makes further accommodation for leaders or teachers.

Stokes Barn is an ideal base for field study groups, schools and walkers. The "Ironbridge World Heritage Site" is only 6 miles away and is part of the national curriculum. The historical market town of Much Wenlock is a walk to shops, pubs and sports facilities. A full or part food service can be provided. We aim to make your stay relaxing and enjoyable.

TELEPHONE/FAX CONTACT Suzanne Hill Tel: (01952) 727293, Fax: (01952) 728130
OPENING SEASON All year
OPENING HOURS 24 hours with prior notice
NUMBER OF BEDS 40
BOOKING REQUIREMENTS Essential with 50% deposit.
PRICE PER NIGHT £8, special rate for groups of 20 plus.

PUBLIC TRANSPORT
Nearest train stations are in Teleford (10 miles) and in Shrewsbury (10 miles). National Express coaches call at Shrewsbury from London, call (0839) 142 348 for information. Local Midland Red buses stop in Much Wenlock, call 01952 223766 for details.

DIRECTIONS
GR 609 999. When driving from the M6 take M54 Telford following Ironbridge Gorge signs. A4169 to Much Wenlock, joining A458 for Shrewsbury. Stokes Barn is then signposted 1 mile from Much Wenlock on the Shrewsbury Road.

INTERNATIONAL YOUTH HOUSE PROJECT

Upperton Road, Bede Island
Leicester, LE2 7AU

Situated within easy walking distance of the city centre the Youth House is close to sports clubs, De Montfort University, The National Space Science Centre and Leicester's busy nightlife. The International Youth House Project provides the only tourist hostel accommodation in the city centre. The building has an attractive riverside location providing comfortable lodgings in four and six person bunk bed dormitories, each with a hand basin and individual lockers (towels not supplied). Showers and toilets are adjacent to the dormitories. The whole building is wheelchair friendly with appropriate shower and toilet facilities. Facilities include a café with TV, music and games. Breakfast, lunch and evening meals are available at reasonable prices by prior arrangement. There is a live-in warden for security. We are ideally suited for schools, colleges, youth groups and individuals. Other facilities include Music Studio, Photography and Sports Hall, these may be booked in advance at a reasonable cost.

TELEPHONE CONTACT Sarah Morley (0116) 2551554
OPENING SEASON All year, except Christmas and New Year.
OPENING HOURS 1.30am curfew, no room access 11am-2pm weekdays, 11am-5pm weekends.
NUMBER OF BEDS 46
BOOKING REQUIREMENTS Booking preferred. 50% deposit required for groups.
PRICE PER NIGHT £10 pp (under 26 years old), £12 pp (over 26).

PUBLIC TRANSPORT
Leicester has a train station and is served by National Express. The hostel is 15 mins walk from train/bus station. Catch bus 52/52A every 20 mins from the clock tower to Upperton Road.

DIRECTIONS
From tourist information in Town Hall Sq walk to city council offices in Welford Rd. Continue on Welford Rd, past prison on left, take right fork at Granby Halls Leisure Centre into Aylestone Rd. 200yds turn right into Walnut St, 400yds to canal bridge, hostel is immediately on left over bridge.

 1m

DODGY DICK'S
BACKPACKERS HOSTEL
157 Wanlip Lane
Birstall, Leicester
LE4 4GL

Richard's Place, open since 1985, caters for students, international backpackers and cyclists of the 16-30 age group only. This hostel is located in a quite peaceful area, close to Watermead Park. The Park is an excellent place to jog, watch wildlife or picnic. There are shops, takeaways and a pub nearby.

This small warm hostel offers you a welcome and a feast. The very large home-cooked meals cater for meat-eaters, vegetarians or vegans. Full English breakfast (£2), supper (£4), large filled bread rolls 85p and free tea and coffee (DIY). There are picnic tables in the garden. Free conducted tour of Leicester City Centre. The nightly price includes a light breakfast, all bedding and hot showers. No self-cooking or smoking in hostel.

To stay ID is required, passport or NUS student card.

TELEPHONE CONTACT Richard (0116) 2673107
OPENING SEASON Phone for dates
OPENING HOURS No access from 10am to 5pm, but open all day in very bad weather. Key available for long stays.
NUMBER OF BEDS 5
BOOKING REQUIREMENTS Phone to book a bed. Answer phone service before 5pm.
PRICE PER NIGHT £8.50 per person (24% discount for 7+ days)

PUBLIC TRANSPORT
Leicester has a train station and National Express services. Mon to Sat take Bus no 61 from Haymarket bus station stand C4, or from across the road from the train station. Sundays, take Bus No 125 from St Margarets bus station stand B. Ask for a ticket to Wanlip Lane, Birstall, get off second stop past Somerfield store.

DIRECTIONS
Birstall is 3 miles north of Leicester on the A6. In Birstall look for the Somerfield store at No.1 Wanlip Lane.

THE OLD RED LION
Bailey Street
Castle Acre
Norfolk PE32 2AG

Visitors to Castle Acre are entranced by the special atmosphere of this medieval walled town which lies within the outer bailey of an 11th-century castle. Castle Acre is on the Peddars Way, an historic path.

The Old Red Lion, a former pub, is centrally situated and now carries on the tradition of serving travellers who seek refreshment and repose. Guests can stay in private rooms or dormitories where bedding and linen are provided free of charge. There are quiet areas, with wood burning stoves, for reading and meeting other guests and playing. There are two large areas and studio space (one area is self-contained with catering facilities and toilets) which are ideal for group use, courses and retreats. The extension under construction will house a reception area and private space for group leaders. Communally served meals (wholefood) are available. The self-catering facilities are suitable for groups. The entire premises are available for hire. Secure bike store. Drying facilities. NO SMOKING.

TELEPHONE CONTACT Alison Loughlin (01760) 755557
OPENING SEASON All year
OPENING HOURS Free time, by prior negotiation.
NUMBER OF BEDS 20
BOOKING REQUIREMENTS Useful but not essential.
PRICE PER NIGHT With full bedding and breakfast from £12.50.

PUBLIC TRANSPORT
The nearest train stations are at King's Lynn and Downham Market (10 miles). Regular buses from King's Lynn to Swaffham. Daily National Express coach between Victoria Coach Station and Swaffham. Buses to Castle Acre, from Swaffham three times a week and from King's Lynn twice a week. Approx taxi fare from Swaffham £3.50. Norfolk Bus information freecall (0500) 626116.

DIRECTIONS GR 818151. Castle Acre is 3½ miles north of Swaffham (A47). The Old Red Lion is on the left 75 yards down Bailey Street (under Bailey Gate in village centre).

DEEPDALE GRANARY BUNKHOUSE
Deepdale Farm
Burnham Deepdale
Norfolk, PE31 8DD

Deepdale Granary Bunkhouse is the ideal base for exploring the unique Norfolk Coast. It is situated halfway between Hunstanton and Wells-Next-The-Sea on the A149.

The hostel has modern facilities including central heating and hot showers. It also has a good self-catering kitchen.

Phone or fax anytime for a fully descriptive leaflet.

www.burnhamdeepdale.co.uk

TELEPHONE/FAX CONTACT Alister Borthwick, Tel: (01485) 210256, Fax: (01485) 210158, Email: deepdale@zetnet.co.uk
OPENING SEASON All Year
OPENING HOURS All day (collect key from office).
NUMBER OF BEDS 18
BOOKING REQUIREMENTS Pre-booking strongly recommended. 20% deposit with balance due one month in advance.
PRICE PER NIGHT £8.50 per person. £5.75 per person (weekdays) if all 18 beds are booked.

PUBLIC TRANSPORT
Nearest train station King's Lynn (25 miles). Local buses stop at Deepdale Garage - 100yds from hostel.

DIRECTIONS
GR 803 443. On the A149 halfway between Hunstanton and Wells-Next-The-Sea, situated beside a garage.

THE IGLOO
BACKPACKERS HOSTEL

110 Mansfield Road
Nottingham
NG1 3HL

Located within walking distance of the city's historical sights and entertaining sounds, the Igloo is Nottingham's only backpackers' hostel. On offer to backpackers and youth groups is a clean, safe and warm overnight stay in a large, listed Victorian house. Just £10 per night per person buys a whole host of homely comforts; bunk bed dorms, hot power showers, lounge with games, TV & info and fully-equipped kitchen plus free tea, coffee and good company. The hostel also has Internet access. Open in outlook and open all day all year, the Igloo is the ideal home-from-home for hostellers seeking rest and recuperation before pursuing the exploits of local hero, Robin Hood, or enjoying the energetic nightlife of this popular university city. Check out the web site for more details: www.igloohostel.co.uk

TELEPHONE CONTACT Steve, Tel: (0115) 9475250, Email: reception@igloohostel.co.uk
OPENING SEASON All year
OPENING HOURS Open all day. 3am curfew.
NUMBER OF BEDS 36
BOOKING REQUIREMENTS Not essential, but advised for groups. Confirm large group booking in writing (deposit may be required).
PRICE PER NIGHT £10 per person. £45 per week.

PUBLIC TRANSPORT
Nottingham has a mainline train station with direct and regular services to London etc. National Express operates from Broadmarsh bus station. From bus/train stations the Igloo is 20 min' walk, a £3 taxi ride or catch Citybus 90 from opposite the train station to Mansfield Rd, ask for International Community Centre, walk uphill for 1 minute.

DIRECTIONS
From the Tourist Information Centre, Market Square, Nottingham, turn right out of T.I.C, take the next left onto Clumber Street and keep walking straight on for ten minutes, past the Victoria Shopping Centre, until you reach the Golden Fleece Pub. The Igloo is diagonally opposite the Pub.

3m

LETTINGO BACKPACKERS

Byron House
1 Brunswood Road
Matlock Bath
Derbyshire DE4 3PA

Nath and Joolz offer you a warm welcome at their Victorian home in the heart of the Derbyshire Dales and Peak National Park - an ideal location to experience the Great Outdoors in an area steeped with history. Right on the doorstep there's lots to do with 1600 miles of public footpaths including the Limestone Way, horse riding, rock climbing, white water canoeing and some of the best mountain biking in Europe. If you feel like something less strenuous, explore Chatsworth House - Palace of the Peak, Haddon Hall - Britain's finest medieval house, or enjoy a cable car ride to the Heights of Abraham.

LettinGo has mixed or private accommodation with great views. Facilities include shop, laundry, luggage store, Internet, travel mags, games and heaps of local info. Within walking distance are shops, pubs and restaurants. So escape the city, come and explore, let go and do something different... or just put your feet up, kickback and relax!

TELEPHONE CONTACT Nath or Joolz (01629) 580686, Email: N&J@LettinGo.freeserve.co.uk www.backpackers.co.uk/matlockbath
OPENING SEASON All year
OPENING HOURS 24 hours - no curfew
NUMBER OF BEDS 11 (1 double, 1x4 and 1x5)
BOOKING REQUIREMENTS To avoid disappointment telephone or Email booking advised. Deposit may be required.
PRICE PER NIGHT £11.50 to £13 per person (including linen)

PUBLIC TRANSPORT

All trains to Matlock Bath start in Derby (only 30 mins away). Frequent buses from Derby, Manchester, Leicester and Nottingham - ask driver to drop you off at cable car stop.

DIRECTIONS

Matlock Bath is 1 mile south of Matlock on the A6 between Derby and Manchester. Turn off A6 into Holme Road by the County and Station pub. LettinGo is 150m up the hill at the fork in the road.

3m

THORPE FARM BUNKHOUSES

Thorpe Farm, Hathersage
Hope Valley
Via Sheffield
S32 1BQ

Thorpe Farm Bunkhouses are situated a mile northeast of Hathersage, on a family run mixed/dairy farm. It is 2 miles from Stanage Edge and other popular climbing and walking areas are nearby. Castleton is 6 miles up the Hope Valley and Eyam is 6 miles southwest.

The dormitories have individual bunks each with mattress and pillow. There is some sleeping space in the sitting room and room for camping outside. The bunkhouses have heating, drying facilities, hot showers, toilets, electric cooking, fridges, freezers, electric kettles, toasters etc.

TELEPHONE CONTACT Jane Marsden (01433) 650659
OPENING SEASON All year
OPENING HOURS No restriction
NUMBER OF BEDS 60 (2 x 14, 3 x 8, 2 x 4)
BOOKING REQUIREMENTS For weekends it is highly recommended to book or enquire.
PRICE PER NIGHT From £6 per person, or sole use of bunkhouse from £80 per night.

PUBLIC TRANSPORT
There is a train station at Hathersage, 10 minutes' walk from the bunkhouse. Bus service 272 operates from Sheffield to Hathersage. On weekends only bus service 257 operates from Sheffield via Stanage and Snake Pass to Hathersage. For bus details phone Busline (01298) 230980 or (01246) 250450.

DIRECTIONS
GR 223 824. **If walking** from A6187/A625 in Hathersage turn right up Jaggers Lane (just past George Hotel); turn second right up Coggers Lane and fifth turning on left (Signed Thorpe Farm). **If driving** follow the road from Hathersage towards Hope for three quarters of a mile, then turn right into private drive (Signposted Thorpe Farm).

PINDALE FARM
OUTDOOR CENTRE
Pindale Lane
Hope, Nr Sheffield
S30 2RN

The Centre is situated ⅔rds of a mile from Castleton in the heart of
the Peak District. The centre comprises of a farmhouse pre-dating
1340 and lead mine buildings from the 1850s. These have been
completely rebuilt from a near derelict condition in 1988, and opened
by H.R.H. The Prince of Wales. The Centre now offers 5 different
kinds of accommodation. The farmhouse offers traditional bed and (an
AGA cooked) breakfast. The Barn has 6 independent self-catering
units, the lower 3 of these can accommodate people with certain
physical disabilities. The old Lead Mine Engine House, our logo, is
a self-catering unit sleeping 8. The Powder House, originally the
mine's explosive store, is a small camping barn with basic facilities for
up to 4 people. A campsite, adjacent to the Centre, has showers, hot
water, and toilet facilities. The Centre is the ideal base for walking,
climbing, caving, horse riding etc. Instruction is available if required.
Well behaved pets welcome. www.pindale.businessfs.co.uk

TELEPHONE CONTACT Alan, Tel: (01433) 620111, Email:
pindalefarm@tingonline.uk
OPENING SEASON All year (Camping March-October)
OPENING HOURS 24 hours.
NUMBER OF BEDS 64 bunkbeds plus camping and B&B
BOOKING REQUIREMENTS Booking advisable for specific dates.
Early booking is best.
PRICE PER NIGHT All prices are per person, per night. Camping
£3.50, Powder House £5, Engine House and Barn £7, B&B £20, £25
with four poster bed.

PUBLIC TRANSPORT
Hope has a train station. The nearest National Express service is in
Sheffield. Approximate taxi fare to Sheffield is £15-£20. On local
buses ask for Hope. Hope is 15 minutes' walk from the hostel.

DIRECTIONS
GR 163 825 From Hope follow cement works signs, turn off main
road between church and Woodroffe Arms.

THE STABLES
BUNKHOUSE BARN
Ollerbrook Farm
Edale
Hope Valley
S53 7ZG

The Stable Bunkhouse is a recently converted barn, on a working farm, near the start of the Pennine Way and Kinder Scout. The village of Edale is half a mile away, with a Post Office, village store, two pubs serving food and the railway station. A Peak Information Centre is also located in the village. This is ideal walking country, with a pleasant walk over the Mam Tor ridge to Castleton and its caves. Other places of interest include Buxton, Bakewell and Chatsworth which are all within 40 minutes' driving time. Sheffield is 18 miles away.

The bunkhouse has the capacity to sleep 16 in 4 rooms - each with bunks for sleeping four people. Each bunk has a mattress and pillow but please bring a sleeping bag. Fully centrally heated with 2 showers, 2 toilets, drying facilities, dining area and fully equipped kitchen. There is adequate car parking for all. The bunkhouse has few restrictions, a no-smoking policy, no under 16s without supervision and no pets please.

TELEPHONE CONTACT Mr Thornley (01433) 670235
OPENING SEASON All year
OPENING HOURS After 3.00 pm
NUMBER OF BEDS 14 Adult and 2 Child
BOOKING REQUIREMENTS Booking required with £40 deposit
PRICE PER NIGHT £8.00 per person

PUBLIC TRANSPORT
Edale Railway Station is just half a mile away.

DIRECTIONS
GR 128 858. Ollerbrook Booth is marked on the map. 10 minutes' walk from Edale Railway Station.

WOODIES BACKPACKERS

19 Blossom Street
Ancoats
Manchester
M4 6AA

Woodies Backpackers is Manchester's only central, independent hostel, just five minutes from the rail and bus stations. It is close to the trendy shopping and buzzing nightlife of Manchester. Explore the local sights such as Manchester United Football Club, the museums and galleries. You could also try Woodies unique experience - the renowned and extremely good fun 'Pop and Pub Tour'.

The hostel is popular, friendly and relaxed with a cosy and comfortable lounge/chill-out area, nice hot showers, good quality bunks, Internet access, a huge kitchen and lockers for your valuables. Open 24 hours a day with no curfews - come and enjoy the experience.

TELEPHONE CONTACT Andy Lyon (0161) 228 3456
OPENING SEASON All year
OPENING HOURS 24 hours
NUMBER OF BEDS 30
BOOKING REQUIREMENTS For weekend booking is essential - one week in advance, credit card required for deposit.
PRICE PER NIGHT £12pp Dorm, £26 for two in a Double, £16 Single (£59 per weekend) all inclusive of tax.

PUBLIC TRANSPORT
Manchester central train and bus station 5 to 10 minutes' walk. Piccadilly bus terminal for all local buses is 3 minutes' walk.

DIRECTIONS
By car - from the A57(M) take the A6010 (Gt. Ancoats St.). Go past the retail park, turn right into Redhill, this leads to Blossom Street. By foot - from Piccadilly train station walk to Piccadilly Gardens, up Newton Street and then straight across Gt. Ancoats St. into Blossom Street. From Chorlton St. National Express bus station, turn right up Portland Street and go straight up Newton Street and then straight across Gt. Ancoats Street onto Blossom Street. Hostel is next to the Edinburgh Castle Public House.

 5m

PEPPERS BACKPACKERS HOSTEL

17 Great Stone Road
Stretford, Trafford
Manchester
M32 0ZP

Peppers is a small (14 bed) clean, friendly, comfortable and privately run establishment, you might say "home from home". Peppers is a smoke free zone but we provide a second TV lounge for smokers only. Continental breakfasts are available on request at a nominal fee. Tea and coffee are provided free of charge as are the showers. Peppers is close to the Metro which is 8 minutes from the city centre. Manchester United Football Ground and Old Trafford Cricket Ground, pubs, shops, "take aways", are all within a 5 minute walk. Stretford Leisure Centre, tennis courts, swimming pool, park and bus stop are within a 2 minute walk. We offer reduced rates for extended stays / out of season.

TELEPHONE/FAX CONTACT tel/fax: (0161) 848 9770, or 0370 303009
OPENING SEASON All year
OPENING HOURS Open all day, but phone first.
NUMBER OF BEDS 14
BOOKING REQUIREMENTS Advisable in peak season. 1-2 weeks in advance. Deposit secures, phone first for availability.
PRICE PER NIGHT From £8 per person. Weekly rate of £6.50 per night. (Reduced out of season and for extended stays.)

PUBLIC TRANSPORT
Manchester has train stations and is served by National Express. Transpeak buses travel from Nottingham to Manchester every two hours and there is a bus link to the airport (Busline 01332 292200). There are trams and buses from central Manchester to hostel.

DIRECTIONS
Take Metro from city centre to Old Trafford Station (approx 8 mins). From station, exit by crossing under tracks passing Old Trafford Cricket Ground (see sign). Take first left at lights. Pass police station and Trafford College. Take next right onto Great Stone Rd, hostel is 190 metres on right hand side. Opposite Stretford School entrance.

MANCHESTER BACKPACKER'S HOSTEL - (JOAN'S PLACE)

41-43 Greatstone Road
Between Talbot Road and Chester Road
Stretford
Manchester, M32 0ZP

'Joan's Place' is a friendly Home-Hostel with garden and patio area. We are 1½ miles west of the centre of Manchester. Salford Quays (Manchester's Dockland), Manchester United, Lancashire County Cricket Club and White City Megabowl are all only minutes away. There is a sports/swimming centre at the end of the road and cinemas, bars and restaurants nearby. Trafford centre 10 minutes' drive.

We are opening another hostel in the city, close to the railway station with prices from £10 per night. For further details of our new 'Holistic Hostel' contact Joan. The hostel will offer a mixture of accommodation with private rooms and dormitory beds catering for up to 40 visitors. Hope to see you there.

TELEPHONE CONTACT Joan tel; (0161) 8723499 / 0411 556157, fax; (0161) 8659296, Email: manchester.backpacker@good.co.uk
OPENING SEASON All year
OPENING HOURS By arrangement - no curfew
NUMBER OF BEDS 30
BOOKING REQUIREMENTS Always telephone ahead for availability and to arrange check in times
PRICE PER NIGHT £6.50-£10(dorm), £26 (twin), £14 (single)

PUBLIC TRANSPORT

Manchester has two train stations and is served by National Express. There are buses from Nottingham every two hours and from Liverpool every hour. There is also a bus link to the airport (Busline 01332 292200). From central Manchester take a tram and ask for Old Trafford, or take a bus and ask for Stretford Leisure Centre.

DIRECTIONS

Metro (tram) to Old Trafford. Follow signs for football and cricket grounds. Turn left at cricket ground, turn right at college - 1st house. Travelling by road take A56 Chester Rd, this is linked to Talbot Rd by the road of the hostel (Greatstone Rd).

3m

EMBASSIE INDEPENDENT HOSTEL

1 Falkner Square
Liverpool
L8 7NU

The Embassie is a terrace house in an unspoilt Georgian square used in the filming of *'In the Name of the Father'*. The house was built in 1820 and until 1986 it was the Consulate of Venezuela. It is only 15 minutes' walk from the city centre. Liverpool is known for its nightlife, a student population of 70,000 ensures a lively scene, bands start playing at 11pm and bars are regularly open till 2am. Hostellers have a key to come and go, the hostel is clean, safe and staffed 24 hours. Bedding is provided (including sheets) and free coffee, tea, toast and jam are available 24 hours, eat as much as you want.

International, or UK regional travellers only, NO LOCALS.

TELEPHONE CONTACT Kevin (0151) 7071089
OPENING SEASON All year
OPENING HOURS Please book in between 9am and 12am (phone if arriving later). Key given for 24hr access.
NUMBER OF BEDS 32
BOOKING REQUIREMENTS Booking is not essential for individuals. Groups larger then 6 should book (20% deposit).
PRICE PER NIGHT £10.50

PUBLIC TRANSPORT
Liverpool has a train station and is served by National Express Coaches. A £2.50 taxi fare will bring you from the train or bus station to the hostel door, (good idea if you have a heavy rucksack).

DIRECTIONS
From the Anglican Cathedral (the third largest in the world) continue uphill along Canning Street away from the city centre. This will bring you into Falkner Square (10-15 mins). The hostel has a red door and is by a phone box.

HARBOUR GRANGE
BACKPACKERS HOSTEL
Spital Bridge
Whitby
North Yorkshire
YO22 4EF

Harbour Grange is an independent backpackers' hostel beautifully situated on the river Esk, in Whitby itself and only ten minutes' walk from bus and train stations. The hostel has good facilities for self-catering. The accommodation is in five dormitories and family rooms are also available.

Whitby is a beautiful little fishing town surrounded by beaches and moorland. Here you can find stunning views from cliff walks and visit lovely villages like Grosmont where steam trains run to Pickering, and Goathland where *Heartbeat* is filmed. Take a look at where Captain Cook lived, and the Abbey that has stood as a landmark for the last 800 years.

Email Backpackers@HarbourGrange.onyxnet.co.uk

TELEPHONE CONTACT (01947) 600817 Birgitta Ward-Foxton.
OPENING SEASON All year
OPENING HOURS All day. Last check in 8pm.
NUMBER OF BEDS 26
BOOKING REQUIREMENTS Booking advised for weekends and for groups. A deposit of 10% is required
PRICE PER NIGHT From £8 per person. The hostel can be hired for sole use by groups for £160 a night.

PUBLIC TRANSPORT
Whitby has a train station.

DIRECTIONS
From Whitby train and bus stations: cross the bridge and turn right. Follow the river.

 3m

YORK CITY CENTRE
YOUTH HOTEL

NO MEMBERSHIP REQUIRED
NO CURFEW (OPEN 24 HOURS)

Meals Available

Bike Hire

DORMITORIES
4-6 BEDDED ROOMS
TWIN ROOMS
SINGLE ROOMS
FAMILY ROOMS
TV LOUNGE

SHOP
SNACKS
REFRESHMENTS (24 hours)
NIGHT PORTER
INFORMATION SERVICE

Kitchen

Laundry

INDIVIDUALS & GROUPS WELCOME

Telephone

Beds

Bar

Games Room

Showers

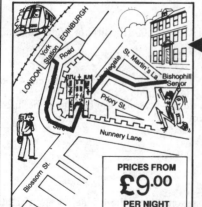

WE ARE HERE

ユース ホステル

YUNGDOMSHARBARGE
OSTELLO
AUBERGE DE JEUNESSE
ALBERGUE JUVENIL
JUGENDHERBERGE

BISHOPHILL HOUSE
11/13 BISHOPHILL SENIOR
YORK YO1 1EF

TEL: (01904) 625904 or
630613

Enjoy the relaxed atmosphere of this early Georgian Residence in the company of fellow Budget Travellers.

PRICES FROM
£9.00
PER NIGHT

Visit our web site at   www.yorkyouthhotel.demon.co.uk

SUE'S PLACE

51 Dijon Avenue
Acomb
York
North Yorkshire
YO24 3DH

This pleasant terraced house has central heating and two spare beds. When I'm around (phone to enquire) you are welcome to stay. Do-it-yourself catering is the order of the day, but B&B is available if required. Come along and share my kitchen and help yourself to a relaxing bath or shower.

The house is opposite a green in a suburb of York, 2 miles from the city centre on frequent bus routes. This makes it ideal for backpackers and those on a tight budget. Walk along the city walls or fascinating medieval streets. Explore York's magnificent Minster and museums, or enjoy the pavement artists, street performers and the vibrant night scene.

Come along and enjoy homely accommodation in the historic city of York. A warm welcome awaits!

No under 16s.

TELEPHONE CONTACT Sue (01904) 782414
OPENING SEASON Phone to enquire
OPENING HOURS By arrangement
NUMBER OF BEDS 2+
BOOKING REQUIREMENTS Advance booking essential.
PRICE PER NIGHT From £8.

PUBLIC TRANSPORT
York has a train station and is served by National Express. Take bus 1,2 or 7 from opposite train station, or from bus station and ask for bus stop by Acomb shops. The hostel is 2 miles from the town centre, approx taxi fare from station £3.50.

DIRECTIONS
Please telephone for full directions.

 3m

WEST END OUTDOOR CENTRE

Whitmoor Farm, West End
Summerbridge, Harrogate
HG3 4BA

Situated in the Yorkshire Dales amidst stunning landscape overlooking Thruscross Reservoir in a designated Area of Outstanding Natural Beauty on the edge of the Dales National Park, this self-catering accommodation centre offers excellent facilities for up to 30 people in 9 bedrooms with bunk beds. Leaders' en-suite accommodation has private catering, dining and lounge facilities. The centre is fully centrally heated. There are 4 showers, 4 hand basins and 4 toilets. There are no extra charges for heating, lighting and hot water. The well-equipped kitchen includes a 4-oven Aga cooker, two fridges and a freezer, together with all the cooking utensils and equipment. Ideal for Team Building Courses, Schools, Scouts, Guides and family parties etc. Located only 12 miles from Harrogate and Skipton, 30 miles from the City of York. Tourist Board inspected and managed by the owners. All teenagers must be accompanied by an adult (25+). Ask for one of our brochures or find us on the web.

Web page : www.yorkshirenet.co.uk/accgde/westend

TELEPHONE CONTACT (01943) 880207, Email: m.verity@virgin.net
OPENING SEASON All year
OPENING HOURS Flexible
NUMBER OF BEDS 30
BOOKING REQUIREMENTS Advisable at weekends
PRICE PER NIGHT £7.50 pp. Sole use £170 (Sat/Sun/Bank Hol), £150 any other night, £500 for 4 nights midweek. Sunday night - if staying for more than 2 nights (not bank holidays) £100.

PUBLIC TRANSPORT
Nearest train stations are at Harrogate and Skipton, both 12 miles from the hostel. Taxi fare from either station would be approximately £15.

DIRECTIONS
GR 146 575. Leave A59 at Blubberhouses, signed West End 2½ miles. Do not turn off, centre is on left side.

AIRTON QUAKER HOSTEL
The Nook
Airton, Skipton
North Yorkshire
BD23 4AE

Airton Quaker Meeting house was built in 1690 by William Ellis and the adjoining hostel was originally a stable for the Quakers attending the meetings. The stable was converted into a wartime evacuee hostel in 1940 and used as a holiday hostel from 1943 with a modernisation in 1983. The meeting house is still used for worship. The hostel is situated in the centre of Airton, a typical Yorkshire Dales village on the banks of the River Aire. The Pennine Way passes the village and Malham Cove, Janet's Foss and Gordale Scar are within walking distance.

The hostel has a self-catering kitchen/common area, and three rooms of 8,4,2 bunks. Blankets and pillow are provide but you must bring your own sheets/sleeping bag liners. There is no shop at Airton, the nearest supplies are in Gargrave. Parties of children (except families) must be accompanied by two adults.

TELEPHONE CONTACT Mr or Mrs Parker (01729) 830263
OPENING SEASON All year
OPENING HOURS No Restrictions
NUMBER OF BEDS 14
BOOKING REQUIREMENTS Advanced booking is recommended with a deposit of 10%
PRICE PER NIGHT £5 (adults) £3 (Children under 16). Exclusive use of the hostel is available for a supplement charge.

PUBLIC TRANSPORT
Nearest train stations Gargrave (4½miles), Skipton (8½miles). Buses from Skipton to Malham pass through Airton. Approx taxi fare from Skipton £5.

DIRECTIONS GR 904 592 Block of buildings at the end of Airton Village on the top of the hill leading down to the river bridge.

HILL TOP FARM
BUNKBARN

Hill Top Farm
Malham, Nr Skipton
North Yorkshire
BD23 4DJ

Hill Top Farm Bunkbarn adjoins a 17th-century farmhouse in the village of Malham. Malham is one of the most popular of all Craven's tourist areas, in close proximity to the Pennine Way, Malham Cove, Gordale Scar and Malham Tarn. Situated in perfect walking country, local amenities include pubs, restaurants, shops, post office and a tourist information centre.

The Bunkbarn is Regional Tourist Board Inspected. It is centrally heated with radiators in all rooms and there is a large drying room. Sleeping accommodation is provided in six bedrooms of 11,8,6,3,2 and 2 beds. There are toilets, washbasins, showers and a well equipped kitchen with electric cooking, fridge etc. The large dining and recreation room has magnificent views of Malhamdale. Milk is delivered daily and freezer food can be ordered before your stay. Hill Top Farm Bunkbarn is ideal for family parties, school parties, youth groups and walkers. Some of the facilities are suitable for the disabled.

TELEPHONE CONTACT Annie Heseltine (01729) 830320
OPENING SEASON All year
OPENING HOURS 24 hours
NUMBER OF BEDS 32
BOOKING REQUIREMENTS Booking is not essential but is advised. Deposit is required with a letter of confirmation.
PRICE PER NIGHT £7.50 per person or £190 sole use.

PUBLIC TRANSPORT
There are train stations at Skipton (11 miles) and Settle (6 miles). National Express coaches stop at Skipton. There are some buses from Skipton to Malham.

DIRECTIONS GR 899 631 The Bunkbarn is in the village of Malham on the Pennine Way, 11 miles from Skipton and 6 miles from Settle.

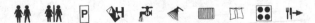

THE GOLDEN
LION BUNKROOM
Horton-in-Ribblesdale
Nr. Settle
North Yorkshire
BD24 0MB

The Golden Lion Bunkroom is part of the Hotel and is situated in the Yorkshire Dales overlooking Pen-y-ghent. It makes an ideal base for the adventurous who are tackling the 'Three Peaks' or a welcome break for Pennine Way Walkers. It is believed that The Golden Lion was a coaching inn during the sixteenth century and the old coach highway can still be followed on foot.

Three public bars provide a good selection of real ales and The Flag Floored Tap Room makes an ideal place for people who enjoy outdoor activities - even in wet weather there is no need to remove boots to enjoy a refreshing drink. At weekends this bar is used extensively by the local pothole clubs and singing sessions are not uncommon. Visitors with musical instruments and plenty of enthusiasm are welcome! A variety of food can provide anything from a beefburger to an a la carte menu. Vegetarian meals are also available.

TELEPHONE/FAX CONTACT Michael Johnson, Tel/Fax: (01729) 860206, Email The.Golden.Lion@kencomp.net
OPENING SEASON All year (except Christmas Day)
OPENING HOURS 11.00 am to 11.00 pm
NUMBER OF BEDS 15
BOOKING REQUIREMENTS Booking recommended with deposit of £3.50 per person
PRICE PER NIGHT £7.00

PUBLIC TRANSPORT
Nearest train stations are Settle (6 miles) and Horton (½ mile). Three buses a day stop near to the Golden Lion Hotel. Taxi fare to Settle is approximatly £5-£6.

DIRECTIONS
Follow signs from Settle to Horton-in-Ribblesdale. We are opposite the Church.

DUB COTE BUNKHOUSE

Dub Cote Farm
Horton in Ribblesdale
Nr. Settle
North Yorkshire
BD24 0ET

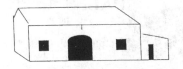

Dub Cote is located on the flanks of Pen-y-gent, it lies half a mile from Horton in Ribblesdale. Situated in a quiet location with fantastic views of Pen-y-ghent, Ingleborough and Whernside, it is ideally situated for the Three Peaks, Pennine Way, caving, cycling (CTC reg) and walking.

The barn was tastefully converted in 1982 to provide civilised self-catering accommodation for up to 14 people. Upstairs there is a fully equipped kitchen, washing and toilet facilities, including ladies' and gents' washrooms, separate toilets and shower. Downstairs there are four bedrooms with bunkbeds with full size spring interior mattresses, pillows and over blanket (sleeping bag required) plus a heated drying room with tumble dryer. In nearby Horton in Ribblesdale there are two pubs to enjoy, cafe and post office shop. No dogs please.

www.yorkshirenet.co.uk/ydales/bunkbarns/hortoninr

TELEPHONE CONTACT (01729) 860238
OPENING SEASON March to January
OPENING HOURS 24 Hours
NUMBER OF BEDS 14 beds (4 rooms accommodate 2,2,4,6 people)
BOOKING REQUIREMENTS Essential only at weekends.
PRICE PER NIGHT £7.25per person (reductions for mid-week block bookings). Price includes electricity.

PUBLIC TRANSPORT
Three quarters of a mile to the nearest railway station at Horton in Ribblesdale (Settle to Carlisle line).

DIRECTIONS
GR 819715. The bunkhouse is signposted from the B6479 Settle to Horton in Ribblesdale Road.

SKIRFARE BRIDGE DALES BARN

Northcote
Kilnsey
Skipton, North Yorkshire
BD23 5PT

Skirfare Bridge Dales Barn is a traditional stone barn and is a distinctive feature of the beautiful Dales landscape, standing at the confluence of Upper Wharfedale and Littondale with the Climbers' Challenge, Kilnsey Crag, providing a spectacular backdrop. The area has long been famous for walking, cycling and touring with several footpaths easily accessible from the barn including the Dales way. Kilnsey is nearby where you can find The Kilnsey Park providing day fishing and food as well as The Tennant Arms Hotel for those who prefer a bar snack. Pony trekking is available at Conistone, and at Long Ashes there is an indoor sports centre.

Although altered little on the outside, internally the Barn has been converted to provide centrally heated accommodation in six ground floor bedrooms with fully equipped kitchen, common room, drying room and showers on the upper floor.

TELEPHONE CONTACT Mrs J Foster (01756) 752465
OPENING SEASON All year round
OPENING HOURS 4.00 pm to 10.30 am
NUMBER OF BEDS 25 in 6 bedrooms
BOOKING REQUIREMENTS Booking essential, up to 6 months in advance for weekend block bookings (Friday, Saturday nights)
PRICE PER NIGHT £7.00 pp or £150 for full Barn booking

PUBLIC TRANSPORT
Skipton Railway Station is 12 miles away. There are also buses from Bradford, Keighley and Harrogate. Infrequent up-Dales bus service runs directly past the Barn, phone (01132) 457676 for details.

DIRECTIONS
From Skipton take B6265 to Threshfield then the B6160 towards Kettlewell for 3 miles. Past the farm the Barn is a further 400m North. 1 mile from the Dales way at Conistone-with-Kilnsey, turn into the Barn just before Arncliffe T junction.

THE BARNSTEAD

Stacksteads Farm
Ingleton
Carnforth
Lancs. LA6 3HS

The Barnstead is situated in the beautiful Yorkshire Dales, one mile from Ingleton village centre. It has panoramic views of Ingleborough and Whernside, and is within easy access of the Lake District and Lancashire coast. Local attractions include rambling, fell walking, pot-holing, climbing and geological and historic sites.

The Barnstead provides bunk-style self-catering accommodation, in two separate units, for individuals, families or groups. Both units are centrally heated, sleeping bag liners, duvets and pillows are provided, inclusive of price. <u>Unit One</u> has:- 22 beds in 4 dorms, large lounge/dining area, drying room, large fitted kitchen (with cookers, fridges, freezer, crockery and utensils) and male & female washrooms with showers. <u>Unit Two</u> has:- One 6 bed dorm, kitchen/lounge and washroom with shower. No extras. Tourist Board Inspected with full N.I.C.E.I.C certificate.

TELEPHONE/FAX CONTACT Wendy/Steve Moorhouse
Tel: (015242) 41386, Fax: (015242) 42407,
Email: stackstead@ingleton90.freeserve.co.uk
OPENING SEASON All year
OPENING HOURS 24 hours
NUMBER OF BEDS (Unit 1) 22 beds (Unit 2) 6 beds.
BOOKING REQUIREMENTS Pre-booking advised with as much notice as possible. Deposit required.
PRICE PER NIGHT (Unit 1) £8 per person or £145 for exclusive use. (Unit 2) £8 per person (minimum of 4).

PUBLIC TRANSPORT
Nearest train station (Bentham) 3 miles. Nearest buses (Ingleton) 1 mile.

DIRECTIONS
GR 686 724. On main A65 Kirkby Lonsdale to Settle road. When travelling south turn right at Masons Arms pub in Ingleton. In 300 yards turn right into farm.

WEST VIEW

Thornton-in-Lonsdale
Ingleton
Via Carnforth
Lancashire
LA6 3PJ

Situated in the Yorkshire Dales National Park, and set amongst peaceful woodland and dramatic limestone fells, West View is the ideal place to stay to sample some of the finest unspoilt countryside and caving Britain has to offer.

West View is a newly converted barn providing comfortable, centrally heated overnight or holiday accommodation for individuals and groups. There are two separate bedrooms with bunk beds, each sleeping up to 7 people, shower-rooms and a fully fitted kitchen. A delightful sitting room with colour TV, doubles as a work room for groups, and can be used as an overspill sleeping area if desired. There are also storage areas for rucksacks and equipment and a heated drying room. All supplies may be found locally in Ingleton. Local attractions include Thornton Force Waterfall Walk, the Three Peaks Walk, Whitescar Show Cave, Clapham Cave, the Ribblehead Viaduct and the Settle to Carlisle Railway.

TELEPHONE CONTACT Geoff or Hazel (015242) 41624
OPENING SEASON All Year
OPENING HOURS All hours
NUMBER OF BEDS 14+
BOOKING REQUIREMENTS Advisable (£50 deposit)
PRICE PER NIGHT £9.00 per person.

PUBLIC TRANSPORT
Nearest train station is at Bentham. The station is 4 miles from the hostel. Taxis are usually available.

DIRECTIONS
On A65, turn right ½ mile past Ingleton heading toward Lake District. In ½ mile turn left to Marton Arms, then turn right up the hill towards Dent. West View is ½ mile on left, (sign on the gate).

THE STATION INN
BUNKHOUSE

The Station Inn
Ribblehead
Ingleton, Via Carnforth
North Yorks. LA6 3AS

The Station Inn and Bunkhouse - often referred to as 'the Three Peaks pit stop' - is at the centre of the Three Peaks and at the crossroads of many well known walks including the Dalesway, Pennine Way, Ribbleway, Centurian Way and others. It is set amongst the beautiful and spectacular North Yorkshire Dales National Park at the foot of Whernside, alongside the Settle/Carlisle Railway and the magnificent Ribblehead Viaduct.

The recently refurbished Bunkhouse offers self-catering accommodation comprising of two units sleeping 6 and one unit sleeping 9 with toilets and showers. There is also a self-contained unit, the Bunk Cottage, which sleeps 11. The Pub next door provides bed and breakfast accommodation, bar meals and by prior arrangement will provide breakfasts for the Bunkhouse residents.

TELEPHONE CONTACT Neil or June (015242) 41274
OPENING SEASON All Year
OPENING HOURS 11.00am-4.00pm,6.30pm-11.00pm (pub hrs)
NUMBER OF BEDS 32
BOOKING REQUIREMENTS Booking recommended a month in advance, deposit is required.
PRICE PER NIGHT From £7 per person - Bunk Cottage £8 per person.

PUBLIC TRANSPORT
Ribblehead Station, on the Leeds to Carlisle line, is 100 metres from the hostel.

DIRECTIONS
GR 764792. From A65 at Ingleton take the B6255 towards Hawes. 6 miles from Ingleton the Settle/Carlisle Railway crosses the B6255, the Station Inn is on the left.

COWPERTHWAITE FARM
BUNKHOUSE

Cowperthwaite Farm
Lowgill, Kendal
Cumbria
LA8 9AZ

At the foot of the beautiful Howgills in a peaceful setting, this Bunkhouse Barn is on the edge of the Yorkshire Dales and the Lake District. The Dalesway walk runs past the Farm.

We provide comfortable bunks with clean linen (sleeping bags required), a self-catering kitchen, eating and recreation area, hot showers and toilets in same building, and large drying space.

Free tea and coffee is provided at all times and basic food stuffs are available at the Farmhouse. Packed lunches are always available. Above all we offer a warm welcome to all our guests.

TELEPHONE CONTACT (01539) 824240 Brenda Stokes
OPENING SEASON All Year (Winter - Bookings Only)
OPENING HOURS All day
NUMBER OF BEDS 16
BOOKING REQUIREMENTS Booking only essential in Winter. No deposit required.
PRICE PER NIGHT £8.00 pp (reductions for groups)

PUBLIC TRANSPORT
The nearest train station is in Kendal which is 6 miles from the hostel. It is possible to arange for a lift from the station for a charge of £2 per person. Please phone the hostel to arrange.

DIRECTIONS
GR 609 966 Leave M6 Junction 37. Take Sedbergh Road for quarter of mile. Turn left towards Lambrigg. Railway bridge 2 miles along on left. Across the bridge and we are next turn on the right - over the cattle grid.

THE WALKER'S HOSTEL

Oubas Hill
Ulverston
Cumbria, LA12 7LB

The Walker's Hostel has 30 beds in shared rooms, with between 2 and 7 to a room. One room is a family room with a cot. Breakfasts and evening meals are home cooked and meat free. We have a book exchange, local maps and games and toys for children. We have a no smoking policy in the house, a cycle lockup, a drying room and an open fire. We play good music and the hostel recently won a Green Apple Environment Award.

Ulverston is on the edge of the Lake District. It is an old market town with plenty of good pubs. The Cumbria Way starts at Ulverston and there are street markets on Thursdays and Saturdays as well as other attractions. The lighthouse on Hoad Hill is a famous land mark. The Walker's Hostel is ideally suited for long and short walks. We are happy to give advice on how to get the most from your visit.

TELEPHONE CONTACT Jean Povey (01229) 585588
OPENING SEASON All year
OPENING HOURS Flexible
NUMBER OF BEDS 30
BOOKING REQUIREMENTS Booking is advisable but not essential.
PRICE PER NIGHT £10 Bed and Breakfast; £6 for evening meal. Reductions for children.

PUBLIC TRANSPORT
Ulverston has a good train service, phone 0345 484950 with your train travel enquiries. National Express coaches come from London via Lancaster (phone 0990 808080). Stage coach buses come from the Lake District

DIRECTIONS
From M6 Jn 36 take the A590. On the edge of Ulverston there is a roundabout. Turn left, and left again. From the bus or train station, walk towards town. Turn right down A590. We are just beyond the second roundabout.

ROOKHOW CENTRE
Rusland
Grizedale
South Lakeland
Cumbria
LA12 8LA

Perhaps the best situated small hostel in the Lake District. Peaceful, in 12 acres of its own woodland, but close to the heart of the Lakes, ten minutes from Lake Coniston and Windermere, and on the edge of the famous Grizedale Forest Park with its trails, sculptures and theatre. Superb area for walking, cycling and all outdoor activities. Also for quiet retreat, relaxation, study and artistic pursuits.

The Rookhow Centre was recently created within the former stables of the nearby historic and unique Quaker meeting house which is also available for conferences and group sessions. Guests find the centre warm, comfortable and well equipped. There are three sleeping areas, a self-catering kitchen/dining area and picnic tables and barbecue for warm days.

TELEPHONE CONTACT Warden (01229) 860231
OPENING SEASON All year
OPENING HOURS All day
NUMBER OF BEDS 30 (including meeting house)
BOOKING REQUIREMENTS Booking is essential (deposit).
PRICE PER NIGHT Adult £7.50, half price for under 16s.

PUBLIC TRANSPORT
Nearest train station (Windermere) is 8 miles from the hostel. Daily post bus to the hostel door. Taxi fare from station would be £10.

DIRECTIONS GR 332 896. **From A590** leave at Greenodd (A5092) junction and follow sign for Workington for ¼ mile. Take minor road to right signed Oxen Park. Continue through Oxen Park for a further 2 miles more, Rookhow is on left. **From Ambleside** : to Hawkshead, then to Grizedale. Continue through Grizedale for 3½ miles (Satterthwaite to Ulverston Road). Rookhow is on the right.

FORTYWINX
22 Gillinggate
Kendal
Cumbria
LA9 4JE

Fortywinx is a new hostel located within five minutes' walk from Kendal town centre. There are seven pubs and six takeaways all within 200 metres. Kendal is an old market town in South Cumbria and makes an excellent base for exploring the beautiful Lake District. Easily accessible by public transport, the main line station of Oxenhome is 1½ miles and the National Express Coach stop is ten minutes walk. Local buses 100 metres.

The centrally heated hostel provides accommodation in comfy dorms with all bedding provided. Hot drinks and a light breakfast are included in the prices. Packed lunches, evening meals and laundry facilities can be provided for a small charge. There are a fully equipped kitchen, drying room, lock up for valuables, yard for bicycles and a cosy lounge with games and all local information.

TELEPHONE CONTACT Camilla (01539) 720576
OPENING SEASON All year
OPENING HOURS Flexible
NUMBER OF BEDS 24
BOOKING REQUIREMENTS Advisable
PRICE PER NIGHT £10.00 per person (includes bedding & light breakfast) reductions for Groups and long stays.

PUBLIC TRANSPORT
Oxenholme main line station 1½ miles. Taxis and buses to town - ask for Gillinggate. Bus station and National Express 10 minutes' walk.

DIRECTIONS
GR 514 922. By foot: from Bus St. head for TIC continue down main st. for approx 300m Gillinggate on right. By car: from the south turn left after 2nd traffic lights. Hostel is 50m on right. From north follow south signs, keep in left hand lane, right at roundabout, right at traffic lights and left after next lights, hostel 50m right. Map can be provided.

GRASMERE INDEPENDENT HOSTEL

Broadrayne Farm
Keswick Road, Grasmere
Cumbria LA22 9RU

Opening early 2000, this small friendly independent hostel is set dramatically on the edge of this beautiful valley, at the centre of the Lake District and entirely surrounded by either National Trust or our land. There are many walks from here including the 'Coast to Coast' which is just 100 metres away. We can arrange contacts for all outdoor activities including mountaineering and watersports or try something different like sheepdog training or learning to drive a JCB! This deluxe hostel is ideally suited for individuals, families and small groups. The accommodation is in cosy bunk bedrooms with good views and sleeping from 2 to 5 people, each with wash hand basins. There are separate private shower/wash cubicles. The hostel is fully centrally heated with efficient drying rooms, self-catering kitchen, bike store, television, payphone, BBQ area and good parking. There is a pub just 400 metres down the road serving real ales and hearty food. Visit our website http//:www.broadraynefarm.freeserve.co.uk

TELEPHONE/FAX CONTACT Bev Dennison, Tel: (015394) 35055 (please don't phone after 10pm), Tel/Fax: (015394) 35733, Email: jodennisondrake@broadraynefarm.freeserve.co.uk
OPENING SEASON All year
OPENING HOURS 7.30-10am 4-9pm, other by prior arrangement
NUMBER OF BEDS Approximately 20
BOOKING REQUIREMENTS Please check availability before arriving. Booking with a credit card will secure your bed.
PRICE PER NIGHT £10 to £14 (inc. bedding)

PUBLIC TRANSPORT
Train to Windermere Station (11 miles from hostel), catch 555 bus, get off at Travellers Rest Pub or catch 556 bus to Grasmere, get off at Swan Hotel (open top service in summer).

DIRECTIONS
GR 336 094. 1⅓ miles north of village of Grasmere, off A591 (or 400m north of Travellers Rest Pub). Turn in Broadrayne Farm drive and take 2nd left.

STICKLEBARN
BUNKHOUSE
Sticklebarn Tavern
Great Langdale
Cumbria
LA22 9JU

The Sticklebarn is beautifully situated amidst some of the finest mountain scenery in England. It is at the very foot of the famous Langdale Pikes and Dungeon Ghyll waterfalls and seven miles north west of Ambleside.

The Sticklebarn is unique to Lakeland as it is privately owned and is available to the general outdoor public and traveller on foot. The bunkhouse has no common room or self-catering facilities but there is a TV room and meals service provided in the pub. Sorry no pets. A brochure is available on request.

TELEPHONE CONTACT Peter Ingham (015394) 37356
OPENING SEASON All year
OPENING HOURS Open all day. Food served all day, breakfasts available between 8.00am and 10.30am.
NUMBER OF BEDS Winter 20, Summer 16
BOOKING REQUIREMENTS Pre-booking is advised for weekends and groups (at least 7 days in advance) and requires a deposit or booking form.
PRICE PER NIGHT £10 per person.

PUBLIC TRANSPORT
Bus service 516 to Great Langdale from Ambleside, ask for Old Dungeon Ghyll Hotel, walk 5 mins (phone 01946 632222 for timetable).

DIRECTIONS
From the A591 Windermere to Keswick road at Ambleside take the A593 turn to Coniston / Torver. After two miles take the B5343 to Great Langdale via Chapel Stile. The Bunkhouse is adjacent to the Sticklebarn Tavern.

REST EASY
BUNK HOUSE
2 Central Buildings
Shap, Penrith
Cumbria
CA10 3NG

Rest Easy Bunk House is situated on the edge of the Lake District National Park, and is a suitable stopping point on the Coast-to-Coast long distance footpath. The Bunk House has rooms of 6 beds, 4 beds and 2 beds.

Facilities include showers, a drying room and laundry. Breakfast can be provided, and evening meals are available locally in Shap.

In Shap there are pubs, a cafe, a fish & chip shop, and grocery stores all within 100 yards of the Bunk House.

TELEPHONE CONTACT Hilda (01931) 716538
OPENING SEASON All year
OPENING HOURS Flexible
NUMBER OF BEDS 16
BOOKING REQUIREMENTS Booking advisable, but not essential.
PRICE PER NIGHT £8.00 per person.

PUBLIC TRANSPORT
Nearest train stations are Penrith (approximately 10 miles from the hostel) and Kendal (approximately 15 miles away).

DIRECTIONS GR 563 153   On the A6 10 miles south of Penrith, 2 miles from Junction 39 off the M6.

THE HUDEWAY CENTRE

Stacks Lane
Middleton-in-Teesdale
Co Durham
DL12 0QR

The Hudeway Centre is a converted farmstead situated in two acres of land. Near the Pennine Way in the picturesque Tees valley, it is an excellent base for outdoor pursuits offering superb opportunities for walking, canoeing, sailing, mountain biking and underground exploration.

Courses can also be arranged through the centre with experienced and qualified staff. Alternatively enjoy the abundance of wildlife and have a relaxing countryside holiday. There are also ample resources for field studies work and local industrial visits. Within a quarter of a mile, the village offers shops, pubs and a restaurant. Nearby lies the attractive historic market town of Barnard Castle. Over 18 year olds only unless accompanied by an adult. Families welcome.

TELEPHONE CONTACT Andy or Barbara (01833) 640012
OPENING SEASON All Year
OPENING HOURS 24 hour
NUMBER OF BEDS 24
BOOKING REQUIREMENTS Advisable. 25% deposit required for groups.
PRICE PER NIGHT £10 per person self-catering. Groups of 12+ £8.50 per person.

PUBLIC TRANSPORT
Nearest train station and National Express coach service are in Darlington. Local bus service stops in Middleton-in-Teesdale.

DIRECTIONS GR 943 257. When leaving Middleton-in-Teesdale, follow the B6277 towards High Force. At the Ford garage turn right through two stone gate posts. At the top of the lane turn left past a bench into Stacks lane. The centre is 200m on the lefthand side

THE HAYLOFT BUNKHOUSE

Eden Ostrich World
Langwathby Hall Farm
Langwathby
Penrith
CA10 ILW

The Hayloft Bunkhouse is a tastefully converted sandstone barn situated at Langwathby Hall Farm in the village of Langwathby. The farm also hosts the award winning Eden Ostrich World Visitor Centre. An ideal base to explore the picturesque Eden Valley, the Hayloft is within walking distance of Langwathby Railway station on the scenic Settle to Carlisle Line.

Popular with backpackers and C-2-C cyclists, the bunkhouse provides B&B accommodation. Packed lunches and evening meals are also available on request or simply relax and enjoy a bar meal in the pub next to the village green. There is an abundance of picturesque walks that are accessible for Langwathby which lies at the foot of the Pennines. The Hayloft is an ideal base for school parties. Key Stage 1, 2 & 3 are available for Eden Ostrich World and educational visits to other attractions can be arranged and booked centrally.

TELEPHONE CONTACT (01768) 881771
OPENING SEASON All Year except Christmas and New Year
OPENING HOURS 24 hrs
NUMBER OF BEDS 36 (4 Dormitories)
BOOKING REQUIREMENTS Booking preferred. 50% deposit required.
PRICE PER NIGHT £13 per person B&B. Reductions for stays of two or more nights.

PUBLIC TRANSPORT
Hostel is 400m from Langwathby Railway station. The nearest National Express service is in Penrith (5 miles from hostel).

DIRECTIONS
M6 junction 40. Take A66 east for 1 mile. At roundabout take A686 for Alston. Follow signs for Eden Ostrich World.

1m

THE MINERS ARMS BUNKHOUSE

Nenthead
Alston
Cumbria
CA9 3PF

At 1500ft above sea level, the Miners Arms can probably lay claim to be the highest village pub in England. If you like excellent food (National Prize Winning Cuisine), great beer (guest ales changed weekly), and friendly family hospitality or you just like drinking at altitude - you must try The Miners Arms in Nenthead, it's well worth a visit.

Accommodation is in a bunkhouse which sleeps 12 in four 3 tier bunks, with washing and changing facilities which include 2 sinks and shower/toilet rooms. All bedding is provided, but there are no cooking facilities. Family, double, twin and single accommodation is available for bed and breakfast in the main house. Each room has a colour TV. Tea and coffee are available on request. The Hostel has a secure lockup for bikes and underground equipment. We are the official Stamping Post in Nenthead for the C2C Cycle route, and the Alternative Pennine Way passes through the village.

TELEPHONE CONTACT Alison Clark (01434) 381427
OPENING SEASON All year
OPENING HOURS All day
NUMBER OF BEDS 12
BOOKING REQUIREMENTS Booking recommended, Group bookings must have 50% deposit.
PRICE PER NIGHT £6.50 bed, £10 B+B, Accomodation in the main house £15.

PUBLIC TRANSPORT
There are train stations at Penrith and Hexham. There are National Express services at Carlise and Newcastle. For details of local buses phone Wrights Bus Co (01434) 381200.

DIRECTIONS
On the main road A689 between Durham and Brampton.

HADRIAN'S WALL BACKPACKERS

Hadrian Lodge, North Road
Haydon Bridge, Hadrian's Wall
Northumberland, NE47 6NF

Set in 18 acres of open pasture, bordered by pine forest and overlooking lakes, Hadrian's Wall Backpackers at Hadrian Lodge is only 1½ miles from the most complete section of Hadrian's Wall. Built from the same local stone, this high quality conversion of a large hunting/fishing lodge offers a licensed bar, tea room with hot and cold food, self-catering kitchen, games area with pool table, launderette, drying room and trout fishing on its own private lake (rods available for hire). The accommodation ranges from bunks in cosy dormitories to fully equipped private rooms with TV and video, or even self-catering cottages.

Hadrian Lodge is safe, clean, friendly, comfortable and fun. Its location is ideal for walking, climbing, bird-watching, fishing, cycling or exploring the many historical sites of England's border country. An ideal diversion from the London to Edinburgh east coast mainline by taking the branch line at Newcastle-upon-Tyne, to Haydon Bridge.

TELEPHONE/FAX CONTACT Lyn Murray, Tel: (01434) 688688, Fax: (01434) 684867, Email: hadrianlodge@hadrianswall.co.uk
OPENING SEASON Open every day, April-October (inclusive). Nov-March telephone booking only.
OPENING HOURS 24 hr access. Staffed 8am to midnight.
NUMBER OF BEDS 40
BOOKING REQUIREMENTS Telephone Booking is essential Nov-March. Also advised at peak times.
PRICE PER NIGHT £10 (dorm), from £12.50 (B&B) per person. Group packages and self-catering cottages also available.

PUBLIC TRANSPORT
Haydon Bridge train station is 2 miles below hostel on North Rd. National Express coaches drop off in Haydon Bridge village.

DIRECTIONS
From A1 or M6 take A69 Newcastle to Carlisle rd. Turn north at Railway Hotel in Haydon Bridge. Hostel is 2½ miles on left.

SHITLINGTON CRAG BUNKHOUSE
Near Wark
Hexham
Northumberland
NE48 3QB

Shitlington Crag is a south-facing outcrop lying at the edge of open moorland above the North Tyne Valley in Northumberland. The bunkhouse is in a converted barn adjoining the proprietor's home in an isolated situation on the Pennine Way, and provides self-catering facilities for walkers and others who enjoy wild, open countryside. The accommodation comprises a living-room/kitchen (with wood-burning stove), bathroom, a double bedroom and an upper dormitory. There is limited space for camping (2 tents). In addition to the Pennine Way and the surrounding moorland and upper Tyne Valley, local attractions include Kielder Water and Forest (10 miles away), Hadrian's Wall (12 miles) and the historic market town of Hexham (15 miles).

TELEPHONE CONTACT Keith Turnbull, (01434) 230330
OPENING SEASON All year
OPENING HOURS 8.00am-11.00pm.
NUMBER OF BEDS 6
BOOKING REQUIREMENTS Pre-booking not essential.
PRICE PER NIGHT £5.50 - group bookings negotiable.

PUBLIC TRANSPORT
Train/National Express to Hexham (15 miles). Then Tyne Valley Coaches route 880 (Bellingham) to Billerley Gate, (for information phone 01434 602217 or 01670 533128. Then walk along gated road (ignore two left turns),through farm yard, turn left and follow track (can be muddy) under crags to bunkhouse (1½miles).

DIRECTIONS
GR 829 808 **Walkers**: on Pennine Way between Greenhead (17miles) or Once Brewed (11miles) and Bellingham (2½miles). **Drivers**: Park at TV mast (GR 833 813) and walk south along Pennine Way for 600yds.

JOINERS SHOP BUNKHOUSE

Preston
Chathill
Northumberland
NE67 5ES

The Joiners Shop Bunkhouse is an attractive 17th-century building retaining much of its historical charm and character. It is situated in a quiet hamlet only seven miles from Alnwick, the seat of the Duke of Northumberland, 5 miles from the beautiful Northumberland Coast and 10 miles from Wooler and the Cheviot Hills. The area offers opportunities for walking, climbing, mountain biking, all water sports or simply sightseeing.

The Joiners Shop Bunkhouse has full cooking facilities and a dining area along with a log fire and cosy sitting area. The 18 large pine beds are in heated dormitories of two's and three's and there is a separate unit with its own facilities which sleeps four or five. Lock up is available for bikes and other equipment and there is ample parking for boats, trailers etc. Dogs welcome.

TELEPHONE CONTACT Jacquie Hall, Tel: (01665) 589245, Email: jacquiehall@yahoo.co.uk
OPENING SEASON All year
OPENING HOURS No Restrictions
NUMBER OF BEDS 18 + 4/5
BOOKING REQUIREMENTS Advised for weekends and holidays.
PRICE PER NIGHT £7.50 and £8.50

PUBLIC TRANSPORT
There are train stations at Chathill (1½ miles - limited service) and Alnmouth (10 miles). There are National Express services at Alnwick (10 miles) and Berwick (24 miles). The local Bus company is called ARRIVA and the nearest stop is Brownieside on the A1 (1½ miles).

DIRECTIONS
GR 183 254 Seven miles north of Alnwick on the A1 to Brownieside. Turn off A1 at sign for Preston Tower, hostel is 1½ miles on the left.

1m

THE OUTDOOR TRUST BUNKHOUSE

Windy Gyle
Belford
Northumberland
NE70 7QE

The Outdoor Trust Bunkhouse is in an ideal location with the Cheviot Hills, Northumbrian Heritage Coast, Farne Islands, Rivers Till and Tweed, and many fine crags and forests nearby. Located in village of Belford in North Northumberland with easy access to the A1.

The property is double glazed, has mains gas central heating and is carpeted throughout. A rear extension comprises a kitchen and dining room on the ground floor with shower and toilet facilities above. The dormitories range from 3 to 12 beds.

Exclusive group use and catering service can be arranged. A full range of outdoor activities and instruction are available at the bunkhouse including Canoeing, Kayaking, Climbing/Abseiling.

TELEPHONE CONTACT Helen, (01668) 213289
OPENING SEASON All Year
OPENING HOURS 24 hours
NUMBER OF BEDS 43
BOOKING REQUIREMENTS Booking in advance by phone is preferred.
PRICE PER NIGHT £7.50

PUBLIC TRANSPORT
The hostel is 15 miles from Berwick Upon Tweed train station. There is a bus service 505/501 from Berwick and Newcastle (alight near the Black Swan).

DIRECTIONS
Take the Belford turning off the A1 and we are located near the centre of Belford. Turn down West Street opposite the Spar Supermarket. The Windy Gyle building is 300 metres on the right. Nearest train station Berwick-upon-Tweed.

WALES

All phone numbers are given with the national code required to phone from anywhere in the UK. To phone from overseas remove the first 0 and add 44.

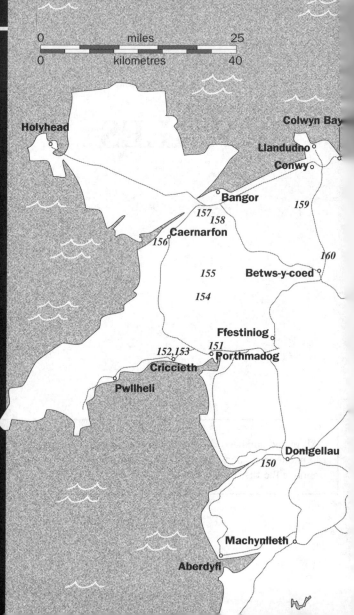

0   miles   25

0   kilometres   40

Holyhead

Colwyn Bay

Llandudno

Conwy

Bangor

157

158

Caernarfon

156

159

160

155

Betws-y-coed

154

Ffestiniog

152,153   *151*

Porthmadog

Criccieth

Pwllheli

Dolgellau

150

Machynlleth

Aberdyfi

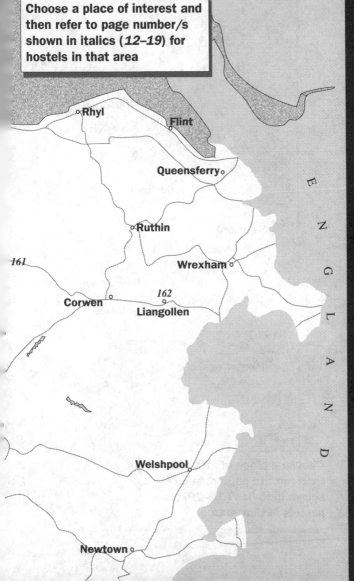

Choose a place of interest and then refer to page number/s shown in italics (*12–19*) for hostels in that area

Rhyl

Flint

Queensferry

Ruthin

161

Wrexham

Corwen

162

Liangollen

Welshpool

Newtown

ENGLAND

North Wales

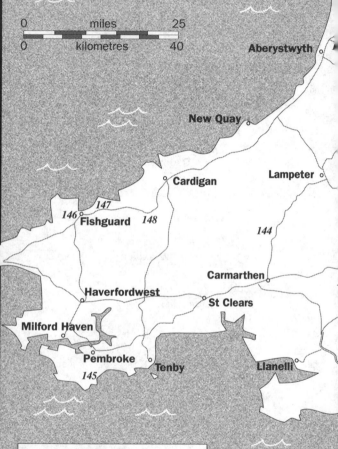

South Wales

0 — miles — 25

0 — kilometres — 40

Aberystwyth

New Quay

Cardigan

Lampeter

147

146 148

Fishguard

144

Carmarthen

Haverfordwest

St Clears

Milford Haven

Pembroke Tenby

Llanelli

145

Choose a place of interest and
then refer to page number/s
shown in italics (*12–19*) for
hostels in that area

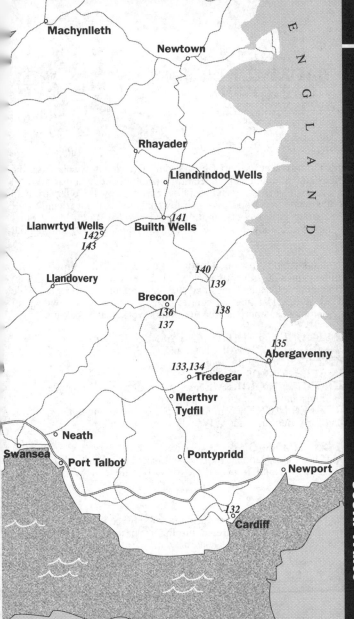

Machynlleth

Newtown

E
N
G
L
A
N
D

Rhayader

Llandrindod Wells

141
Builth Wells

Llanwrtyd Wells
142
143

Llandovery

Brecon
136
137

140
139

138

135
Abergavenny

133,134
Tredegar

Merthyr
Tydfil

Neath

Swansea

Port Talbot

Pontypridd

Newport

132
Cardiff

South Wales

CARDIFF BACKPACKER CAERDYDD

98 Neville Street
Riverside
Cardiff
CF11 6LS

Cardiff's only central tourist hostel, only five minutes walk from the stations and all municipal and central amenities. Enjoy a warm Welsh welcome, whilst relaxing and socialising with fellow travellers from all over the world in Europe's youngest capital city. All our friendly staff are experienced travellers; multilingual in Welsh, English and other languages; and knowledgeable about sights and activities throughout Wales.

Accommodation is in a combination of twin/double and group rooms. Facilities include reception/breakfast area with *essentials* shop; information desk; telephones and fax; comfortable lounge with cable and big screen TV; Internet centre; roof garden; guest bar with pool table and amusements; bicycle and motorcycle secure lock-up.

TELEPHONE CONTACT (029) 20 345577
OPENING SEASON All year round
OPENING HOURS 24 hours
NUMBER OF BEDS 80
BOOKING REQUIREMENTS Booking recommended for individuals and essential (with deposit) for groups.
PRICE PER NIGHT From £13 per person, including light breakfast. Phone for group discounts. Weekly rates available.

PUBLIC TRANSPORT
Cardiff has train, National Express and local bus services all calling at the central bus and train station (5 to 10 minutes' walk from the hostel).

DIRECTIONS
From Cardiff Central Station, turn left crossing the River Taff. Follow the river embankment upstream, turning left past the Riverbank Hotel. We are on the roundabout ahead of you.

1m

BRYN BACH PARK

The Visitor Centre
Merthyr Road
Tredegar
Gwent, NP2 3AY

Set in 600 acres of beautiful country park, Bryn Bach offers self-catering accommodation within our own Countryside Centre. All rooms have heating and washing facilities with a fully fitted kitchen/diner. Breakfasts and packed lunches can be ordered from our excellent lake-side cafe as well as using our on-site information display to plan the rest of your holiday. Other facilities include showers, toilets, laundry, drying room and telephone.

The location is very central and ideal for walking, climbing, caving, canoeing (can be done on site) and pony trekking. The use of a qualified instructor for activities can be booked. The park contains a 36 acre lake, adventure playground, picnic area, orienteering courses and BBQ hire. Camping is also available with a heated shower block.

A warm Welsh welcome awaits any group - large or small.

TELEPHONE CONTACT Rose Bowen (01495) 711816
OPENING SEASON All Year
OPENING HOURS 9am - very flexible
NUMBER OF BEDS 18 +
BOOKING REQUIREMENTS Booking is preferred - phone for availability.
PRICE PER NIGHT £10 per adult. £5 per junior/UB40/oap. 10% reductions for groups of 14 plus.

PUBLIC TRANSPORT
Nearest train stations are at Rhymney (3 miles from hostel) and Merthyr Tydfil (8 miles) on the railway line from Cardiff. Buses from Newport, Cardiff, Brecon and Abergavenny call at Tredegar (3 miles).

DIRECTIONS
GR 126 100. From M4 Junction, follow signs to Tredegar. Well signposted from A465 'Heads of the Valley' road and Rhymney or Tredegar roundabouts.

5m

HOBO BACKPACKERS
Plas y gwely
Central Chambers
Morgan Street
Tredegar NP22 3NB

Tredegar is on the edge of the Brecon Beacons National Park and is ideally placed for walking, mountain biking, caving, waterfall walking, rafting, kayaking, paragliding and more... The Welsh International Indoor Climbing Centre is nearby. We can help organise activities and equipment hire. For 'Culture Vultures' go back in history, explore a coal mine, ride on a steam train or visit a castle or two!

In a hurry! HoBo is an ideal stopping point when travelling between England and Ireland or North and South Wales. Come and explore some 'Welsh valleys' humour and singing. HoBo has a fully equipped kitchen and dining area, with secure storage for bikes etc. The hostel is run by experienced travellers. HoBo is a non smoking building.

HoBo where B&B means Bike's and Boot's welcome

TELEPHONE   CONTACT   (01495)   718422,   Email: hobo_backpackers@hcliff.freeserve.co.uk
OPENING SEASON All year
OPENING HOURS Flexible
NUMBER OF BEDS 30 (in five rooms)
BOOKING REQUIREMENTS Phone to check availability. Groups of 6+ require 20% deposit
PRICE PER NIGHT £10 per person (including linen). Discounts for groups of 12+ and sole use.

PUBLIC TRANSPORT
Nearest mainline station is Cardiff. The Valley Line Railway runs from Cardiff to Rhymney station and there is a connecting bus to Tredegar. National Express coaches run from London to Cardiff, Merthyr and Brecon. There is a Stage Coach bus service from Cardiff (X40) and Brecon (X43) to Tredegar.

DIRECTIONS   From M4 Junction 28, follow signs to Tredegar. From A465 follow the second sign to town centre, or find the town clock, we're just downhill from it!

3m

SMITHY'S BUNKHOUSE

Lower House Farm
Pantygelli
Abergavenny
Monmouthshire
NP7 7HR

Located on a working hill farm, Smithy's Bunkhouse lies in the Black Mountains within the Brecon Beacons National Park, some two miles from the historic market town of Abergavenny. Designed to accommodate a maximum of 24 persons in two dormitories of 12 bunks, additional space is available above the common room if required. The bunkhouse is equipped with showers, toilets, fully equipped kitchen, drying area (with coin operated washer and dryer), public telephone and a common room with wood burning stove. It is heated during the winter by night storage heaters, hot water and electricity are supplied at no extra cost, some firewood is provided and extra may be purchased. A 16th-century coaching inn is located at the top of the farm drive which serves bar snacks, restaurant meals and traditional ales. The area is ideal for walking, climbing, caving, mountain biking, canoeing, water sports, pony trekking.

TELEPHONE/FAX CONTACT Neil or Katy Smith tel; (01873) 853432 fax; (01873) 859833
OPENING SEASON All year
OPENING HOURS 24 hours by arrangement
NUMBER OF BEDS 24
BOOKING REQUIREMENTS Booking is advised with £50 deposit for groups. Cheques payable to Smithy's Bunkhouse.
PRICE PER NIGHT £7 per person, Group bookings £6pp.

PUBLIC TRANSPORT
Nearest train station Abergavenny (2 miles). Taxi fare from station £3 maximum. No local buses.

DIRECTIONS
GR 304 178. Pantygelli village is located two miles north of Abergavenny just off the old Hereford Road. The bunkhouse is down the farm track opposite the Crown Inn.

1m

CANAL BARN

(Ysgubor Camlas)
Ty Camlas
Canal Bank
Brecon
Powys
LD3 7HH

This is different! A quality bunkhouse in a rural setting but actually within a lively market town. Nestling between the river Usk and the canal, Canal Barn is surrounded by fields, and yet is just a short walk from the centre of Brecon, in the heart of the Brecon Beacons National Park. Canal Barn is the base from which to have fun and enjoy the numerous exciting activities available in and around the Park. It is on many walking and cycling routes (on and off road) that criss-cross the Park, including the Taff Trail and Sustrans Lon Las Cymru Route 8, and is an ideal stopover point. Brecon town offers a range of pubs, restaurants, takeaways and entertainment to satisfy most tastes and pockets. Accessible by disabled people, Canal Barn gives excellent value; featuring 6 bedrooms, 5 shower/toilet rooms, centrally heated, unlimited hot water, drying facilities, kitchen, secure equipment store, workshop for cycle/equipment repair, phone/Internet access and a large garden for outdoor games, barbecues or just crashing out.

TELEPHONE CONTACT Ralph or Liz, Tel: (01874) 625361, Email: Ralph@antur-camlas.u-net.com
OPENING SEASON All year
OPENING HOURS All day
NUMBER OF BEDS 24 (in 6 rooms)
BOOKING REQUIREMENTS Advanced booking advised.
PRICE PER NIGHT From £10

PUBLIC TRANSPORT
Hourly train service to Merthyr Tydfil (20 miles) with connecting bus to Brecon. Daily bus service from Cardiff to Brecon (arrives 18:20).

DIRECTIONS
GR SO 052 279. On the canal towpath a short walk from Brecon town centre. Vehicular access is via the canal bridge situated next to the BP Petrol Station on the nearby Abergavenny to Brecon road (B4601).

THE HELD BUNKHOUSE

Cantref, Brecon
Powys
LD3 8LT

Thousands of visitors have already enjoyed staying at The Held Bunkhouse since it opened in 1988. Its isolated situation with spectacular views to the mountain tops makes it a superb base for a wide range of outdoor adventurous activities, expedition training, residential courses or simply for family recreation.

The Bunkhouse has a spacious common room with fully equipped kitchen. There are 24 sleeping spaces in 5 bedrooms (2,4,4,6,8); five individual washrooms each with W.C. and power shower; lashings of hot water; central heating throughout - all included in the price. There is a balcony from the common room with a stairway leading to the barbecue terrace. Groups large or small are welcome on either a 'willing-to-share' or 'sole occupancy' basis. Individuals, families and couples are also welcome. The price is the same for everyone; £8.50 per person per night. Sorry no dogs allowed. More information? Phone for a brochure.

Under new ownership and refurbished

TELEPHONE CONTACT Christina Mitchell (01874) 624646
OPENING SEASON All year
OPENING HOURS 24 hours by arrangement
NUMBER OF BEDS 24
BOOKING REQUIREMENTS Always phone in advance.
PRICE PER NIGHT £8.50 per person

PUBLIC TRANSPORT
Train stations and National Express service at Abergavenny and Brecon. Approximate taxi fare to hostel from Brecon £3.

DIRECTIONS
GR 036 266. Situated 2 miles south of Brecon town and 2 miles from the foot of the central Brecon Beacons. Phone for more detailed directions.

TREKKERS' BARN
The Castle Inn
Pengenffordd
Near Talgarth
Powys. LD3 0EP

The Trekkers' Barn is a traditional stone barn some 200 years old. Located at over 1,000 feet above sea level in the rural heart of the Black Mountains which make up the northern half of the Brecon Beacons National Park. There are spectacular views of the surrounding hills.

The barn is divided into 2 rooms, one with 6 bunks, the other with 4 bunks, chairs, benches and tables - several fold up beds are also available. In addition at one end of the barn there are male and female toilets both with sinks with hot and cold water. At the other end the shower block contains 2 showers and 2 wash hand basins. The whole barn and adjoining rooms are fully centrally heated and hot water is plentiful. The Barn is unique in that it is part of the Castle Inn, which is a traditional style country inn. In the evenings you can relax by an open log fire and replenish yourself with an economically priced meal or choose from a selection of Real Ales.

TELEPHONE/FAX CONTACT Paul (01874) 711353, fax (01874) 711353, Email: castlepen@aol.com
OPENING SEASON All year
OPENING HOURS 8.00 am to 12 midnight
NUMBER OF BEDS 20
BOOKING REQUIREMENTS Credit Card number
PRICE PER NIGHT £12 B&B without linen - or £14 B&B with linen and towels.

PUBLIC TRANSPORT
Nearest train station is at Abergavenny. Taxi fare from Abergavenny to hostel is approximately £10. Local bus runs from Brecon to Talgarth which is then 4 miles' walk from the hostel.

DIRECTIONS
Part of Castle Inn alongside A479, 4 miles south of Talgarth, 8 miles north of Crickhowell.

 3m

JOE'S LODGE
Hay Road
Talgarth
Nr Brecon
Powys, LD3 0AL

Joe's Lodge is a non-smoking bunkhouse offering warm and dry budget accommodation for individuals or groups. Exclusive use can be offered to groups of 18+ at weekends (15+ during the week). Breakfast can be provided by arrangement, and there is plenty of good value pub grub (& real ale) nearby.

Joe's Lodge is situated at the foot of the Black Mountains, between the River Wye and the Brecon Beacons. It is ideal for walking, cycling and horse riding. The river Wye offers canoeing, kayaking or white water rafting in the winter. Sailing and wind surfing are available on Llangorse Lake, and qualified instructors can be arranged for caving, abseiling and gorge walking. An international indoor rope climbing centre is 5 miles away. We have a drying room, bike storage and ample parking.

TELEPHONE CONTACT Janet (01874) 711845
OPENING SEASON All year
OPENING HOURS By arrangement
NUMBER OF BEDS 28
BOOKING REQUIREMENTS No later than one week in advance with 10% deposit.
PRICE PER NIGHT Self catering £7, B&B £10 per person.

PUBLIC TRANSPORT
Rail services to Abergavenny (18 miles) or Hereford (20 miles). National Express coaches from London to Brecon. Good bus service from Hereford and Brecon to Talgarth. Phone Talgarth Tourist Information Centre for transport details (01874) 711044.

DIRECTIONS
GR 155 340 (sheet 161). Talgarth is on A479 between Crickhowell and Bronllys. From town square, walk 150yds past MACE shop (on left), Joe's Lodge is on left.

TRERICKET MILL BUNKHOUSE

Erwood
Builth Wells
Powys
LD2 3TQ

Across the stream from Trericket Corn Mill this stone bunkhouse in an old cider orchard overlooks the river Wye. It is particularly suitable for small groups and individuals with two rooms sleeping four people each and an additional en-suite bunkroom for two in the mill. The bunkhouse is clean and cosy; heating, hot water and showers are all inclusive. Limited self-catering facilities are provided in a covered outdoor kitchen. Alternatively breakfasts and packed lunches can be provided and good pub meals are available locally. There are heated drying and common rooms in the mill. Camping is also available.

Situated on the Wye Valley Walk and National Cycle Route Eight. An ideal stop-over for walkers, cyclists and for others wishing to spend time in the beautiful countryside of Mid Wales. Canoeing, pony trekking, gliding, mountain bikes, rope centre and white water rafting all available locally. Brochure on request.

TELEPHONE/FAX CONTACT Alistair/Nicky Legge, Tel: (01982) 560312, Fax: (01982) 560768
OPENING SEASON All year
OPENING HOURS 24 hour access
NUMBER OF BEDS 10 bunks plus 6 veggie B&B beds
BOOKING REQUIREMENTS Advanced booking advised.
PRICE PER NIGHT £8.50 pp, £9.50 pp en suite.

PUBLIC TRANSPORT
Train stations at Builth Wells (10 miles), Hereford (30 miles) and Merthur Tydfil (30 miles) with daily bus service - ask to be dropped at Trericket Mill. National Express coaches drop off at Hereford and Brecon (13 miles). Taxi charges approximately £1 per mile. For transport enquiries phone (01597) 826678 (office hours).

DIRECTIONS
GR SO 112 414. We are set back from the A470 Brecon to Builth Wells road between the villages of Llyswen and Erwood.

🚶🚶 🚶🚶 ⚲ 🚿 ⛺ 🛏 🛏 ⠿ 🍴 ⇥ 🚲 1m

THE LION HOTEL
2, Broad Street
Builth Wells
Powys
LD2 3DT

The Lion Hotel is situated in the small market town of Builth Wells, which is an ideal place to explore the outstanding countryside of Mid Wales, including the world famous Elan Valley Dams and the Brecon Beacons. A wide range of outdoor pursuits and activities are available in the vicinity and our staff will be pleased to offer you any assistance and advice you may require. The routes of both National Cycleway No. 8 and the Wye Valley Walk pass by our front door.

On weekends, the Hotel gets very lively with a disco held in our function room/weekend bar. Added to that there is the Poachers Bar which is open every night, and a restaurant serving everything from bar snacks to à-la-carte. The bar closes when the last resident is incapable of ordering another!

So for an unforgettable experience, come and stay at the Lion Hotel.

TELEPHONE CONTACT James, Dai or Paul (01982) 553670
OPENING SEASON All Year
OPENING HOURS Register between 8am and 11pm
NUMBER OF BEDS 70 (40 bunks/30 single, twins, doubles)
BOOKING REQUIREMENTS Booking not essential but advised to avoid disappointment.
PRICE PER NIGHT Including breakfast, Bunks £15 per person, Private Rooms £20 per person.

PUBLIC TRANSPORT
Llandrindod Wells is the nearest train station (7 miles from hostel). Approx taxi fare to station £4. National Express drop ¼ mile away. For information on local buses phone Roy Brown Coaches (01982) 552597 or Crossgate Coaches (01591) 851226

DIRECTIONS
On Junction of A483 and A470 in middle of Builth Wells, opposite bridge over the River Wye, on route of National Cycleway No.8.

STONECROFT HOSTEL AND HOUSE

Dolecoed Road
Llanwrtyd Wells
Powys
LD5 4RA

Stonecroft Hostel and House are two self-catering guesthouses situated in Llanwrtyd Wells, "The Smallest Town in Britain". Surrounded by the green fields, mountains and glorious countryside of Mid Wales, Llanwrtyd is renowned as Red Kite country, and is a centre for mountain biking, pony trekking, walking, photography and bird watching. The town hosts numerous special events including Man V Horse Marathon, World Bog Snorkelling Championships and the Mid Wales Beer Festival.

The Hostel and House offer a warm Aussie welcome and a comfortable stay. We are WTB graded and have private or shared accommodation with fully made up beds (no bunks). We also offer fully equipped kitchens, TV rooms, free laundry and drying facilities, full CH, large riverside gardens and ample parking. The hostels adjoin Stonecroft Inn (CAMRA Good Beer Guide) and are truly your "home away from home", offering the very best of everything for your stay.

TELEPHONE/FAX CONTACT Diane Lutman, Tel: (01591) 610327, Fax: (01591) 610304
OPENING SEASON All year
OPENING HOURS All day - phone on arrival
NUMBER OF BEDS 52 (including 7 doubles)
BOOKING REQUIREMENTS Welcome, 50% deposit.
PRICE PER NIGHT £12.50 (private room), £11 (shared accommodation). Exclusive Use rates are available.

PUBLIC TRANSPORT
Llanwrtyd Wells Station on the Heart of Wales line is a few minutes walk from the hostel. Nearest National Express service is at Builth Wells, 12 miles from the hostel.

DIRECTIONS
GR 878 468. From Llanwrtyd town centre (A483) take Dolecoed Road towards Abergwesyn. Hostels 100 yds on left.

CABAN CWMFFYNNON

Cefn Gorwydd
Llangammarch Wells
Powys
LD4 4DW

Situated in the Heart of Wales, Caban Cwmffynnon is a century old stone barn, converted into a comfortable bunkhouse. It is an ideal base for field studies, residential and management courses.

The Caban is easily accessible to the Brecon Beacons and the Elenydd Range of hills, and activities include hill walking, pony trekking, mountain biking and expedition training. It can be an ideal base for the many events held in nearby Llanwrtyd Wells. The Caban will also be on the new National North/South Cycle Route. Hill walks, guided walks and bird watching breaks can be organised through Dinefwr Treks for groups and individuals. Self-catering or full meal service. BBQ area, limited camping and secure bike storage.

CABAN CWMFFYNNON   Escape to our beautiful landscapes

www.dinefwr-treks.co.uk

TELEPHONE/FAX CONTACT   Bryan or Antoinette. Tel/fax (01591) 610638. Email cabantreks@btinternet.com
OPENING SEASON All year
OPENING HOURS No access from 10am to 5pm.
NUMBER OF BEDS 20
BOOKING REQUIREMENTS Essential. Deposit required.
PRICE PER NIGHT £8 per person (discounts for groups).

PUBLIC TRANSPORT
Train stations at Llanwrtyd Wells (one hours' walk to Caban) and Llangammarch Wells (40 mins' walk to Caban).

DIRECTIONS
GR 907 439 (Landranger map 147). Three miles south east of Llanwrtyd Wells.

THE LONG BARN

Penrhiw, Capel Dewi
Llandysul
Ceredigion
SA44 4PE

The Long Barn is a traditional stone barn providing comfortable and warm bunkhouse accommodation. It is situated on a working farm in beautiful countryside, with views over the Teifi Valley. The stunning Ceredigion Coast and the Cambrian Mountains are both an easy drive away and the busy small town of Llandysul (1½ miles away) has all essential supplies.

The barn's location is ideal for exploring, studying or simply admiring the Welsh Countryside. Activities enjoyed by guests in the surrounding area include: horse riding, fishing, swimming, climbing, abseiling, canoeing, farm walks and cycling. The barn is open all year, having adequate heating with a lovely warm Rayburn, log fire, roof insulation and double glazing throughout.

TELEPHONE/FAX CONTACT Tom or Eva (01559) 363200
OPENING SEASON All year
OPENING HOURS All day
NUMBER OF BEDS 34
BOOKING REQUIREMENTS Booking is essential, deposit required.
PRICE PER NIGHT £6 (adult), £4 (Under 18s). Discount of 10% for groups of 20 or more.

PUBLIC TRANSPORT
Carmarthen (16 miles) has a train station and National Express service. Taxi fare from Carmarthen is approximately £16. Llandysul (1½ miles away) has a local bus service, phone (01267) 231817 for details.

DIRECTIONS
GR 437 417. In Llandysul, at the top of the main street, take right hand lane. Turn sharp right down hill. After 100 yds turn sharp left. Another ½ mile turn first right. Continue for 1 mile and the Long Barn is on your right.

BARN AT THE BACK OF BEYOND

Lower Lamphey Park
Lamphey
Sir BenFro
SA71 5PD

Barn At The Back of Beyond is situated in the heart of a medieval deer park on The Ridgeway, which is on The Celtic Trail section of the Sustrans network. The Barn is situated just east of Lamphey Village, a mile inland from the Pembrokeshire Coast Path and some of the most beautiful beaches in the area. With superb views towards the coast the quiet location makes the hostel a perfect base for backpackers climbers, walkers, cyclists, surfers and artists etc.

The accommodation is in four rooms each sleeping four in bunk beds. The hostel is fully self-catering. Meals can be provided for groups by prior arrangement. Extra space is available for workshops, teaching and lectures. Sorry the hostel cannot accept dogs

TELEPHONE CONTACT Max or Sheila, Tel: (01646) 672047, Email: barnatbeyond@dial.pipex.com
OPENING SEASON All year
OPENING HOURS Book in 4.30 pm onwards. Rooms to be vacated by 10.30 am.
NUMBER OF BEDS 16
BOOKING REQUIREMENTS Book ahead if possible. 50% deposit required for groups.
PRICE PER NIGHT £9.50pp

PUBLIC TRANSPORT
The nearest railway stations are Lamphey (½ mile) and Pembroke (1 mile). Coaches stop in Pembroke (1½ miles). Pembroke Ferry (2½ miles).

DIRECTIONS
GR 025 012. From A477 turn left at Milton road to The Ridgeway, turn right to Lamphey. At bottom of hill continue for 400yds, Hostel is 1st turning on right - signposted. From A4139 to Lamphey village. Turn right at church (approach east or south), continue straight from west. Hostel is 1st turning on left along The Ridgeway, about ½ mile.

HAMILTON BACKPACKERS LODGE

21/23 Hamilton Street
Fishguard
Pembrokeshire
SA65 9HL

Hamilton Backpackers Lodge is an excellent overnight stop on the stunning Pembrokeshire Coast Path. It is also an ideal overnight stay five minutes from the ferries to Rosslare in Ireland. Pembrokeshire has a wealth of natural beauty and local history and many beautiful secluded beaches. The Backpackers Lodge is a very comfortable and friendly hostel with small dormitories and double rooms, all centrally heated. There is a dining room and TV lounge with Sky. The garden at the back of the hostel has a hammock, barbecue and picnic tables. We provide free tea, coffee and light breakfast. There is parking close by and the hostel is in the centre of town near to a number of pubs serving good meals. There is no curfew. Smoking is permitted only in the Garden Patio. To view web page see: http://fishguard-backpackers.com

TELEPHONE CONTACT Steve Roberts (01348) 874797, Email: Steve@fishguard-backpackers.com
OPENING SEASON All year
OPENING HOURS 24 hours
NUMBER OF BEDS 23
BOOKING REQUIREMENTS Booking advised to confirm beds. 50% deposit required from groups.
PRICE PER NIGHT £10 (bunk), £12 (double) per person.

PUBLIC TRANSPORT
Fishguard ferry port has a train station and ferries to Rosslare in Ireland. The port is 1 mile from the hostel (approx taxi fare £3). National Express coaches call at Haverfordwest (15 miles). For details of local buses in Wales phone Richard Bros (01239) 613756.

DIRECTIONS
From Haverfordwest (A40) to Fishguard Square, across first right by tourist office, 50 yds on left. From Cardigan A487 (NT Wales Road) up hill and first left. From Harbour 1 mile to Fishguard Square, left, first right, 50 yards on left.

FELIN HESCWM REFUGE

Dinas, Newport
Pembrokeshire
SA42 0XL

Where the Preseli Hills tumble down to the sea, you will find a small country cornmill powered by the mountain streams, a stone's throw from lonely Aberbach Cove. The Refuge is really a cottage with the flexibility of a hostel in a simple conversion from the stable using colourful limewashes, slate slabs, wooden shutters and a big cosy stove. There are 3 twin bedrooms upstairs, overlooking the millpond. Sheets and continental breakfast materials are provided free, including home baked bread. There is a fully equipped kitchen for self-caterers, or meals available in the village (½ mile). Spend a night whilst walking the coast path; or stay longer, explore the Preseli Hills, swim, go birdwatching or rockclimbing, or just sit on the point watching the sun go down. Park up in the village for free or on site for £1.50 a car.

TELEPHONE CONTACT (01348) 811289 John/Jo (7am-11pm)
OPENING SEASON Closed Jan 6th to Feb 11th.
OPENING HOURS Flexible
NUMBER OF BEDS 6
BOOKING REQUIREMENTS Phone first.
PRICE PER NIGHT £12 per person per night.

PUBLIC TRANSPORT

Train station is at Fishguard Harbour (port for Stena Line ferries from Ireland), 4 miles from hostel. From Harbour catch bus to Fishguard centre. Then 412 Haverfordwest to Cardigan bus which stops in Fishguard, ask for Council Houses in Dinas (Richard Bros 01239 820751). Taxi fare from Harbour to hostel approx £6.50. Nearest National Express drop is at Haverfordwest (20 miles).

DIRECTIONS

GR 997 386, On foot, from coast path turn up to Felin Hescwm at Aberbach. By car or bike, from Fishguard take A487 towards Newport. In Dinas, pass green and tennis courts. Take 2nd left(300yds). From Newport take A487 towards Fishguard. In Dinas take 1st right after petrol station(400yds). In each case take left turn 400yds after Tabor Chapel signed Aberbach. Hostel at bottom on right.

BRITHDIR MAWR
Cilgwyn Road
Newport / Trefdraeth
Pembrokeshire
SA42 0QJ

Brithdir Mawr Hostel is a converted barn with two lofts and a family rooms as sleeping accommodation. There is an open plan self-catering kitchen and dining area with stone flagged floor, gas cooker and wood burning stove. There is a shower/bathroom with solar/wood heated water. The lighting is provided using 12 volt renewable sources and there are hygienic smell-free compost toilets.

The hostel is run by a small community on a beautiful organic farm with wild flower meadows, woodlands' a lake and streams. We aim to live simply, using sustainable methods wherever possible. Visitors can participate in farming or gardening activities if they wish.

Brithdir Mawr is in the Pembrokshire Coast National Park between the Preseli mountains and the sea. Newport (Pembs) is two miles away and is on the Pembrokeshire Coastal Path.

website: www.brithdirmawr.freeserve.co.uk

TELEPHONE CONTACT Anja (01239) 820164
OPENING SEASON All year
OPENING HOURS All day
NUMBER OF BEDS 12
BOOKING REQUIREMENTS   Always phone in advance.
PRICE PER NIGHT £5 per person

PUBLIC TRANSPORT
Haverfordwest is the nearest train station. Then take 412 bus to Newport (1 hour journey). Hostel is 2 miles from Newport.

DIRECTIONS
GR 074 373. Take road to Cilgwyn signposted from A487 Fishguard to Cardigan Road at the edge of Newport. Go 2km towards Cilgwyn and the hostel drive is on your left.

 5m

PLAS DOLAU
Lovesgrove
Aberystwyth
Ceredigion
SY23 3HP

Plas Dolau is set in quiet countryside just 3 miles from the popular coastal town of Aberystwyth. Ideal for exploring West Wales, walking, cycling, riding, fishing and golf etc. The holiday centre includes a warm country mansion (WTB 3 star hostel) with dormitory style accommodation, with adjoining scandinavian style modern farmhouse guesthouse (WTB 2 star farm guesthouse) set on a 22 acre smallholding.

Plas Dolau includes meeting rooms, dining rooms, games room, small tuckshop and walks and sports areas. The centre can accommodate groups of up to 40 people. Various options for accommodation, provision of food, cooking facilities, etc are available. We are ideally suited for youth groups, field courses, retreats, house parties and many other groups or individuals. Please phone or visit to discuss your requirements.

TELEPHONE CONTACT (01970) 617834 Tony or Pat
OPENING SEASON All year round
OPENING HOURS 24 hours
NUMBER OF BEDS 40
BOOKING REQUIREMENTS Booking is recommended, especially for large groups.
PRICE PER NIGHT £6 to £20 per person per night. £350 per night for the whole mansion. Meals extra.

PUBLIC TRANSPORT
Nearest train station is in Aberystwyth. Taxi fare from the station to the hostel will coast around £4. National Express coaches and local buses (501 and 531) will set down at the end of the hostel drive.

DIRECTIONS
GR 623 813 OS map 135. On the A44, 3 miles from Aberystwyth, 1 mile from Llanbadarn railway bridge, 0.6 miles from turning to Bow Street. Sign on roadside says "Y Gelli", B+B. We are about 250 yards along the drive. Reception in "Y Gelli".

CABAN
CADER IDRIS
Islawrdref
Dolgellau
Gwynedd, LL40 1TS

Caban Cader Idris is a listed building in a secluded wooded valley within walking distance of Cader Idris and the Mawddach Estuary in Snowdonia National Park. It is in an ideal setting for field work and outdoor pursuits with wonderful unspoilt mountain, valley and estuary walks from the doorstep. Local activities include:- climbing, hill walking, pony trekking, biking, canoeing, rafting and fishing. The area is also ideal for the study of geology, geography, local history, industrial archaeology and ornithology (RSPB woods adjoin grounds). Nearby are slate mines, dry ski slope, narrow gauge railways and beaches. There is a large kitchen/dining room, two dorms sleeping 6 and 10, a lounge (with 3 beds), toilets, hot showers and a drying room. It is heated and has a payphone, car park and fire safety certificate. Camping by arrangement. This self-catering bunkhouse is ideal for groups but also open to individuals. Phone for a brochure or take a look on the web, http://www.barmouth.net/cabancaderidris

TELEPHONE CONTACT (01248) 600478 / (07887) 954301
OPENING SEASON All year
OPENING HOURS No restrictions
NUMBER OF BEDS 19
BOOKING REQUIREMENTS Booking is essential. Always phone before arrival. £15 per night deposit for group bookings. Last minute enquiries welcome from individuals or groups.
PRICE PER NIGHT £6 per person. Sole use:- £80 per night in the week, £100 on Friday and Saturday.

PUBLIC TRANSPORT
Nearest train station is Morfa Mawddach (4 miles). Nearest bus stop is Abergwynant (¼ mile). For local bus info call (01341) 422614

DIRECTIONS
GR 682 169. From Dolgellau take the A493 Fairbourne road on south of Mawddach estuary. One mile beyond Llynpenmaen/Penmaenpool take left hand turn just before Abergwynant Bridge. The bunkhouse is on left in 300 yds.

1m

SNOWDON BACKPACKERS

Lawrence House, Tremadog
Nr Porthmadog
Gwynedd, LL49 9PS

Snowdon Backpackers is a Grade 2 listed building, famous as the house in which Lawrence of Arabia was born in 1888. It has recently been totally modernised to provide the ultimate in clean, comfortable and secure accommodation for backpackers. There is a choice of dormitories or private rooms, with full central heating, wash basins in every bedroom, personal lockers and extra storage for valuables and baggage, a large dining room, fully equipped kitchen, lounge/TV room with real log fires in winter and a private car park leading to extensive woodland walks.

We are ideally positioned just 10 miles from Snowdon, yet only 2 miles from beautiful sandy beaches, and only a few minutes' walk from the train station, National Express coaches, and many pubs and restaurants. Within a mile are the Ffestiniog and Welsh Highland railways, the famous Tremadog rocks for climbers, and virtually every other outdoor activity one could wish for. Snowdon Backpackers is the perfect base from which to explore Snowdonia and the Lleyn Peninsula.

Hostel open to backpackers only.

TELEPHONE CONTACT Lynda or Roger, Tel: (01766) 515354, Fax: (01766) 515364, Email: snowdon@backpackers.fsnet.co.uk
OPENING SEASON All year
OPENING HOURS No restrictions
NUMBER OF BEDS 35
BOOKING REQUIREMENTS Booking is recommended and essential for groups. 50% deposit required.
PRICE PER NIGHT From £11.50 including light breakfast and linen. Group discounts available.

PUBLIC TRANSPORT
Half a mile from Porthmadog train station and 250 yards from National Express coach stop.

DIRECTIONS
Half a mile from Porthmadog on Caernarfon road (A487).

BUDGET ACCOMMODATION
11, Marine Terrace
Criccieth
Gwynedd
LL52 0EF

Budget Accommodation is in a large Victorian residence located on the seafront close to Criccieth Castle with beautiful views of Harlech and the Lleyn Peninsula. The beach is great for fishing, swimming, paddling or simply for skimming stones. The house is close to the Snowdonia National Park and is an area ideal for watersports, climbing and walking. The Sustrans cycle route passes in front of the house.

The accommodation comprises of twin rooms with hot and cold water. Sheets, blankets and towels plus tea and coffee making facilities are provided free of charge. There is a dining room with cutlery, crockery, toaster, kettle and microwave for making drinks and snacks and a continental breakfast can be provided if requested for an extra £1.00 per person. Cycles can be housed in the back-yard.

Smoking is not allowed anywhere in the accommodation.

TELEPHONE CONTACT Bob or Sue (01766) 523098
OPENING SEASON May - September inclusive
OPENING HOURS 8.00 am - 12 midnight
NUMBER OF BEDS 4
BOOKING REQUIREMENTS Advanced booking advisable with 50% deposit.
PRICE PER NIGHT £9.50 per person £5.00 for child sharing.

PUBLIC TRANSPORT
Criccieth village has a train station and National Express coach service.

DIRECTIONS
Turn off A497 at the centre of Criccieth and go over the level crossing. Follow the road, bearing right. Turn right at 'T' junction opposite Cadwaladers Ice Cream Parlour, past Castle. We are 100m past corner shop on sea front.

 1m

STONE BARN AND STUDIO
Tyddyn Morthwyl
Criccieth
Gwynedd
LL52 0NF

The Stone Barn and Studio are converted farm buildings at Tyddyn Morthwyl Farm and Caravan Park near Criccieth on the fringe of Snowdonia. The farm provides a good centre for climbing and walking in Snowdonia and the Lleyn Peninsula. Tremadog Rocks (an all year rock climbing venue) is only 7 miles away. Canoeing and wind surfing nearby.

The Barn has an alpine style sleeping platform. Hot showers and toilets are shared with the caravan park. There is a wood burning stove for heating and clothes drying (wood provided free) and a kitchen area with fridge and running water. The Studio is a small stone building with two single beds, washbasin and cooking facilities. There is also a static caravan to let.

Several pubs in the locality serve good bar meals.

TELEPHONE CONTACT Mrs Trumper (01766) 522115
OPENING SEASON All year
OPENING HOURS Flexible
NUMBER OF BEDS 12
BOOKING REQUIREMENTS 48 hrs advanced booking required, with one night's fee as deposit.
PRICE PER NIGHT £5 per person in the Stone Barn including wood (discount for groups). £8 per night in the Studio.

PUBLIC TRANSPORT
Criccieth has a train station and National Express coach service. The hostel is 1¼ miles from Criccieth and the taxi fare to or from the station is approximately £2.50.

DIRECTIONS
1¼ miles from Criccieth on B4411 Caernarfon road.

BRYN DINAS BUNKHOUSE

Bryn Dinas
Nant Gwynant
Caernarfon, LL55 4NH

Bryn Dinas Bunkhouse / Hostel is situated in the magnificent Gwynant Valley right at the foot of Snowdon on the south side. The village of Nant Gwynant is flanked on two sides by the twin lakes of Llyn Gwynant and Llyn Dinas and is only three miles from the picturesque village of Beddgelert. There is a good selection of pubs, cafes and restaurants in Beddgelert.

The accommodation is fully fitted for self-catering and catering for large groups can be arranged. There are two grades of accommodation. The Farmhouse has twenty five bunk beds arranged dormitory style in six bedrooms, and the Cabins have twenty seven bunk beds in twelve separate wooden cabins in the centre grounds. Outdoor activity tuition/holidays can be arranged to include all grades of mountain-craft, navigation, ropework, scrambling and snow/ice skills. Please write/ring for a leaflet.

TELEPHONE CONTACT Vince/Annette Webb (01766) 890234
OPENING SEASON Open all year
OPENING HOURS Totally flexible
NUMBER OF BEDS 52
BOOKING REQUIREMENTS Advanced booking (with deposit) is recommended.
PRICE PER NIGHT From £6.50 per person.

PUBLIC TRANSPORT
Nearest train stations are at Porthmadog and Betws-y-coed. Snowdon Links runs from Porthmadog to Betws-y-coed and stops outside hostel.

DIRECTIONS
GR 625 503. Turn left off the A5 at Capel Curig on to the A4086. At the Pen-y-Gwryd Hotel turn left onto the A498. Descend into the Gwynant valley and into Nant Gwynant. Pass the car park at the base of the Watkin Path and 300 yards on the right is Bryn Dinas, just past the post office.

THE HEIGHTS HOTEL
74 High Street
Llanberis
Gwynedd
LL55 4HB

THE HEIGHTS HOTEL, LLANBERIS. <u>The</u> meeting place for climbers and mountaineers.

Ideally situated in the heart of Snowdonia.

Backpackers dormitory accommodation available for groups or individuals. £10.50 B&B or £7.50 bed only.

Ensuite rooms available.

Facilities include bar, restaurant, video screen, music, pool room, and climbing wall.

Rock climbing tuition available.

Open all year round.

TELEPHONE CONTACT (01286) 871179
OPENING SEASON All year
OPENING HOURS Access from 8am to 12 midnight
NUMBER OF BEDS 24
BOOKING REQUIREMENTS Booking is not essential, but recommended to save disappointment.
PRICE PER NIGHT £9(bed) or £12.50 (bed and breakfast) per person.

PUBLIC TRANSPORT
Nearest train station is in Bangor. Nearest National Express service calls at Caernarfon. Local bus service from Llanberis to Caernarfon and Bangor.

DIRECTIONS
Situated in the centre of Llanberis, very easy to find.

 5m

"TOTTERS"

Plas Porth Yr Aur
2 High Street, Caernarfon
Gwynedd. LL55 1RN

'Totters' is situated in the heart of the historic castle town of Caernarfon. Sheltered by the castle's town wall, we are only 30 metres from the shores of the Menai Straits and get to see some fantastic sunsets. The town not only offers the visitor a huge selection of pubs and restaurants to choose from, but also acts as the perfect base for trips into the Snowdonia National Park. There is very good public transport in and out of the National Park.

The hostel is a 200 year old, five floored town house, which is fully heated with all the comforts of home. Continental breakfast and all bedding is provided in the overnight charge. We have a common room with TV and games, drying room, book exchange, dining room, bicycle hire and a secure left luggage facility. The bedrooms sleep either 4 or 6 and can be arranged as mixed or single sex dorms. There is also a separate family room. We're easy going, flexible and WTB approved. Check us out !!

TELEPHONE CONTACT Bob or Henryette (01286) 672963
OPENING SEASON All year
OPENING HOURS All day access. Book in by 10pm.
NUMBER OF BEDS 30
BOOKING REQUIREMENTS Booking is essential for groups in June, July, August and September, 25% deposit required.
PRICE PER NIGHT £9.50 per person (includes breakfast and all bedding). Discounts for groups and long stays.

PUBLIC TRANSPORT
Bangor train station is 7 miles from the hostel. Catch a bus from outside the station to Caernarfon (fare £1.50). National Express coaches drop off in Caernarfon 200m from the hostel.

DIRECTIONS
Coming by road:- follow signs for town centre, turn right 200m after the big Celtic Royal hotel, keep going and Totters is the last house on the left (if you fall in the sea you've gone just too far!) The hostel is beside the castle wall next to the Royal Welsh Yacht Club.

JESSE JAMES' BUNKHOUSE

Penisarwaen
Nr Llanberis
Gwynedd, LL55 3DA

Established by Jesse in 1966, Snowdonia's Original Bunkhouse, a comfortable base for non-smokers. Once an Activity Centre, it now provides a range of self-catering accommodation suitable for outdoor people who want to do their own thing, or perhaps just soak up the peace. Perfectly situated between the mountains and the sea, there is a whole world to explore and enjoy - mountains and moorlands, rock climbing and scrambling, woodlands and beaches, with easy walks starting from the bunkhouse. Cyclists can experience everything challenging from lovely quiet lanes to mountain bridleways and passes, where the views can be breathtaking and the silence deafening. There are two bunkhouses, like simple hostels and an apartment and flat. All self-catering, with fully equipped kitchens and dining areas. There's a drying room, some camping space and off road parking. All you need is your sleeping bag and your food, even these could be provided, by arrangement. Jesse is a retired instructor/guide and a mountain rescue leader, who'll readily chat over a brew and maybe his famous flapjack! This is a centre of Lo-Tech Pragmatism - keep it simple so long as it works. Here it really does. Ring or write for a leaflet.

TELEPHONE CONTACT Jesse James (01286) 870521 24hrs
OPENING SEASON All year, but enquire first.
OPENING HOURS All day
NUMBER OF BEDS 36, plus more in other grades
BOOKING REQUIREMENTS Ring or write, casuals take their chance. 50% deposit for two night weekends, less for longer.
PRICE PER NIGHT £7.50 to £15. Negotiable discounts for groups.

PUBLIC TRANSPORT
Train and coach services to Bangor (7 miles). From Bangor take bus (bus enquiries 01286 870484) 76 or 77 to Deiniolen turn off below Beran Garage, then walk downhill 700yds to find bunkhouse on right.

DIRECTIONS
GR 566 638. 3½ miles from Llanberis on Bangor road B4547 (not in the village of Penisarwaen).

3m

BREDE ARKLESS BUNKHOUSE
Buarth
Deiniolen
Gwynedd, LL55 3NA

Brede Arkless Bunkhouse is a long established family run bunkhouse which has been converted from an old barn. At 1000ft it has superior views overlooking the Irish sea with a 3000ft mountain on the doorstep. Ideal for mountaineers, climbers, walkers and all watersports. This makes it the first choice for all outdoor people.

The bunkhouse is open plan with two bunk-rooms, one of nine and a smaller one of six beds. Heating is by a wood burning stove with back boiler and immersion heater. Everything is provided for self-catering - all you need are food and sleeping bags.

Please write or ring for further details.

TELEPHONE CONTACT (01286) Jim 870518 / John 871672
OPENING SEASON All year
OPENING HOURS 24 hours
NUMBER OF BEDS 15
BOOKING REQUIREMENTS Pre-booking preferred to avoid disappointment. 20% deposit in advance. There are usually some last minute beds available.
PRICE PER NIGHT From £5.50 per person. Sole use of whole bunkhouse £55.

PUBLIC TRANSPORT
Nearest train station and National Express service are at Bangor (9 miles from hostel). There is a bus station at Deiniolen ½mile away. Holyhead ferry port (34 miles away) has connections to Dublin in Ireland.

DIRECTIONS
GR 592 634. From B4547 turn off towards Deiniolen. Take first left (before village) up a steep hill and continue for 1 mile. Bear right at T junction towards Marchlyn Mawr Dam. Buarth is the first house on the right after the forest plantation. The house is named on most Ordnance Survey maps.

3m

CONWY VALLEY BACKPACKERS
Pyllau Gloewon Farm
Tal-y-bont, Conwy
Gwynedd
LL32 8YX

Conwy Valley Backpackers is situated on a peaceful working farm, in the heart of the beautiful Conwy Valley with excellent access to Snowdonia. This Backpackers is a tasteful conversion, purpose built with you in mind. Centrally heated, small dorms, fully equipped self-catering kitchen, log fires, hot showers and a fire alarm system. We also provide secure bike/canoe storage, grazing for horses and tourist information. Beside the barn is a small stream and guests may picnic and BBQ on the river bank or swing lazily in the hammock - ideal space for restoration, relaxation and retreat.

There are some great pubs and eating places within walking distance. Ample activities available from paragliding, fishing or hiking to white water rafting and mountain biking. The Backpackers is unsuitable for children. Groups are welcome and a genuine Indian Tipi (sleeps 6-8) is available. Payphone available.

TELEPHONE/FAX CONTACT David, Claudia, Glyn or Helen; Tel/Fax: (01492) 660504
OPENING SEASON All year
OPENING HOURS All day
NUMBER OF BEDS 20
BOOKING REQUIREMENTS Not essential but recommended.
PRICE PER NIGHT £10 pp (including all linen and light breakfast). Special rates for groups of 14 or more people who are self-catering.

PUBLIC TRANSPORT
Nearest train stations and National Express coach services are at Llandudno Junction and Conwy. Local bus 19 or 19a runs every 20 minutes from Conwy and Llandudno Junction, ask driver to drop you at Pyllau Gloewon farm gate.

DIRECTIONS
GR 769 697. Six miles south of Conwy on the B5106, look for Backpackers sign just before entering Talybont.

BRON RHEDYN BUNKHOUSE

FSC Rhyd-y-Creuau
The Drapers' Field Centre
Betws-y-Coed
North Wales
LL24 0HB

Bron Rhedyn Bunkhouse is part of a nineteenth-century stone house set in woodland and belongs to the Field Studies Council at Rhyd-y-Creuau. The bunkhouse is a pleasant walk of less than a mile, from the town of Betws-y-Coed. It provides excellent access to Snowdonia, a superb area for hill-walking, scrambling, climbing, mountain biking, canoeing and many other outdoor activities.

Bron Rhedyn is fully heated with four comfortable modern sleeping rooms with en-suite facilities, each with two bunkbeds. There is a cooking area with a four ring electric hob, kettle, toaster, fridge and microwave, along with a dining/lounge area and a payphone. Meals and packed lunches can be provided at the field centre across the road with prior arrangement. Also pubs, restaurants, shops and tourist information are available in Betws-y-Coed.

TELEPHONE CONTACT Lorna Shipp, (01690) 710494
OPENING SEASON All year
OPENING HOURS Office open 9am - 5pm. Duty member of staff available till 11pm.
NUMBER OF BEDS 16
BOOKING REQUIREMENTS Essential, 2 days minimum and preferably six weeks in advance
PRICE PER NIGHT £7per person or £85 a night for entire bunkhouse. Breakfast £3 pp. Other meals by arrangement.

PUBLIC TRANSPORT
Betws-y-Coed train station (1 mile) has six trains a day. Frequent Buses from Llandudno and Llandudno Junction stop outside the hostel.

DIRECTIONS
A470 - 3 miles south of Llanrwst or 1 mile north of Betws-y-Coed. On bend by sign indicating a School.

TYDDYN BYCHAN
Cefn Brith
Cerrig y drudion
Corwen
LL21 9TS

Tyddyn Bychan is an 18th-Century traditional Welsh farmhouse, set in two and a half acres of private grounds surrounded on all sides by farmland with a large parking area well away from the road. Situated in an excellent location for fieldwork in Hiraethog and Snowdonia, climbing, fishing and numerous watersports including whitewater rafting, and many local walks. The Bunkhouse is luxurious with two sleeping areas containing 8 and 10 bunks which are of a very high standard. There are showers, washbasins and toilets for each room and a well equipped kitchen/dining room. Additional room is available in a small cottage. All bedding, heating and electricity are included, but bring your own towels. We can provide delicious homemade food in our licensed dining room and make up packed lunches. The bunkhouse and cottage are also equipped for self-catering.

TELEPHONE CONTACT (01490) 420680 Lynda
OPENING SEASON All year
OPENING HOURS All day
NUMBER OF BEDS 24
BOOKING REQUIREMENTS Booking is advisable
PRICE PER NIGHT £8.50 pp including bedding, discounts for groups and longer stays.

PUBLIC TRANSPORT
Nearest train station is at Llanrwst. Nearest National Express service at Colwyn Bay and Llandudno. Local bus service 'Conwy Clipa' to Cefn Brith from Llanrwst, Llandudno, Corwen, Llangollen, Wrexham, Bala, and Denbigh. Phone (01492) 575412 for details.

DIRECTIONS
GR 931 504. Turn off A5 at Cerrig y drudion. Take B4501 out of village for Llyn Brenig, take the turning on left for Cefn Brith. After about 2 miles you will see a phone box on left, chapel on right and the road widens for a layby. The gate for Tyddyn is on the left directly opposite junction on the right.

CANOE INN
Riverside Cafe and Accommodation
Mile End Mill
Berwyn Road, Llangollen
Denbighshire
LL20 8AD

The Canoe Inn is situated on the banks of the River Dee, a short walk from the picturesque town of Llangollen in North Wales. The Inn is part of a watersports and activity centre which provides white water rafting, canoeing, climbing, abseiling, archery, laser clay shooting and other activities. Ideally placed for walking in the Berwyns, Arans, Arenig Hills, Worlds End and Offa's Dyke Trail.

An old Flannel Mill has been converted to provide inexpensive accommodation with all rooms looking directly over the river. Duvets, sheets and tea/coffee facilities are all included in the price. The Cafe is open 9am to 6pm with a comprehensive breakfast, lunch and afternoon tea menu, as well as an extensive vegetarian menu. Llangollen has a wide variety of options for evening meals.

www.jjraftcanoe.com

TELEPHONE/FAX CONTACT Steve Batham (01978) 860763
OPENING SEASON All year
OPENING HOURS All day (booking 9.00am - 6.00pm)
NUMBER OF BEDS 14
BOOKING REQUIREMENTS Booking advisable with 50% deposit though not essential on weekdays.
PRICE PER NIGHT £7.00 bunk, £8.00 en suite

PUBLIC TRANSPORT
Nearest local bus service is Llangollen. The nearest train station with connecting bus service is Wrexham on Chester/Birmingham line.

DIRECTIONS
Situated on the A5. Three quarters of a mile west of Llangollen. From the centre of Llangollen, turn right onto the A5 signposted Corwen. Pass a large hotel on the left hand side, the Mill is 100m further on right. Follow the driveway down into the carpark. The Centre office is on the Riverside.

SCOTLAND

All phone numbers are given with the national code required to phone from anywhere in the UK. To phone from overseas remove the first 0 and add 44.

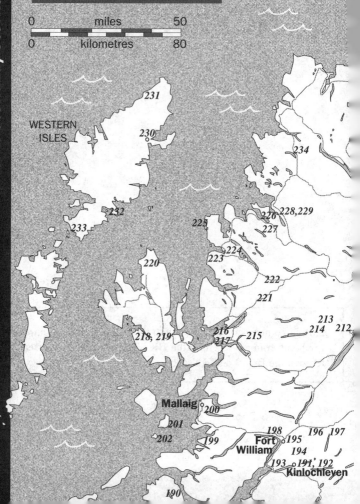

Choose a place of interest and then refer to page number/s shown in italics (*12–19*) for hostels in that area

| | miles | | 50 |
| 0 | kilometres | | 80 |

WESTERN ISLES

231

230

234

232

233

225

226   *228,229*
227

220

224
223

222

221

213
214   *212*

218, 219

216   *215*
217

Mallaig   *200*

201

202   *199*

198   *196*   *197*
195
Fort William   *194*

193   *191*, *192*

Kinlochleven

190

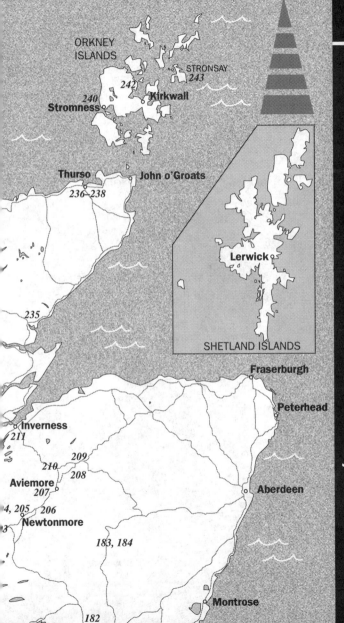

ORKNEY
ISLANDS

STRONSAY
243

242

240
Stromness

Kirkwall

Thurso

John o'Groats

236–238

235

Lerwick

SHETLAND ISLANDS

Fraserburgh

Peterhead

Inverness
211

210   *209*

208

Aviemore
207

4, 205   *206*

3

Newtonmore

183, 184

Aberdeen

182

Montrose

North Scotland/Scottish Isles

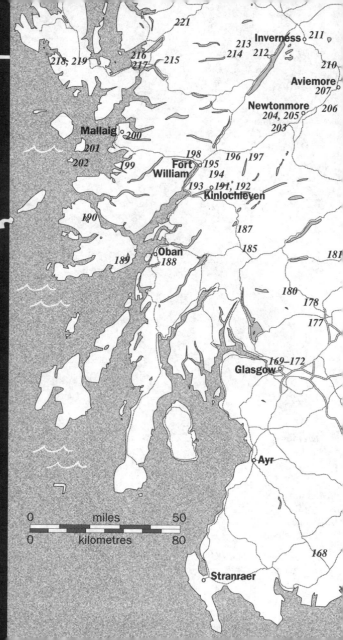

221

213   Inverness   211
214   212

210

Aviemore
207

216   215
217

218, 219

Newtonmore
204, 205   206
203

Mallaig   200
201
202   199

198   196   197
Fort   195
William   194
193   191, 192
Kinlochleven

190

187

185   181

Oban
189   188

180
178
177

169–172
Glasgow

Ayr

0   miles   50
0   kilometres   80

168

Stranraer

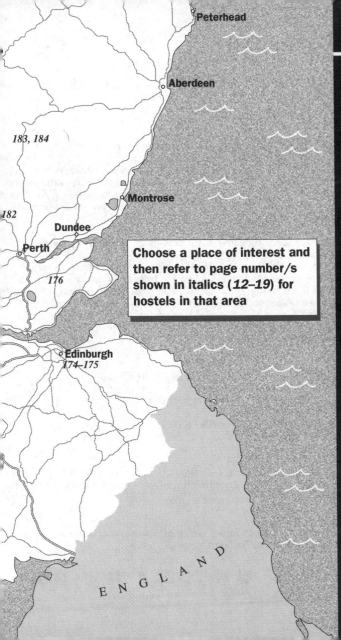

Peterhead

Aberdeen

183, 184

182

Montrose

Dundee

Perth

176

Choose a place of interest and
then refer to page number/s
shown in italics (*12–19*) for
hostels in that area

Edinburgh
174–175

E N G L A N D

GALLOWAY
SAILING CENTRE
Parton
Loch Ken, Castle Douglas
DG7 3NQ

The centre is family owned and run and our aim is to give you a memorable holiday in a friendly family atmosphere. Learn to sail, windsurf, kayak or powerboat on a safe non-tidal inshore loch with our qualified instructors. We also offer quad biking - the best fun on four wheels - as well as gorge scrambling and raft building for those prepared to get wet! We offer special rates for groups including disabled groups.

Guests are accommodated in our new lodge. Built last year, this well-appointed chalet has all the creature comforts you want after a hard day on, or off, the water! Rooms are spacious and newly-furnished. There is a well appointed kitchen for making your own meals, and a lounge for relaxing and chatting with your fellow guests. For your meals, home-cooked Scottish fare is available, served around the Great Table by a member of staff. Use of the Lodge is not restricted to those taking our sailing courses. It is available as a peaceful haven for those exploring Galloway.

TELEPHONE CONTACT (01644) 420626
OPENING SEASON All year
OPENING HOURS 9.00 a.m - 9.00 p.m.
NUMBER OF BEDS 20
BOOKING REQUIREMENTS N/A
PRICE PER NIGHT £9.50 per person (£150 sole use)

PUBLIC TRANSPORT
Nearest train station is at Dumfries (25 miles from hostel). Local bus service delivers to the door five times a day, phone (0345) 090510 for details.

DIRECTIONS
A713 (Ayr Road) 2 miles north of Parton, large brown signs on roadside 'Galloway Sailing Centre'

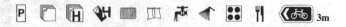

BLUE SKY
65 Berkeley Street
Glasgow
G3 7DY

Glasgow, Britain's third most visited city has so much to explore. Its excellent commuter services can whisk you to Ayr, Loch Lomond, Stirling, Edinburgh and Lanark in less than an hour, making it the ideal centre from which to tour. Arran and Bute isles are just an hour away by train.

The Blue Sky is the most central of the city's all-year-round backpackers' accommodation and our welcome two minute map tours are legendary and make you feel Glaswegian. There are twin rooms, family rooms and dorms ranging from 6-12 beds. Well equipped kitchen, two lounges and Sky TV. We cater for all tastes and provide free tea, toast, jam and marmalade.

With us your stay will be carefree with no curfew and our staff, who are well travelled themselves, will advise on trips, tickets (including teletext last minute bargains), jobs, bicycle and car hire. You can even start any Haggis tour here.

TELEPHONE CONTACT (0141) 221 7880
OPENING SEASON All year
OPENING HOURS All day. No curfew but night coded entry
NUMBER OF BEDS 30
BOOKING REQUIREMENTS Recommended in high season.
PRICE PER NIGHT £9.50 (dorm) plus 7th night free. Twins from £11.75. Under 12's half price, small children free in twin rooms.

PUBLIC TRANSPORT
Glasgow has train and coach services. Take bus from bus stop outside Charing Cross station to hostel. Taxi fare from station is around £2.

DIRECTIONS
From Central or Queens Street station walk up the hill to Bath Street. From bus station walk two blocks down the hill to Bath Street. Walk west along Bath St. Berkeley St is a continuation of Bath St. We are six doors past the library.

STRATHCLYDE UNIVERSITY CAMPUS VILLAGE

Weaver Street
Glasgow
G1 0NG

Strathclyde University Campus Village is located in the centre of Glasgow, five minutes' walk from Buchanan Street Bus Station and Queens Street Station. The accommodation is in modern flats on an attractively landscaped site. All rooms are singles with access to a comfortable lounge/kitchen area and adjacent to laundry facilities. They are built round the Lord Todd restaurant/bar which also houses a shop. Rooms are available with and without linen and self-catering flats for small groups may be booked for three nights or more. Breakfast and other meals can be arranged in advance.

Glasgow city centre's shops, bars, restaurants, museums and many attractions are within walking distance or are easily reached by underground or bus.

TELEPHONE CONTACT Julie Scouller (0141) 553 4148
OPENING SEASON June to September inclusive
OPENING HOURS 24 hours
NUMBER OF BEDS 200 +
BOOKING REQUIREMENTS Phone in advance, groups should always book.
PRICE PER NIGHT From £10 per person (bed only)

PUBLIC TRANSPORT
Glasgow has two train stations, an underground railway and is served by Citylink coaches. A number of buses run from Queen Street Station to the campus village and will charge around £2. It is only a ten minute walk from Queen Street Station to the campus village.

DIRECTIONS
From Queens Street Station proceed along Cathedral Street. Strathclyde University is on the right hand side and the student village is easy to find. The village office is in the Lord Todd Restaurant - turn right opposite the Clydesdale Bank, through the archway.

1m

A FREE ICECREAM
Top Floor
136 Holland Street
Glasgow Scotland
G2 4NB

As the name says, an endless supply of FREE ICECREAM is available
to our guests and even though the hostel is right smack in the heart of
the City Centre with all the pubs, clubs, discos, restaurants, etc. just
around the corner, it is a small, cosy place and is surprisingly quiet
and peaceful. We are planning to offer five different daytrips this year
around and about in our ex-Highland Postbus to some of the most
beautiful places in the area. We also enjoy hill-walking, so often you
can cadge a lift from one of us or we hire out bikes for the day.

The hostel is carpeted throughout and the only restriction we have is
a no smoking policy. Unfortunately we are in a building dating from
1859 (don't worry - the central heating and showers are new!) so there
is no disabled access. Accommodation comprises of a large bright and
airy dormitory which sleeps 8 when it is full and a nicely furnished
family room. Full Scottish breakfast is £2.50. If we are full we can
often point you to other places- we have never disappointed anyone.

TELEPHONE/FAX CONTACT Irena, Tel: (0800) 279 4736
Fax: (0141) 248 6290
OPENING SEASON May to September inclusive
OPENING HOURS All day - new bookings between 8am-10pm
NUMBER OF BEDS 8 (plus another 10 available with neighbours)
BOOKING REQUIREMENTS Phone or turn-up. Photographic ID
(eg Passport) essential.
PRICE PER NIGHT £8.00 in dormitory, £12.50 in private room.

PUBLIC TRANSPORT
The Charing Cross Station 100m and Buchanan St Bus Station 800m.

DIRECTIONS
Leave M8 on right J17. Turn left Sauchiehall St. 1st right Elmbank
St and 2nd left Bath Lane. From Central or Queen St Station, walk
north to Bath St (From bus station walk south) then west along Bath
St and Holland St will be on your left.

 1m

CAIRNCROSS HOUSE
20 Kelvinhaugh Place
Glasgow
G3 8NH

Cairncross House is in an excellent location within walking distance of the trendy West End and City Centre and is close to public transport. The West End is great for pubs and restaurants and has lots of good value places to eat. Nearby you will find some of Glasgow's top visitor attractions: Art Gallery and Museum, Transport Museum, University of Glasgow and its Visitor Centre, Hunterian Museum and Art Gallery (with a replica of the home of Charles Rennie Mackintosh - one of the best Mackintosh attractions in Glasgow). The City Centre offers all that you would expect - great shopping, clubs and pubs. Have fun!

The Hostel offers great value for money and is part of the University of Glasgow's student residence. It is modern and well equipped with bed linen, wash hand basin in room, use of cooking facilities, showers, laundry facilities and common room.

TELEPHONE CONTACT (0800) 0272030 or (0141) 2219334
OPENING SEASON 3rd July - 21st September
OPENING HOURS 8.00 am - 10.00 pm
NUMBER OF BEDS 242
BOOKING REQUIREMENTS Advised but not essential
PRICE PER NIGHT £10.50 per person

PUBLIC TRANSPORT
Buchanan Street Bus Station, Central Station and Queen Street Station are all 2 miles away. The nearest underground station is Kelvinhall ($^1/_2$ mile). From George Square take buses 6 or 16 and disembark at the stop nearest to KelvinHaugh/Radnor Street (ask driver).

DIRECTIONS
From George St. take St.Vincent St. which becomes Argyle St. after 1 mile. Through traffic lights take third left into Kelvinhaugh St. - Cairncross House is on the right. From M8 J19 take A814 to Finnieston. Turn right into Finnieston St. Continue to traffic lights and turn left into Argyle St. Kelvinhaugh St. is third on the left.

P ══ ▦ 🚕 🚿 ⠿ ▐AM ▌▶ ◉ 🚲 3m

BELFORD HOSTEL

6-8 Douglas Gardens
Edinburgh
EH4 3DA

Situated in the centre of Edinburgh, this unique converted church provides quality budget accommodation in a fun and friendly atmosphere. Accommodation is in either dormitories or double/twin rooms. Facilities include cable TV lounge, wide screen TV, pool table and darts, internet access, large self-catering kitchen and dining area, tours and travel booking service, book-a-bed-ahead service, free linen, coin-op laundry, employment board, garden and great music.

Breakfast and bar meals are available plus all guests receive a 10% discount for our stylish *new* Edinburgh bistro *Southern Cross Café*. Regular party nights, pool competitions, and bar specials plus summer weekly pub crawls. Packages for New Year, Edinburgh Festival/Tattoo, Rugby etc. Weekly rates available in low season. No curfew.

TELEPHONE CONTACT Advance booking (0800) 096 6868 or (0131) 221 0022, Reception (0131) 225 6209
OPENING SEASON All year
OPENING HOURS 24 hours
NUMBER OF BEDS 106
BOOKING REQUIREMENTS Booking essential for groups with 25% deposit. Individuals advised to book during summer.
PRICE PER NIGHT From £11 per person. Discounts for following card holders ISIC, ISE, NUS/Matriculation, VIP Backpacker, Young Scot/Euro26, plus more (ask for details).

PUBLIC TRANSPORT
Edinburgh Waverley train station 20 minutes' walk from hostel. Bus station with Citylink and local buses 20 minutes' walk from hostel. Haymarket train station 5 minutes' walk from hostel. Local buses from Princes Street to Haymarket. Taxi fare from Waverley train station £4.

DIRECTIONS
From Waverley train station, proceed to the west end of Princes St past Shandwick Pl until you reach Palmerston Pl on the right. Follow road to the end and the hostel is on the right. From bus station turn left to Princes Street then follow directions as above.

1m

EDINBURGH
BACKPACKERS HOSTEL

65 Cockburn Street
Edinburgh, EH1 1BU

Best located hostel in Edinburgh! Only two minutes from the train station and right in the heart of the historic Old Town close to attractions, pubs, clubs and restaurants. The dormitories are clean and bright and offer unrivalled views of the city. Double/twin accommodation is provided in a private apartment equipped with kitchen and bathroom. Hostel facilities include self-catering kitchen, cable TV, Internet access, pool table, breakfast bar, dining area, tours and travel booking service, book-a-bed ahead service, free linen and secure storage for valuables. World style food and drink is available at our *new* bistro *Southern Cross Café* next door, with a 10% discount for all hostel guests. Summer pub crawls and packages for New Year, Edinburgh Festival/Tattoo, Rugby etc. Our friendly and helpful staff are on hand to offer advice and information on what to see and do, and with 24 hour access and no rules or curfews, you are free to come and go as you please.

TELEPHONE CONTACT Advance booking (0800) 096 6868 or (0131) 221 0022, Reception (0131) 220 1717
OPENING SEASON All year
OPENING HOURS 24 hours
NUMBER OF BEDS 105
BOOKING REQUIREMENTS Booking essential for groups with 25% deposit. Individuals advised to book in summer.
PRICE PER NIGHT From £11.50 per person. Discounts for following card holders ISIC, ISE, NUS/Matriculation, VIP Backpacker, Young Scot/Euro26, plus more (ask for details).

PUBLIC TRANSPORT
Edinburgh Waverley train station 2 minutes' walk from hostel. Bus station with Citylink and local buses 5 minutes' walk from hostel.

DIRECTIONS
From Waverley train station turn left on Waverley Bridge, walk to mini roundabout and up road straight ahead Cockburn St. Hostel at the top on the left.

1m

FALKLAND BACKPACKERS
Back Wynd, Falkland
Fife, KY15 7BX

Feel good in Fife! The charming historic village of Falkland has pubs, peaks, paths and a splendid Renaissance Palace formerly frequented by Mary Queen of Scots. Falkland offers a rural getaway for travellers tired of the city, yet is within an hour of Edinburgh, Perth, Stirling, Dundee and St. Andrews. On the Kingdom of Fife Millennium Cycleways route it is an ideal place from which to explore the surrounding countryside. Falkland Backpackers is clean, spacious and centrally located with safe free parking nearby. Expect a genuine welcome, free tea and coffee and ridiculously comfy sofas in front of a log fire. Step outside and walk up East Lomond for an inspiring view. Fully-equipped kitchen, but if you're too tired to cook the local pubs and restaurants are highly recommended. Budget-priced beds with a bit of style! There is a major upgrade taking place between January and Easter 2000, adding: drying room, heating, private rooms, disabled access and Internet facilities. No smoking.

TELEPHONE/FAX CONTACT Anne (01337) 857710
email: Falkland@Backpackers.connectfree.co.uk
OPENING SEASON Open from Easter till November, (open by arrangement only from Nov to Easter 2000).
OPENING HOURS 8.30 am - 11.00 pm (late keys available)
NUMBER OF BEDS 36
BOOKING REQUIREMENTS Booking is recommended.
PRICE PER NIGHT £10.00 first night £9.00 thereafter

PUBLIC TRANSPORT
Nearest train station is Markinch 6 miles away. Regular buses from Glenrothes and approx. 2-hourly from Perth. From Dundee to Freuchie (approx. 3 miles to Falkland) connect to local services.

DIRECTIONS
From North, On M90 exit at Junction 9 (Bridge of Earn), follow signs to Gateside, Strathmiglo and Falkland. **From South,** On M90 exit Junction 8, signposted St Andrews and Falkland Palace. **On entering village** go past palace on right and immediately turn left at Bank of Scotland. Falkland Backpackers on left at entrance to free carpark.

WILLY WALLACE HOSTEL
77 Murray Place
Stirling
FK8 1AU

Stirling's only independent backpacker hostel, the Willy Wallace is bang in the middle of the thriving historic market town at the centre of *Braveheart* country. It is two minutes from the train and bus stations and is surrounded by nightclubs and pubs, and opposite a cybercafe which does a special deal for Willy Wallace guests. There is masses of sightseeing in the area including Stirling Castle and the Wallace Monument, with Loch Lomond and the Trossachs National Park within easy reach.

The hostel is in a fine Victorian Building and has 7 dormitories, a large common room, a well equipped kitchen, plenty of showers and loos, a great atmosphere with wacky historical theme, and no curfew. There is a free history guide on special days.

Every 2000th guest wins a night for 2 in an historic Scottish castle with a 4-poster bed.

TELEPHONE CONTACT The manager (01786) 446773
OPENING SEASON All year - from April 2000
OPENING HOURS 24 hours
NUMBER OF BEDS 56
BOOKING REQUIREMENTS Booking is not essential.
PRICE PER NIGHT £10 per person. Various special deals available, please enquire.

PUBLIC TRANSPORT
Stirling is well connected by rail and coach services. The hostel is conveniently situated, the location having been chosen for proximity to public transport.

DIRECTIONS
From train station:- go up Station Road towards the town centre and turn right into Murray Place. Willy Wallace is on the left, on the corner of Friar Street (2 minutes walk). **From Bus Station**:- turn right into train station, then follow directions (above) from there.

RED LION HOSTEL
Balkerach Street
Doune
Stirling
FK16 6DF

The Red Lion Hostel, Doune, is situated in the centre of Scotland. On the edge of the Trossachs it is only 40 minutes from Glasgow or Edinburgh.

Opened in August 1998, it is centrally heated and has two rooms with six bunks in each. There are excellent hot showers and a drying room. There are no self-catering facilities but the hostel is situated behind the Red Lion Hotel which offers good bar snacks, meals and beer. The hostel also has facilities for the disabled.

Local attractions include Doune Castle, a variety of shops, antique centre, hillwalking, fishing, golf and a safari park.

TELEPHONE CONTACT Margaret (01786) 842066
OPENING SEASON All Year
OPENING HOURS 24 hours
NUMBER OF BEDS 24
BOOKING REQUIREMENTS Essential in July and August. Deposit required.
PRICE PER NIGHT £8.50. Reductions for groups. Breakfast available for £3.

PUBLIC TRANSPORT
Stirling has a train station. Citylink coaches stop at Dunblane and Stirling. Phone (0990) 505050 for details of Citylink coaches.

DIRECTIONS
The hostel is situated behind the Red Lion Hotel in the centre of Doune. Doune is on the A84 halfway between Stirling and Callander and close to the M8.

I.B.H.S

Independent Backpackers Hostels Scotland

This association represents over 100 hostels in Scotland, many of which are featured in the Independent Hostel Guide. The hostels range from historic town houses to converted barns and a leaflet is produced which lists details of all the IBHS hostels.

All the hostels in IBHS are inspected annually and comply with the following standards:-

* No membership required *
* No minimum period of stay *
* Privately owned, most are family run *
* Open and facilities available all day *
* No curfews or late pass key available *
* All have fully equipped kitchens *
* Hot Showers *
* Minimum of rules *
* Prices as stated in leaflet *

For a copy of the leaflet please send a SAE to:- Pete Thomas, Croft Bunkhouse, Portnalong, Isle of Skye, IV47 8SL.
www.hostels-scotland.co.uk

TROSSACHS BACKPACKERS
Invertrossachs Road
Callander
Perthshire, FK17 8HW

Trossachs Backpackers has been purpose-built on its own 8 acre site, set amidst beautiful scenery (on Sustrans route 7c) just outside the bustling tourist town of Callander. The Hostel, which is the only one in the Trossachs area, opened in August 1997 and is finished to a very high standard, hence its nickname "*Posh*tel" The rooms are all en-suite and are either 8,4 or single, the 4 bed family rooms have their own private kitchen/dining facilities. There is a spacious Dining/Common Room, well equipped kitchen, a laundry and drying room. A large Meeting/Recreation Room is also available and may be booked separately for conferences, parties, etc. We have an on-site Cycling Centre, which also sells basic provisions. Other activities available locally include Hill Walking, Pony Trekking, Canoe Hire/Instruction, Fishing, Sailing and much much more. Find more information on:-

www.scottish-hostel.co.uk

TELEPHONE CONTACT Mark or Janet, Tel: (01877) 331200, Email: mark@scottish-hostel.co.uk
OPENING SEASON All year
OPENING HOURS 24 hours, (Reception 08.00 to 23.00)
NUMBER OF BEDS 30
BOOKING REQUIREMENTS Booking advised for weekends. Groups must pre book. (deposit required)
PRICE PER NIGHT £10 - £15 including linen & continental breakfast. Group discounts on request.

PUBLIC TRANSPORT
Nearest train station is at Stirling (15 miles). Nearest Citylink coach stop is at Callander (1½ miles). Taxi fare to Callander is approx £3.

DIRECTIONS
GR 606 072. The hostel is situated one mile up Invertrossachs Rd from its junction with the A81 (Glasgow Rd) in Callander.

BRAINCROFT BUNKHOUSE
Braincroft
Crieff
Perthshire, PH7 4JZ

Braincroft Bunkhouse is a high standard conversion of a 19th-century farmstead. Accommodation is provided in two, four, six and eight bedded rooms (some are family rooms), many with private en-suite facilities. The bunkhouse has a large well equipped kitchen with excellent cooking and eating facilities. It also has a lounge, laundry, drying room and shop. Breakfast is available on request and we can provide transport. Recent additions include a conference/meeting room for up to 50 people, along with an indoor games room.

This area of Perthshire is extremely popular with visitors. Glenturret Distillery, Auchingarrich Wildlife Centre, Drummond Fish Farm and Trout Fishery and Drummond Castle are all within 15 minutes' drive of Braincroft. There are numerous walks of varying degree, watersports at Loch Earn, golfing on 31 different courses and fishing on some of Scotland's finest rivers. Guests at the bunkhouse also have access to the surrounding land, our own mountain bike course (with bike hire) and private fishing.

TELEPHONE/FAX CONTACT Neill, Tel: (01764) 670140, Fax: (01764) 679691
OPENING SEASON All year
OPENING HOURS All day - no curfew
NUMBER OF BEDS 56
BOOKING REQUIREMENTS Booking is not essential but is recommended during June, July and August.
PRICE PER NIGHT £8.50 to £9.50 pp, group rates available

PUBLIC TRANSPORT
Nearest train station is at Gleneagles (14 miles). Nearest Citylink coaches service is in Perth (23 miles). Catch local bus No 15 from Perth, ask the driver to drop you off at Braincroft and he will stop at the bunkhouse. Bunkhouse transport available.

DIRECTIONS
The bunkhouse is situated just off the A85 between Crieff (5 miles) and Comrie (2 miles).

WESTER CAPUTH
INDEPENDENT
HOSTEL
Wester Caputh Steading
Caputh, By Dunkeld
Perthshire, PH1 4JH

Wester Caputh Hostel sits in rural Perthshire near to the River Tay. There are quiet roads for cycling and excellent woodland and river walks. Nearby forgotten castles, forts and Pictish stones can be explored. Canoeing, climbing and skiing are also close. The medieval cathedral town of Dunkeld is four miles upstream. Full of character, it has plenty of places to eat and drink. Join a traditional music session at Dougie MacLean's Real Music bar or even at the hostel with us!

The hostel itself is intimate and friendly. There are various sizes of bedroom and spaces to be either sociable or alone. A good place as a base for indoor or outdoor interests, or as a welcome place to rest and relax on a longer journey. Transport available to or from buses and trains.

TELEPHONE/FAX CONTACT tel/fax (01738) 710617, tel 710449
OPENING SEASON All year
OPENING HOURS All day, no curfew
NUMBER OF BEDS 18
BOOKING REQUIREMENTS Booking advisable
PRICE PER NIGHT £8.00 (1 free night if you stay 7 nights)

PUBLIC TRANSPORT
Nearest train station and Citylink stop are in Birnam which is 5 miles from the hostel. Phone for a lift from Birnam. Stagecoach operate a bus service from Perth (Mill Street), ask for Caputh Village.

DIRECTIONS From north: From A9 take A923 into Dunkeld. Take 1st right onto A984 into Caputh (4.5 miles). After church on right turn right (onto B9099) then 1st right at foot of hill. 2nd house on right (long white building). **From south**: From A9 take B9099 though Luncarty, Stanley and Murthly. Cross river and into Caputh. Turn left at foot of hill (signposted Dunkeld). 2nd house on right.

THE BUNKHOUSE
SPITTAL OF GLENSHEE HOTEL

A93 Glenshee
Blairgowrie
Perthshire

The Spittal of Glenshee is situated at the junction of four glens with dramatic views in every direction. The Spittal is arguably the oldest operating Inn site in Britain, first chronicled in 961AD. Glenshee is an ideal touring location for the Eastern Highlands of Scotland, particularly popular with skiers and walkers, situated close to the Glenshee ski slopes with 21 Munros within a 14 mile radius of the Cairnwell pass. Suggested 12 walks area guide available on request.

The Bunkhouse is attached to the hotel and provides budget-priced accommodation with excellent food. Accommodation is in three rooms (2,4 and 12 beds), with all bedding provided. There are no self-catering facilities but full buffet breakfast in the hotel is included, packed lunches are available on request, and a choice of soup/sandwiches, bar meals and carvery buffet in the evening. The Hotel facilities are available for Bunkhouse guests including bar, TV lounge, sauna, sunbed and games room.

TELEPHONE CONTACT (01250) 885215
OPENING SEASON All year except 4th - 20th January 2000
OPENING HOURS 7am - midnight
NUMBER OF BEDS 18
BOOKING REQUIREMENTS Recommended deposit £4.00 pppn.
PRICE PER NIGHT £13.50 per person including full breakfast (£8.10 children 7-12 years), discount for groups.

PUBLIC TRANSPORT
Nearest train station & National Express is Perth (36m). There are buses from Perth to Blairgowrie once an hour during the day, every 2-3 hours in the evening. Taxi fare Blairgowrie to Spittal approx £20.

DIRECTIONS
GR 111699, OS Sheet 43. From Perth follow A93 through Blairgowrie and look for signs to ski slopes. Spittal of Glenshee is approx 18 miles north of Blairgowrie.

GULABIN LODGE
Spittal of Glenshee
By Blairgowrie
PH10 7QE

Gulabin Lodge is beautifully situated in the heart of Glenshee at the foot of Beinn Gulabin offering the nearest accommodation to the Glenshee ski slopes which offer roller, nordic, alpine and telemark skiing and snowboarding. Gulabin is also an ideal base for climbing, walking or mountain biking - whether you are a beginner or an expert. Also on your visit you can try some of the other activities available which include hang-gliding, paragliding, orienteering, survival or canoeing. There is a nine-hole golf course and pony trekking nearby. Five minutes' walk from the hostel is the Spittal of Glenshee Hotel, which with its friendly bar, can provide meals and usually has entertainment on Saturday evenings. The lodge offers comfortable, reasonably priced accommodation for individuals, families and groups. Now under new ownership it has been extensively renovated with a new accommodation wing. There are free hot showers and all rooms are equipped with wash basins and linen. We offer packages to suit all types of groups. Ski hire and ski servicing facilities are available in-house.

http://members.tripod.co.uk/cairnwell/flyer.htm

TELEPHONE/FAX CONTACT Gustar, Tel/Fax: (01250) 885255, Fax: (01250) 885256, Email: cairnwell.h@virgin.net
OPENING SEASON All year
OPENING HOURS 24 hours
NUMBER OF BEDS 30
BOOKING REQUIREMENTS Booking advisable with 50% deposit
PRICE PER NIGHT £10pp or £13pp B&B, Family rooms £36. Reduced rates for group of over 10.

PUBLIC TRANSPORT
Train and bus stations at:- Pitlochry (22 miles), Blairgowrie (20 miles), Glasgow (100 miles), Edinburgh (70 miles).

DIRECTIONS
Gulabin Lodge is on the A93 road at Spittal of Glenshee - 20 miles from Blairgowrie and 19 miles to Braemar. Transport can be arranged.

STRATHFILLAN WIGWAMS
Auchtertyre Farm
Tyndrum, Crianlarich
Perthshire
FK20 8RU

The Strathfillan Wigwams are located on the A82, 3 miles north of Crianlarich, surrounded by spectacular views within easy reach of a number of Munro mountains (Ben Lui, Ben More, Ben Dorain). The Wigwams makes an ideal base for hill walking, canoeing, pony trekking, fishing and skiing (the Glencoe Ski-Centre is just 30 minutes away). Tyndrum and Crianlarich villages are within easy access of the farm, where there are a number of restaurants and local shops.

The wooden wigwams offer self-catering facilities and are suitable for families, groups or individuals. All units are large enough to stand up in and can accommodate 4/5 people. They are comfortably equipped with mattresses and each have electric light and heating, giving you that great feeling of camping outdoors but still providing you with that extra comfort. **No restrictions, Dogs welcome.** *Absolutely Great Fun*

TELEPHONE/FAX CONTACT Rena Baillie Tel: (01838) 400251 fax: (01838) 400248
OPENING SEASON All year
OPENING HOURS 8am - 11pm
NUMBER OF BEDS 48 (in 12 Wigwams)
BOOKING REQUIREMENTS Booking recommended for large groups. Deposit required
PRICE PER NIGHT £9 adults, £4.50 children under 15 years. Groups from £7 (depending on number)

PUBLIC TRANSPORT
Nearest train station and Citylink drop off at Tyndrum 1½ miles from hostel. Phone number for Taxi/minibus (01838) 400279

DIRECTIONS
On A82 3 miles north of Crianlarich. Opposite Strathfillan Church, 1½ miles south of Tyndrum.

HIGHLAND HOSTELS

Come stay awhile with us in the Highlands of Scotland. Choose from a unique variety of hospitable, independently run Bunkhouses, Hostels and Bothies, mostly set amongst remote, stunning scenery.

Europe's premier outdoor activity and wildlife arena is at our doorsteps, steeped in Pictish and Celtic culture & history - all year round. Cycle, Walk, Pony Trek, Rock Climb, Ski, Sail, Canoe or Kayak on sea, river and loch ~ or quite simply relax.

www.highland-hostels.co.uk
email info@highland-hostels.co.uk
tel (01397) 712900

For a brochure contact: Gavin Hogg, Àite Cruinnichidh, 1 Achluachrach, by Roy Bridge, INVERNESS-SHIRE, PH31 4AW.

WEST HIGHLAND WAY SLEEPER

Bridge of Orchy Station
Bridge of Orchy
Argyll PA36 4AD

A new bunkhouse for a new Millennium. The West Highland Way Sleeper rests at the foot of the famous Beinn Dorain on the West Highland Way. With well over 35 Munros, a ski centre, winter climbs, fishing, the spectacular Glencoe, Glen Etive and Glen Orchy all within easy reach, the hostel offers a myriad of choices and is ideally suited to cater for all types of outdoor pursuits.

Opening April 2000 - please telephone for confirmation. The hostel is housed in the old station building built circa 1894. It is category B listed and has been renovated to include modern features whilst still incorporating much of the original design. We offer good food, good crack but best of all, good value. Traditional style bunk accommodation in two rooms with en-suite toilets/showers, common room, cooking facilities. Licensed restaurant offers quality meals/budget snacks/packed lunches. Unusual malts can be enjoyed by the fire. Laundry facilities are housed in the old signal box. Locked cycle shed for cycle maintenance with spare parts available.

Opening April 2000

TELEPHONE CONTACT Marion or Keith (01855) 831381
OPENING SEASON All year after April 2000
OPENING HOURS 8.00 am to Midnight
NUMBER OF BEDS 15
BOOKING REQUIREMENTS Recommended during high season 50% deposit. Large parties at least 2 weeks advance booking.
PRICE PER NIGHT £8.00 pp - special rates for large parties

PUBLIC TRANSPORT
Hostel is the Bridge of Orchy Station on the Glasgow-Fort William-Mallaig train line. Excellent bus service from Glasgow/Edinburgh.

DIRECTIONS
Travelling north on A82 turn right at hotel follow road for 300 mtrs to station car park. Travelling south turn left. Station is signposted.

JEREMY INGLIS HOSTEL

21 Airds Crescent
Oban
Argyll
PA34 4BA

Jeremy Inglis Hostel is only 150 yards from the station and the bus terminus in Oban. Prices include a continental breakfast with muesli, toast and home made jams, marmalade and Vegemite, etc. Tea and coffee are available at any time. The rooms are mostly double and family size so you have some privacy, all linen is included in the price. Kitchen facilities are provided and the hostel is heated by meter. Smoking is not allowed in the rooms.

Please phone for bookings (01631) 565065 or 563064 if no reply.

TELEPHONE CONTACT Jeremy Inglis (01631) 565065/563064
OPENING SEASON All year
OPENING HOURS No curfew, access with key.
NUMBER OF BEDS 12 to 14
BOOKING REQUIREMENTS Booking preferred. Deposit in certain circumstances.
PRICE PER NIGHT From £7 per person (in a shared room), including breakfast.

PUBLIC TRANSPORT
Nearest train and city link drop off 150 metres from hostel. Ferries to Islands 200 metres. For ferry enquiries phone (01631) 562285

DIRECTIONS
Office hours 9-5 Mon-Fri, From the train station turn right away from the sea into Argyll Square (the tourist office is on the right hand side of the square). 50 metres up on left hand side of the square, is a small bakery and jewellers shop (Charms). Between the two is the entrance to McTavish's Kitchens Office (upstairs). Please ask for Jeremy. **Non-Office hours** If office is closed continue up the left hand side of the square turn first left into Airds Crescent, first doorway, second floor, to the pink door. If Jeremy is not in he's often to be found at Mctavish's Kitchens in George Street next to Woolworths and Boots (Tel (01631) 565065).

SHIELING HOLIDAYS
Craignure
Isle of Mull
PA65 6AY

We're right on the sea, with views to Ben Nevis. There are regular sightings of seals and otters, and sometimes of porpoises, dolphins and eagles. You can hire boats and canoes on site. Stroll to the ferry, pubs, shops, and miniature steam railway. Walk to Torosay and Duart Castles. Catch the bus for Tobermory; for Iona (where Columba brought Christianity to Scotland) and for Staffa (home of puffins, and inspiration for Mendelssohn's overture "Fingal's Cave").

Your accommodation is in Shielings, unique carpeted cottage tents, made by us on Mull, which are clean, bright and spacious, and have real beds for 2, 4, or 6. There are super showers, and communal Shielings with woodburner, TV, payphone and launderette. Our campsite is rated " 5 stars, exceptional, World Class" by the Scottish Tourist Board.

www.holidaymull.org/members/shieling.html

TELEPHONE CONTACT David Gracie, Tel: (01680) 812496, Email: graciemull@aol.com
OPENING SEASON April to October
OPENING HOURS 24 hours (Reception 0800 - 2000)
NUMBER OF BEDS 18
BOOKING REQUIREMENTS Booking advisable. Phone bookings held to 6pm
PRICE PER NIGHT £7 - £8

PUBLIC TRANSPORT
From Glasgow, rail (01631 563083) or bus (0990 505050) at 12.00, ferry (01680 812343) at 16.00 from Oban, arrive Mull 16.40; back by 11.00 ferry, arrive Glasgow 15.45. From Edinburgh, 09.14 bus, 14.00 ferry; back 13.00 ferry, arrive Edinburgh 18.15.

DIRECTIONS
GR 724 369 From the ferry, turn left on the A849 to Iona. After 400 metres, left opposite church past the old pier to reception - 800 metres in all.

ARLE FARM LODGE
Aros
Isle of Mull
Argyle
PA72 6JS

Situated overlooking the sound of Mull on a working farm, Arle Farm Lodge is the ideal base from which to explore the beautiful Hebridean Isle of Mull. This modern well equipped lodge has a large fitted kitchen with cooker, microwave, fridge and ample hot water. All crockery and cutlery are provided and basic provisions may be purchased on the premises. The large sitting room doubles as a lecture room which makes Arle Farm Lodge the perfect location for study groups. The sleeping quarters consist of six twin rooms, two three bedded rooms and two four bedded rooms. There are ample hot showers, a large drying room and laundry facilities which include a hosedown/open air storage for wet suits etc.

Disabled access is easy throughout the ground floor. We have motor access to the shore. There are adequate parking facilities. Children under 5 by prior arrangement only. No dogs.

Graded 3 Star

TELEPHONE/FAX CONTACT Geoff and Mags Williams (01680) 300343
OPENING SEASON All year
OPENING HOURS All day
NUMBER OF BEDS 26
BOOKING REQUIREMENTS Booking (with deposit) required in high season.
PRICE PER NIGHT £12pp reducing to £11 for large groups.

PUBLIC TRANSPORT
Ferries operate from Oban on the mainland to Criagnure and also from Lochaline to Fishnish. The hostel is situated on the main island bus route which operates from Craignure to Tobermory.

DIRECTIONS
On the A848, halfway between Salen and Tobermory, approx 15 miles from Craignure ferry terminal on right hand side of road.

WEST HIGHLAND LODGE BUNKHOUSE
Kinlochleven
Argyll, PA40 4RQ

The West Highland Lodge Bunkhouse is a traditional family run bunkhouse, and as such is non exploitative to visitors and a warm welcome is offered to all. Situated in the heart of the Western Highlands the bunkhouse is ideal for the Mamores, Glen Nevis to the north and Glencoe to the south. The village of Kinlochleven lies at the head of Loch Leven and this beautiful glen provides a unique diversity of walks, scrambles and climbs all year round, it is also a night stop for the West Highland Way. The Glen has a rich abundance of local and natural history. The village is off the A82, the main road through the Highlands and all locations throughout Scotland are easily accessible from nearby Fort William, however Kinlochleven is well serviced by local shops, pubs and a hotel so you can either self cater or eat out. The Bunkhouse sleeps 32 in rooms of four. Amenities include fully equipped kitchen, dining room, lounge with TV, showers and drying room. All rooms are heated and linen and breakfast are available on request. Prices from £6 per night no hidden extras.

TELEPHONE/FAX CONTACT Kevin/Tracey Beard (01855) 831471, fax (0870) 052 4462, Email whl@adl.demon.co.uk
OPENING SEASON All year
OPENING HOURS Flexible
NUMBER OF BEDS 32
BOOKING REQUIREMENTS Booking is advised
PRICE PER NIGHT £6 per person, breakfast is available for an additional £3.50. Reduced rates for groups in the low season.

PUBLIC TRANSPORT
Nearest train station is at Fort William and Citylink coaches drop off in Glencoe.

DIRECTIONS
From the A82 Glasgow to Fort William road take the turn at Glencoe or at North Ballachulish signed to Kinlochleven. The hostel is 100 yards south from the centre of Kinlochleven village.

BLACKWATER HOSTEL
Lab Road
Kinlochleven
Argyll

Blackwater Hostel is in the centre of the scenic village of Kinlochleven surrounded by the Mamore mountains midway between Glencoe and Ben Nevis. An ideal stopover for families, walkers, climbers or those who enjoy the outdoors. There are high- and low-level, half-hour to full-day walks, all with great views, or if you prefer there is a regular bus service from the village to Glencoe, Ballachulish and Fort William. Most water sports are available nearby. The hostel can arrange fishing permits for the River Leven and hill lochs as well as bike hire. Pony trekking is available at Appin and at the nearby Nevis Range and Glencoe there are a range of winter sports to participate in. The hostel offers very comfortable, high-quality bunkhouse accommodation. All rooms have en-suite facilities, TV and central heating. Facilities include self-catering kitchens, lounge, dining and conference area, drying room and laundry. Breakfast and packed lunches can be arranged on request. There are supermarkets, pubs and restaurants within two minutes' walking distance.

TELEPHONE CONTACT Caroline (01855) 831253, Email: black.water@virgin.net, Web: www.scotland2000.com/blackwater
OPENING SEASON All year
OPENING HOURS 24 hours
NUMBER OF BEDS 39 - 2,3,4,8 bedded rooms
BOOKING REQUIREMENTS Not essential
PRICE PER NIGHT £10.00 pp including bed linen

PUBLIC TRANSPORT
The nearest train station is Fort William and National Express travels from Glasgow to Glencoe and Fort William. Regular bus service to Kinlochleven all day from Glencoe, Ballachulish and Fort William.

DIRECTIONS
From A82 Glasgow to Fort William road - turn at Glencoe right to Kinlochleven. The hostel is situated near the centre of Kinlochleven. Just past the Co-op you will see our large sign with an arrow to point you in the direction of the Hostel.

INCHREE
HOSTELS
Onich, Fort William
Highlands, PH33 6SD

Inchree Hostels is a friendly, family run centre, located midway between Ben Nevis and Glencoe, in a peaceful country setting. It is an ideal base for all outdoor acitivites, such as hill-walking, rock/ice climbing, skiing and canoeing; or for simply touring the Western Highlands with ease. There are scenic waterfall and seal watching walks nearby, whilst the adventure sports of mountain-biking, canyoning, canoeing and also mountain guiding are run from the centre. Accommodation consists of two modern, purpose built hostels. Both have full s/c facilities, one for up to 23 persons, and the other for 32 persons in ensuite rooms. Group/family/twin and double rooms are all available. Groups are most welcome, fully catered for if requested. There are laundary/drying facilities, and a technical climbing wall and barbeque area are on site. Local maps, touring guides and useful holiday tips are all provided. Relax in our pub and bistro which has real ales, real fire and real food. Holiday chalet accomodation, each for 4-6 persons, is also available, with fine mountain and loch views.

TELEPHONE/FAX CONTACT Paddy Heron (01855) 821287, Email: inchreecentrel@lineuk.net Web: www.inchree-scotland.com
OPENING SEASON All year
OPENING HOURS All day
NUMBER OF BEDS 23 + 32 +42
BOOKING REQUIREMENTS Booking not required but recommended in summer season. Credit cards accepted.
PRICE PER NIGHT £7 to £11 pp (inc VAT)

PUBLIC TRANSPORT
Citylink coach from Glasgow to Fort William passes by bunkhouse. On all buses (local and long distance), ask for Corran Ferry stop. Bunkhouse sign is 100yds south of bus stop. Nearest train station is in Fort William.

DIRECTIONS
Situated at the north end of the village of Onich, 8 miles south of Fort William and 4 Miles north of Ballachulish Bridge. Turn right off A82 (signposted Inchree) up side road for 300 metres to site entrance.

BEN NEVIS BUNKHOUSE
Achintee Farm
Glen Nevis, Fort William
Inverness-shire, PH33 6TE

Ben Nevis Bunkhouse is a converted stone barn overlooking Glen Nevis. It is situated at the start of the Ben Nevis footpath and at the end of the West Highland Way. Walking, climbing, mountain biking, canoeing and skiing are all available locally.

The main bunkhouse is well equipped for 20 people and is centrally heated. The beds are comfortable and the showers are hot. There is a self catering kitchen and a separate drying room. The kitchen is fully equipped and there is ample seating in the dining area. There is also a smaller self-catering bunkhouse with two twin rooms. Bed and breakfast is provided at the farmhouse and there is a traditional stone cottage and self-catering apartment available for people staying a minimum of 3 nights.

www.glennevis.com

TELEPHONE CONTACT Scot or Heather, Tel: (01397) 702240, Email: achintee.accom@glennevis.com
OPENING SEASON All year
OPENING HOURS Closed for cleaning at midday.
NUMBER OF BEDS 24
BOOKING REQUIREMENTS Booking advised - is essential (with deposit) for groups.
PRICE PER NIGHT Dorm £9.00 per person. Twin £11 per person

PUBLIC TRANSPORT
Nearest train station and Citylink coach services are in Fort William. A local bus operates to Glen Nevis in the summer only, catch it beside Fort William train station and get off at the Visitors Centre.

DIRECTIONS
By Car, follow A82 north out of Fort William - just before the traffic lights take turn into Claggan - at Spar shop look for sign "Achintee-Ben Nevis Footpath" - follow road to end (1 mile). **By Foot**, take A82 north out of Fort William and follow signs to Glen Nevis - at Visitors Centre (1 mile) take foot bridge over river, we are the farm on the other side.

3m

CALLUNA
Heathercroft
Fort William
Inverness-shire
PH33 6RE

Situated within fifteen minutes' walk of Fort William High Street this accommodation is ideal for short or long stays. **Free transport from the town centre is available if we are at home, just give us a call**. The modern accommodation consists of one flat and two new apartments. Bedding is supplied, along with spacious kitchen and comfortable lounge. Very efficient drying rooms. On the spot advice about Ben Nevis from Alan Kimber (Mountain Guide) who owns and runs Calluna with his wife Sue.

Calluna is well known for peace and quiet and fine views over Loch Linnhe to the hills of Ardgour. A popular base for climbing and canoeing groups, families and individual globe trotters. Plenty of parking for mini-buses and trailers. **Scottish Tourist Board approved 2/3 star, self-cater.**

TELEPHONE CONTACT Alan or Sue (01397) 700451
OPENING SEASON All year
OPENING HOURS 24 hours (keys supplied)
NUMBER OF BEDS 22
BOOKING REQUIREMENTS Phone up beforehand
PRICE PER NIGHT £9 / £9.50 per person

PUBLIC TRANSPORT
Fort William train and coach stations are 20 minutes' walk from the hostel. Citylink and local bus services operate from the coach station, *phone Tourist Info (01397 703781) for details*. Alan and Sue offer a free lift from the station when convenient (Taxi fare would be £2).

DIRECTIONS
By Vehicle: From roundabout (West End Hotel) go uphill on Lundavra Rd and take third on left (Connochie Rd) between four storey flats. Follow Connochie Rd and do not take any right turns. You should arrive at our back door! **On Foot:** Ask for directions to the West End Hotel which is five minutes from the Tourist Office and follow the route described for vehicles above (15/20 minutes on foot from Tourist Office) Phone if unsure !

         3m

ÀITE CRUINNICHIDH

1 Achluachrach
By Roy Bridge
Near Fort William
Inverness-shire
PH31 4AW

Àite Cruinnichidh, 15 miles north east of Fort William, occupies a unique sheltered spot adjacent to the Monessie Gorge; explore remote glens, mountain passes and lochs. Numerous easy walks within minutes of the hostel and seven magnificent canoeing rivers within 20 miles. The location is also ideal for climbing (rock & ice), mountain biking and skiing.

A warm, peaceful, friendly, country hostel in a converted barn. Àite Cruinnichidh has been renovated to high standards and sleeps 30 in fives rooms of four, one of six, one twin and one double. All bedding supplied. A fully equipped kitchen/dining room, sitting room, excellent showers. **Additional facilities**:- sauna suite, garden, seminar room, dark room, shop, bike hire, use of maps, advice on walking/cycling routes. Groups and individuals welcome.

TELEPHONE CONTACT (01397) 712315 Gavin or Nicola
OPENING SEASON All year
OPENING HOURS 24 hours
NUMBER OF BEDS 28
BOOKING REQUIREMENTS Booking advised, 50% deposit.
PRICE PER NIGHT £8 per person, discounts for groups

PUBLIC TRANSPORT

Roy Bridge train station is 2 miles from hostel and Citylink coaches drop off all year at Spean Bridge, 5 miles away. Bus service 343 (31st May - 26th Sept) from Fort William to Aviemore drops at our door, (01397) 702373 for details. Pick up from local transport available.

DIRECTIONS

From Fort William follow A82 for 10 miles to Spean Bridge, turn right onto A86 for 3 miles to Roy Bridge. Pass though village and continue for 2 miles. The hostel is 100 metres on the right after passing Glenspean Lodge Hotel on left.

STATION LODGE
Tulloch
Roy Bridge
Inverness-shire
PH31 4AR

Station Lodge, once the Tulloch Railway Station, is located in a unique and picturesque setting at the eastern end of Glen Spean. The lodge is surrounded by numerous excellent walks and climbs, including ten Munros within a short distance. Cyclists can enjoy the many tracks available and skiers can visit the Nevis Range and Cairngorm Ski-Centres nearby. For those who prefer something less strenuous, walk the route of the Lochaber Narrow Gauge Railway and see its views!

The Lodge buildings date from August 1894. We offer comfortable sleeping accommodation for 24 people as groups or individuals, good home cooking, packed lunches or self-catering facilities. Both cycle hire and walking/mountain guides are available with notice. Common room with open fire. **No smoking.**

www.stationlodge.co.uk

TELEPHONE/FAX CONTACT Alan Renwick, Tel/Fax: (01397) 732333, Email: info@stationlodge.co.uk
OPENING SEASON All year
OPENING HOURS All day
NUMBER OF BEDS 24
BOOKING REQUIREMENTS Booking is advisable with 25% deposit. Cheque payable to Station Lodge
PRICE PER NIGHT £10-£11 per person

PUBLIC TRANSPORT
Tulloch station is on site. Nearest Citylink is at Speanbridge or Newtonmore. There is a summer only bus service between Fort William and Cairngorm, which stops on demand and calls at Tulloch.

DIRECTIONS
The hostel is off the A86 road, 5 miles east of Roy Bridge. Turn right at telephone box, next to telephone exchange building. The station is ½ mile down this road. From the East it is 1 mile from Laggan Dam, turn left at telephone box.

FARR COTTAGE HOSTEL AND ACTIVITY CENTRE
Farr Cottage
Corpach
Fort William PH33 7LR

Farr Cottage is situated in Corpach, just 4 miles outside Fort William, with breath-taking view of Ben Nevis and across Loch Linnhe, in the outdoor pursuits capital of Scotland.

We specialise in Scottish History and Whisky evenings and there is a full range of in-house facilities including; satellite television, video lounge, licensed bar, pool table, self-catering facilities, Email, laundry and drying facilities, central heating and hot showers. We also organise outdoor pursuits which comprise, white water rafting, canyoning, climbing, abseiling, skiing, snowboarding, fishing, golf and many many more! We can provide evening meals, breakfast, picnic lunches and we will ensure you have the break or holiday of a lifetime with us. Our professional team are geared to meet your needs and requirements.

The FULL Scottish Experience!!

TELEPHONE CONTACT (01397) 772315 Stuart
OPENING SEASON All year
OPENING HOURS 24 hours a day
NUMBER OF BEDS 30
BOOKING REQUIREMENTS Advance booking advised
PRICE PER NIGHT £10 and £11

PUBLIC TRANSPORT
Corpach train station is 400m from the hostel. The nearest Citylink service is four miles away at Fort William. Taxi fare from Fort William is approximatly £3.

DIRECTIONS
Follow the A82 north from Fort William towards Inverness for 2 miles. Turn left at the A830 to Mallaig. Follow this road for 2 miles into Corpach. We are on the right hand side of the road. Look for the flags.

1m

GLENUIG INN & BUNKHOUSE

Glenuig
By Loch Ailort
Inverness-shire
PH38 4NG

The Glenuig Inn and Bunkhouse overlooks the sea, close to a sandy beach and pier. The area is popular amongst walkers, windsurfers and divers. The local wildlife includes deer, buzzards, seals and porpoises and fishing is available in the lochans and larger rivers. You can visit the nearby Castle Tioram, seat of the Clan Ranald Macdonald, or walk to Smirisary, an old crofting community. Or, if you prefer, the Inn is in a beautiful location to just relax and enjoy a dram!

We welcome those who are travelling alone, in small groups or large groups up to 18. A range of accommodation is available comprising of bed and breakfast; self-catering chalet sleeping four with kitchen/living room; or the bunkhouse which sleeps 10 with shared bathroom and shower and includes full Scottish breakfast. The Glenuig Inn has a small traditional bar which serves a range of beers and spirits. Celtic music abounds and can often be heard on an impromptu basis.

TELEPHONE CONTACT (01687) 470219 Mandy or Peter
OPENING SEASON March - October + New Year
OPENING HOURS All day
NUMBER OF BEDS 18
BOOKING REQUIREMENTS Booking advised at weekends and in July and August.
PRICE PER NIGHT From £12.50

PUBLIC TRANSPORT
Nearest train station is at Loch Ailort (8 miles from hostel). There are two buses a day from Fort William.

DIRECTIONS
Take the A830 from Fort William to Mallaig, at Lochailort turn left on A861. The Inn is 8 miles down the road on the right. Or from Corran Ferry from A82 and follow A861

SHEENAS
BACKPACKERS LODGE
Harbour View
Mallaig
Inverness shire
PH41 4PU

The Backpackers Lodge in Mallaig offers a homely base from which you can explore the Inner Hebrides, the famous white sands of Morar and the remote peninsula of Knoydart. Mallaig itself is a working fishing village which makes it very exciting when the boats come in to land. Come and see the seals playing in the harbour waiting for the boats.

The hostel provides excellent budget accommodation with two rooms each with six beds, a drying room, full central heating and fully equipped kitchen/common room with coal fire.

Meals are available during the summer months, with notice.

TELEPHONE CONTACT (01687) 462764
OPENING SEASON All year
OPENING HOURS 24 hour access
NUMBER OF BEDS 12
BOOKING REQUIREMENTS No need to book
PRICE PER NIGHT £9.50 per person.

PUBLIC TRANSPORT
Mallaig has a train station. Nearest Citylink drop off is in Fort William. For information on local buses phone (01967) 431272

DIRECTIONS
From railway station turn right, hostel is two buildings along.

THE GLEBE BARN
Isle of Eigg
Scotland
PH42 4RL

A new conversion of an 18th-Century building, the Glebe Barn has charm and character whilst providing comfortable accommodation with magnificent views. You can enjoy breathtaking scenery along numerous walks; study fascinating geological formations, or explore varied natural habitats with incredible varieties of plant and animal species. Relax on beautiful sandy beaches, listen to the famous singing sands and watch the eagles soar above the spectacular Sgurr of Eigg. Just a mile away there is a well stocked shop and cafe/restaurant with regular traditional music sessions. Facilities at the Barn include a well equipped kitchen, spacious lounge/dining room (polished maple floor, log fire), a combination of twin, triple, family and dormitory rooms, each with wash hand basins (linen provided), central heating, hot showers plus laundry facilities.
http://ourworld.compuserve.com/homepages/glebebarneigg

TELEPHONE CONTACT Karen or Simon (01687) 482417,
Email: glebebarneigg@compuserve.com
OPENING SEASON Individuals April to October, Groups all year
OPENING HOURS All day
NUMBER OF BEDS 24
BOOKING REQUIREMENTS Booking essential prior to boarding ferry. Deposit required for advance bookings.
PRICE PER NIGHT £9.50 pp (£22 twin room) Group bookings for 3 nights or more £8.50 pp

PUBLIC TRANSPORT
Fort William is the nearest National Express Coach stop. The early train from Fort William to Arisaig and Mallaig meets the ferry. Daily summer sailings from Arisaig or Mallaig.

DIRECTIONS
NO CAR FERRY - We generally meet visitors at the pier. Follow tarmac road around the shore and up hill until you cross a small stone bridge over a burn. Continue up hill and take first track on right. Taxi/minibus service available on request.

ISLE OF MUCK
BUNKHOUSE
Isle of Muck
Via Mallaig
Inverness-shire
PH41 2RP

The Isle of Muck Bunkhouse overlooks Port Mor, near the Pier, and invites you to sample life on a small Hebridean island: a working hill farm with just 15 households. Enjoy the stunning sea views, sandy beaches, and the closeness to wildlife and farm animals. The Island has an excellent ferry service and communication links and is a fascinating place to investigate, with signs of an earlier Gaelic community and a Bronze Age fort. Its terrain is mostly low lying, and there is a lot of coastline and an adjoining smaller island to explore. During spring and summer the licensed restaurant serves fresh baking and quality meals using local produce. Visit us in autumn and winter for craft courses, quiet study, star gazing.....

The Bunkhouse can be a self-catering hostel, holiday cottage or base for a camping group. It has a kitchen with gas stove and small fridge, a bath/shower room and a living room. The focal point is the Rayburn stove which emanates constant warmth. There are some board games, cards and a wide range of books.

TELEPHONE CONTACT Rosie 01687.462042
OPENING SEASON All year
OPENING HOURS 24 hours
NUMBER OF BEDS 6 (2 twinbedded and 1 double)
BOOKING REQUIREMENTS Recommended
PRICE PER NIGHT £9.50 (£8.50 with own sleeping bag) reductions for families and larger groups

PUBLIC TRANSPORT
Train stations at Arisaig and Mallaig. Book your boat tickets in advance from Arisaig Marine (summer season only) (01687) 450224; or from Mallaig, Caledonian MacBrayne (all year) (01687) 462403

DIRECTIONS
GR 427 794 By road to Arisaig or Mallaig via Fort William. Ferry details given in Public Transport section above.

POTTERY BUNKHOUSE

Caoldair Pottery
Laggan Bridge
Inverness-shire, PH20 1BT

The Pottery Bunkhouse is situated in the valley of the river Spey looking onto the Monadhliath mountains to the North. See it to believe it! Laggan is a working Highland village with a reputation for adventurous rural initiatives, such as the Laggan Forestry Project. It provides an ideal base for day trips to many places including Loch Ness, or for local exploration of the Monadhliath mountains, Strathmashie forest, Loch Laggan, Creag Meagaidh Nature Reserve, the Corrieyairack Pass, Ben Alder and many tracks and paths.

The Bunkhouse is a purpose built timber building nestling at the rear of the Caoldair pottery and coffee shop. The facilities include two en-suite family rooms and three bunkrooms, disabled shower/toilet, lounge and TV room, kitchen, drying room, central heating throughout. The on-site coffee shop provides excellent home-baking (continental breakfast if required) with a range of clothing and artefacts for purchase (summer season only). The nearest building is the pub (400m) which provides meals and a lively local bar.

TELEPHONE/FAX CONTACT (01528) 544231 Lynda
OPENING SEASON All year
OPENING HOURS All day. No curfew
NUMBER OF BEDS 34
BOOKING REQUIREMENTS Please telephone to check availability especially for weekends and group bookings
PRICE PER NIGHT £9.00 - £10.50 pp, including linen.

PUBLIC TRANSPORT
Nearest train station and Citylink coach stop are in Newtonmore (7 miles from the hostel).

DIRECTIONS
You will find us on the A889, 8 miles from the A9 at Dalwhinnie heading west to Fort William and Skye.

NEWTONMORE INDEPENDENT HOSTEL
Craigellachie House
Main Street, Newtonmore
Inverness-shire, PH20 1DA

Newtonmore, an attractive village in the Central Highlands, is the perfect base for outdoor activities, relaxing or touring. The village has shops, garage and several hotels which serve good value food and drink. The area has a colourful history; follow the Castle or Whisky trails, visit the Folk Museum or the Steam Railway. You can walk, climb, ski, canoe, windsurf, cycle, fish, golf, birdwatch or sail, the choice is yours. The purpose built hostel has lots of showers and toilets, brilliant drying room, well equipped kitchen and lounge/dining area with wood burning stove. **No Meters**. **Smoking is not allowed anywhere in the hostel**, smokers are welcome to smoke outside. Inverness 46, Fort William 50, and Glasgow/Edinburgh 110 miles. *Come and stay in our hostel, the area is unique, you will love it.*

Web Site www.HighlandHostel.co.uk

TELEPHONE/FAX CONTACT Kathryn or Peter, tel/fax (01540) 673360, Email newtonmore@HighlandHostel.co.uk
OPENING SEASON All year
OPENING HOURS All day, no curfew
NUMBER OF BEDS 18
BOOKING REQUIREMENTS   Phone to check availability, especially for weekend and group bookings, 20% deposit.
PRICE PER NIGHT £9 pp, £65 - 8 beds, £130 - sole use.

PUBLIC TRANSPORT
Newtonmore train station ½ mile from hostel. Buses from Inverness and Perth stop in the village (0990 505050).

DIRECTIONS
GR 713 990. The hostel is behind Craigellachie House in the centre of the village at the junction of the A86 and B9150. Look for blue signs.

1m

CROFT HOLIDAYS

Strone Road
Newtonmore
Invernesshire
PH20 1BA

Our newly refurbished croft accommodation, in the foothills of the Monadhliath mountains, has family units and 2 and 4 bedded rooms. From the door explore (by foot or bike) the hills and moor to the north, east and west. Stunning views across the valley of Spey beckon you to the hills of the south. Join the way-marked Wild Cat Trail just 200m from the door. Our traditional highland village has shops, pubs, museums, golf course, tennis, and Waltzing Waters. From its central position there is easy access to several ski areas; a variety of car and bike tours and many tourist attractions including Landmark-Highland Heritage Adventure Centre, the Highland Wildlife Park, the Castle and Whisky trails and the famous Loch Ness. Our well equipped hostel and its cottages have central heating (no meters), TV, drying rooms, lockable bike/ski storage and plenty of parking space. We welcome well behaved pets.

www.newtonmore.com/strone

TELEPHONE CONTACT Mary, Tel: (01540) 673504,
Email: mmakenzie@sprite.co.uk
OPENING SEASON All year
OPENING HOURS 24 hours
NUMBER OF BEDS 18
BOOKING REQUIREMENTS Group bookings essential, individual bookings preferred - please phone for late bookings (deposit required)
PRICE PER NIGHT £9 per person, £90 for 12 beds. Reduced rates for weekly bookings.

PUBLIC TRANSPORT
Newtonmore Train Station 2km away. Citylink Stop 1km (Waltzing Waters). Airports at Inverness (45 miles) and Edinburgh (100 miles).

DIRECTIONS
GR 721 001. Look for Highlander Hotel on A86 at the end of Newtonmore Village. Turn into Strone Road and follow road 500m

GLEN FESHIE HOSTEL

Balachroick House
Kincraig, Inverness-shire
PH21 1NH

Set in beautiful Glen Feshie with immediate access to the Cairngorm National Nature Reserve, this hostel is ideally placed for walking, climbing and cycling. In winter Glen Feshie is the perfect base to try cross-country ski touring. Both Nordic skiing equipment and mountain bikes can be hired from the hostel. Watersports and pony trekking are nearby for those with transport.

The hostel has three bunkrooms each with four beds, a double room and a single room (duvets and linen provided). Hot showers, and good drying facilities are available. The kitchen is fully equipped for self-catering and there is a wood burning stove in the common room/dining area. Porridge is provided free for breakfast and other meals including vegetarian/vegan meals can be provided with notice. There is a small store selling essentials, homemade bread, free range eggs and other goodies.

TELEPHONE CONTACT Jean Hamilton (01540) 651323
OPENING SEASON All year
OPENING HOURS All day - 24 hours
NUMBER OF BEDS 15
BOOKING REQUIREMENTS Booking advised at weekends.
PRICE PER NIGHT £8 per person (including porridge for breakfast), £28 for family bunkroom (4/5 beds), £88 whole hostel.

PUBLIC TRANSPORT
Train stations at Kingussie (15km) and Aviemore (15km). Citylink buses stop at Kingussie and Aviemore and also limited number stopping at Kincraig (7km from hostel). Hostel can collect from buses and trains if contacted in advance.

DIRECTIONS
GR 849 009. From Kingussie take B9152 to Kincraig. Turn right at Kincraig, down unclassified road, after 2km turn left onto the B970 towards Feshiebridge. After crossing the River Feshie in 1.5km, turn right onto a road signposted Achlean and hostel, follow for 4km.

3m

BADENOCH CHRISTIAN CENTRE

Kincraig
Kingussie
Inverness-shire PH21 1NA

The Badenoch Christian centre is situated in Strathspey, set amidst the mountains, woodlands, rivers and lochs of this beautiful region of Scotland. Badenoch makes an excellent base for outdoor activities; within close proximity of the centre there are facilities for pony-trekking, mountain biking, orienteering, golf, canoeing and sailing. The Cairngorm and Monadhliath mountains are only a few miles away and there are many tourist attractions. At the centre we try to present the Christian faith in a warm, friendly, family atmosphere by offering comfortable well equipped self-catering accommodation to our guests. Groups, families and singles are all welcome at the centre which is a single storey building (disabled access) with four-bedded and two-bedded bunkrooms, plus one twin-bedded room, a large fully equipped kitchen and spacious open-plan dining and lounge area. **This is a non smoking centre and alcohol is not permitted.**

Email: badenoch@dial.pipex.com

TELEPHONE CONTACT (01540) 651373 Manager
OPENING SEASON All year
OPENING HOURS All day until 11pm
NUMBER OF BEDS 34
BOOKING REQUIREMENTS Booking recommended with £5.00 per head non-refundable deposit
PRICE PER NIGHT £9.00 reducing to £59.50 for seven nights. 10% reduction for over 25 people. Reductions midweek October to March.

PUBLIC TRANSPORT
Aviemore has the nearest train station and Citylink coach stop. Aviemore is 5 miles from the hostel.

DIRECTIONS
Turn off at the war memorial in Kincraig, pass the Church hall on your left and immediately left into driveway.

LAZY DUCK HOSTEL

Badanfhuarain, Nethybridge
Inverness-shire, PH25 3ED

Beside a stream in a 3 acre forest homestead, the *Lazy Duck* overlooks waterfowl ponds and has clear views south to the Cairngorm mountains, and deer paths to explore starting almost from the door. With adjoining covered garden, barbecue etc, the accommodation is interesting and friendly. *Bothy-style*, it has a choice of sleeping areas and is cosy and relaxing with woodburning stove, music system (no TV), tapes and books. It has a well equipped kitchen, shower room, laundry/drying facilities, frozen food supplies, ready meals, free range eggs (usually), advance groceries and use of telephone or Email by arrangement. Nethybridge, on the *Speyside Way,* has a Post Office/store, butcher, bike and ski hire, ski school, tennis, golf and a choice of pubs with food. The area is also ideal for climbing, hill walking, sailing, canoeing, fishing, bird watching or to relax and enjoy peace amid wonderful scenery. *www.lazyduck.co.uk*

TELEPHONE/FAX CONTACT David or Valery, Tel/Fax: (01479) 821642, Email: lazy.duck@virgin.net
OPENING SEASON All year
OPENING HOURS All day
NUMBER OF BEDS 5 (+ alpine platform)
BOOKING REQUIREMENTS Phone for availability. A deposit guarantees a bed. Phone bookings are kept until an agreed time.
PRICE PER NIGHT £8.50, 10% discount for 7 nights / groups of 5+.

PUBLIC TRANSPORT
Coach to Aviemore by Scottish Citylink or National Express from England. Trains to Aviemore daily from London Kings Cross/Peterborough/York/Newcastle/Edinburgh, overnight sleeper from London Euston via Crewe. Taxi from Aviemore about £10. Local bus service from most local villages and Aviemore. Phone (01479) 811566 for times and pick-up points (ask for Causer crossroads, Nethybridge).

DIRECTIONS
The Lazy Duck is 1 mile from the centre of Nethybridge village. Turn off the B970 at Nethybridge Hotel. Follow the road for ¾ mile to crossroads, go straight across then look for hostel logo on r.h.s. 100 yds past 30mph signs. Local buses stop at crossroads.

SPEYSIDE BACKPACKERS

The Stopover
16 The Square
Grantown-on-Spey
Morayshire, PH26 3HG

The hostel opened in April 1995 when the building was upgraded and adapted for its present use. The building provides self-catering accommodation for 30 people mostly in bunks, but private and double bedded rooms are available. Free hot showers and WC facilities are located on all floors, including excellent facilities for the disabled on the ground floor. All bedding is included in the price and breakfast can be provided for groups by arrangement.

The hostel provides an excellent base for exploring the Strathspey area including the Whisky Trail. For those seeking a more activity-based visit the area offers fantastic opportunities for most outdoor pursuits, the following list is not exhaustive:- walking, climbing, skiing, fishing, mountain biking, golfing, horse riding, watersports, bird watching, canoeing etc. Check out our website www.scotpackers-hostels.co.uk

TELEPHONE CONTACT Stewart or Richard (01479) 873514
OPENING SEASON All year
OPENING HOURS All day
NUMBER OF BEDS 30
BOOKING REQUIREMENTS Advisable in peak season.
PRICE PER NIGHT From £8.50 - £12.50 pp

PUBLIC TRANSPORT
Train stations at Aviemore and Carrbridge. Nearest Citylink stop at Aviemore. Local buses run by Highland Country buses, phone (01463) 222244 for details. Approximate taxi fares:- from Aviemore (14 miles) £14, from Carrbridge (9miles) £10.

DIRECTIONS
The hostel is easy to find, located in the square at Grantown-on-Spey. If travelling from the south the hostel is situated on your left hand side, just past the war memorial.

CARRBRIDGE BUNKHOUSE HOSTEL

Dalrachney House
Carrbridge
Invernesshire
PH23 3AX

Carrbridge Bunkhouse is a cosy wood panelled cabin situated next to the River Dulnain. The village sits nestled in the glorious Spey Valley - famous for its year round attractions and activities to suit all including ski school and ski hire, home of Landmark Centre, golf, pony trekking and an indoor swimming pool with sauna and steam room. In the winter the best of Scottish skiing and climbing is to be found on the snowcovered mighty Cairngorms and in the summer every kind of watersport can be enjoyed within this area of unsurpassed beauty.

The Bunkhouse has a fully equipped kitchen/dining room with wood burning stove, toilets and showers, sauna, drying room and ample secure parking. The village is nearby for provisions and a variety of eating places including restaurants, cafe and fish and chip shop.

TELEPHONE/FAX CONTACT Tom/Alyson 01479.841250
OPENING SEASON All year
OPENING HOURS 24 hours
NUMBER OF BEDS 18
BOOKING REQUIREMENTS Booking recommended
PRICE PER NIGHT £7.00 pp summer £7.50 winter, group discounts.

PUBLIC TRANSPORT
Bus and train service in village. Citylink coach services from London to Edinburgh and Glasgow to Inverness stop at Carrbridge.

DIRECTIONS
GR 896 229 A short walk from the village on the road to Inverness or follow the riverside footpath to Dalrachney House.

        3m

EASTGATE HOSTEL
38 Eastgate
Eastgate, Inverness
IV2 3NA

Eastgate Hostel is a perfect base for backpackers, walkers and cyclists to explore the Highland capital and surrounding area. Loch Ness is only a short drive away, as is Urquhart Castle and Culloden battlefield. Day trips to Skye, Orkney and the north are all possible. Inverness boasts an excellent choice of pubs, clubs and restaurants to suit all tastes, while a large modern shopping centre is located directly opposite us. We are a 5 minute walk from the train and bus stations - find us on the second floor, opposite the "Eastgate Shopping Centre".

Enjoy your stay in a cosy, relaxed atmosphere with friendly staff, who will advise you on travel arrangements, bookings etc. Make full use of all our facilities: large kitchen, lounge/dining room, beer garden, barbecue, ample showers, 2 twin rooms, 1 family room, 5 six bedded rooms, free tea and coffee, no curfew, cycle hire, Email access, book-a-bed-ahead service. Children and groups **most** welcome. Book early for twin/family rooms. Annexe providing extra 60 beds open in July and August.

TELEPHONE/FAX CONTACT Lee, (01463) 718756
OPENING SEASON All year
OPENING HOURS July/August 7am-11pm. Rest of year 8am-11pm. No curfew as late keys are provided.
NUMBER OF BEDS 47 (plus 60 July to August)
BOOKING REQUIREMENTS Booking required 2/3 weeks in advance in summer. 10% deposit for group bookings.
PRICE PER NIGHT £8.90 per person.

PUBLIC TRANSPORT
Inverness has a train station and is served by Citylink.

DIRECTIONS
Turn left outside train/bus station, cross at traffic lights next to taxi rank. Walk to Burger King, turn left, walk 200m you will see Eastgate Shopping Centre on left. We are opposite on the right. Entrance next to Chinese takeaway.

LOCH NESS BACKPACKERS

Coiltie Farmhouse
East Lewiston, Drumnadrochit
Inverness-shire, IV63 6UJ

Loch Ness Backpackers Lodge is the perfect base from which to enjoy the mystic atmosphere and breathtaking scenery which surrounds Loch Ness and Urquhart Castle. The outstanding beauty of the area makes it ideal for walking (we are on the Great Glen Way), cycling, horse riding, fishing, photography, or just cruising on the Loch. All of these activities are within walking distance of the hostel, as are the Loch Ness Exhibition Centre, Restaurants, Bank, Post Office, Bus Stops, and Pubs where you can have a drink and a friendly chat with the locals. The hostel is a cosy and friendly place to unwind in a very relaxed atmosphere. We have two lounges with coal/log fire (one with TV and Video), two fully equipped self-catering kitchens, an excellent BBQ area, hot showers and very comfy beds (linen included). We offer discounts to holders of Scotrail and Citylink passes.

TELEPHONE CONTACT (01456) 450807
OPENING SEASON All year
OPENING HOURS All day, no curfew.
NUMBER OF BEDS 38
BOOKING REQUIREMENTS Booking advised in peak season
PRICE PER NIGHT From £9. Enquire for group discounts.

PUBLIC TRANSPORT

Nearest train (0345 484950) and coach (0990 505050, 808080) stations are in Inverness. From Inverness (15 miles) there is a regular bus service to Lewiston with Citylink, Skyeways and Highland Country Buses. Ask for Backpackers in Lewiston. If a few people are travelling from Inverness a taxi is a good idea. If travelling from Fort William or Skye the buses pass through Lewiston on their way to Inverness.

DIRECTIONS

Hostel is near the A82 Inverness to Fort William road. From Inverness, go through Drumnadrochit to Lewiston, hostel sign first left after Smiddy Pub. From Fort William, hostel turn off is immediate right after the stone bridge in Lewiston.

GLEN AFFRIC
BACKPACKERS HOSTEL
Cannich By Beauly
Inverness-shire
IV4 7LT

Glen Affric Backpackers Hostel offers a high standard of accommodation at a budget price. The bedrooms accommodate one or two people in single beds. We also have larger rooms with four beds which are ideal for families. All bedding is provided in price. The hostel has two common rooms each with log burning fires and an ample supply of wood. One common room has a television and pool table and a large assortment of reading matter. The other common room is a peaceful reading/study area with comfy chairs and a small kitchen area. We have a large dining/kitchen area fully equipped with cookers, fridges and microwave. A chest freezer is also available. There are ample toilet and shower facilities with constant hot water.

The hostel is situated in the village of Cannich which is an ideal base for touring the Highlands. We are surrounded by beautiful scenery with an abundance of walks in the locality.

TELEPHONE CONTACT Kath Gregory (01456) 415263
OPENING SEASON All year (except Xmas and New Year)
OPENING HOURS Access 24 hrs, service between 9am-10pm
NUMBER OF BEDS 70
BOOKING REQUIREMENTS Groups should book in advance with 10% deposit.
PRICE PER NIGHT £6 per person.

PUBLIC TRANSPORT
Nearest train station at Inverness, 26 miles away. Nearest Citylink drop off at Drumnadrochit, 14 miles. Regular bus service (Highland Buses) from Inverness, passes hostel three times a day.

DIRECTIONS
By car:- take A82 out of Inverness to Drumnadrochit, then A831 for Cannich. Upon entering Cannich look for hostel sign on left.

COUGIE LODGE
Cougie,Tomich
Cannich,Beauly
Inverness
IV4 7LY

Cougie is an isolated croft, six miles from Tomich, along a forest track. A wonderful, peaceful place to relax and go for walks in a forest of ancient Caledodian pines. An ideal stopover between Cannich and Glen Affric for walkers, mountain bikers or pony trekkers, on the way to or from the west.

Offering a friendly welcome to families, groups or loners Cougie Lodge provides accommodation in 'Carma Brecka' a cosy, homely timber cabin which sleeps 5/6 in three bedrooms, bathroom, kitchen, sitting room, shower room. Too remote for mains there is a generator for electricity, calor gas and wood stove for cooking, heating and hot water. Meet the Jersey cows, friendly sheep, highland ponies and an assortment of poultry, cats and dogs. Large garden and patio with BBQ and picnic tables. Camping, if hostel full, with use of facilities.

TELEPHONE CONTACT Valerie (01456) 415459
OPENING SEASON April to September inclusive
OPENING HOURS 24 hours
NUMBER OF BEDS 5 (1 double, 2 bunks)
BOOKING REQUIREMENTS Telephone if possible or just turn up.
PRICE PER NIGHT £8.00 pp - discounts for groups of 4+ or stays of 3 nights or longer.

PUBLIC TRANSPORT
Bus from Inverness to Tomich and Cannich. Lifts can be arranged.

DIRECTIONS
GR 245 215. From Cannich take road to Tomich. At end of village follow sign for Plodda falls and small sign to Cougie. Continue following Plodda/Cougie signs to Plodda car park. Over bridge and up hill over cattle grid and on to Cougie which is 6 mile from Tomich.

TIGH ISEABAIL BUNKHOUSE

Camusluinie
Killilan
Kyle of Lochalsh
IV40 8EA

Tigh Iseabail Hostel is set in the beautiful Glen Elchaig in Kintail. 11km from the main road, it is fairly remote and there are amazing walks, including a walk to the Fall of Glomach (the 3rd highest waterfall in Europe). Alternatively hire a bike from the hostel to get further into the hills.

Basic provisions are available from the hostel and self-catering breakfast (made using our own fresh free range eggs) is included in the price. The hostel sleeps 10 people. There is one room which sleeps 6 with toilets and shower. The second room sleeps 4 with its own toilet and shower.

Free transport is available from/to Kyle or Dornie (Eilean Donan Castle).

TELEPHONE CONTACT Willie (01599) 588205
OPENING SEASON All year
OPENING HOURS No curfew
NUMBER OF BEDS 10
BOOKING REQUIREMENTS Block bookings essential
PRICE PER NIGHT £7.50 per person. £6.50 per person for groups of 10. £280 weekly for hostel.

PUBLIC TRANSPORT
Kyle of Lochalsh has a train station and the nearest Citylink drop off is in Dornie (12km from hostel). The hostel will provide a free bus from/to Kyle and Dornie on request.

DIRECTIONS
From the A87 Dornie to Kyle of Lochalsh, 1km past Dornie Bridge, turn off the main road at the junction signposted Camusluinie / Killilan / Sallachy. Follow signs for hostel 11km along to the road end.

STATION BUNKHOUSE

Burnside, Plockton
Ross-shire
IU52 8TF

The Station Bunkhouse is situated adjacent to the Railway Station, only six miles from Kyle of Lochalsh and is ideal for those travelling by train or bus. For hillwalkers with cars, Plockton is geographically ideal for trips to Torridon, Kintail mountain range and Cullins of Skye. There are nearly 50 Munros within an hour's drive of this beautiful west coast village. Plockton is now a thriving place and people from all over the world come to visit what has been called "Britain's Prettiest Village". Because of this popularity, which has been enhanced by "Hamish MacBeth" the hit TV series being made locally, there is an energetic and vibrant community and visitors will always find a warm welcome.

The bunkhouse is fully centrally heated and offers four bedrooms (two sleeping 4 and two sleeping six) all with solid pine bunks. There is a spacious open-plan living/kitchen/dining area with the kitchen being fitted with cooker, separate hob, microwave, fridge and all kitchen utensils.

TELEPHONE CONTACT Tel: (01599) 544235, Email: gill@ecosse.net
OPENING SEASON All year
OPENING HOURS Flexible
NUMBER OF BEDS 20
BOOKING REQUIREMENTS None
PRICE PER NIGHT £8.50 and £10 per person. Reduced rates for Groups staying more than 2 nights.

PUBLIC TRANSPORT
Situated next to Plockton train station. Citylink coaches drop off at Kyle of Lochalsh. Post bus from Kyle of Lochalsh to Plockton.

DIRECTIONS
Situated adjacent to the Railway Station and on the only road into Plockton, six miles from Kyle of Lochalsh.

CUCHULAINN'S BACKPACKERS HOSTEL

Station Road, Kyle of Lochalsh
Ross-shire, IV40 8AE

Centrally situated in Kyle of Lochalsh, Cuchulainn's is a cosy well equipped hostel which provides quality self-catering accommodation at an affordable price. Accommodation is in three rooms (2,4 and 6 beds). There are showers, a fully equipped kitchen, a launderette and plenty of hot water. Bedding is provided and sheets can be hired (50p) if required. Kyle of Lochalsh is at the mainland end of the controversial Skye Bridge, and close to the world famous Eilean Donan Castle. Kyle boasts a small fishing fleet, a swimming pool, a nine hole golf course and a wide variety of shops as well as two banks and a Post Office; all within easy reach of the hostel. Next door to the hostel is a friendly pub and restaurant which provides good home made food in cheery surroundings. Kyle is an ideal place for hill-walkers, climbers and divers, and there is plenty of good fishing. Bike, car and boat (for parties of divers/fishermen) hire is available. Kyle is accessible by car, boat, train and bus and makes an ideal centre for touring Skye and Wester Ross. Boat trips are available in Kyle.

TELEPHONE CONTACT Paul (01599) 534492
OPENING SEASON All year round
OPENING HOURS All day - no curfew.
NUMBER OF BEDS 12
BOOKING REQUIREMENTS Phone bookings held until 6.00pm. Advance payment guarantees bed.
PRICE PER NIGHT £8 - £9 per person per night.

PUBLIC TRANSPORT

Kyle of Lochalsh train station is 150m from the hostel. The Citylink bus stops 50m from the hostel. Buses to main places of interest in Skye pass through Kyle. Phone Skyeways (01599 534862) and Highland County Skye Line (01478 612622).

DIRECTIONS

Entering Kyle on the A87 travelling north, it is the first building on the right after the railway station.

SKYEWALKER
INDEPENDENT
HOSTEL
Old School, Portnalong
Isle of Skye, IV47 8SL

Situated close to the Cuillin hills on the beautiful Minginish Peninsula the old village school has been tastefully converted to very high standards of comfort and has all the normal features and more! The hostel is centrally heated throughout and provides plenty of hot water and more than adequate shower and toilet facilities. The village Post Office and a small shop are housed within the hostel and for those not wishing to use the well fitted kitchen at any time, a good café is situated in the hostel grounds. The pub is 5 minutes' walk away, and beaches and beautiful walks are nearby. All entrances are ramped to provide full wheelchair access throughout the hostel. Bed linen included and no meters! The perfect base for outdoor activities with hill, moors and water combining into spectacular scenery - and a hot shower and comfy bed to finish the day.

Email skyewalker.hostel@virgin.net

TELEPHONE/FAX CONTACT Trevor or June (01478) 640250, fax (01478) 640420
OPENING SEASON All year
OPENING HOURS 24 hour access
NUMBER OF BEDS 36
BOOKING REQUIREMENTS In peak season booking 4 weeks in advance is advised (deposit required)
PRICE PER NIGHT From £7 per person.

PUBLIC TRANSPORT
Two local buses run each weekday. Running from Portree via Sligachan to Portnalong (hostel) and back. Citylink coaches (from the mainland and north Skye) drop off at Sligachan. We will provide free transport from/to Sligachan outside of bus hours.

DIRECTIONS
GR 348 348. From Sligachan take A863 then B8009 through Carbost and Fernilea to Portnalong. At the bus stop turn left onto Fiskavaig Road, walk 500m to hostel.

CROFT BUNKHOUSE AND BOTHIES
Portnalong
Isle of Skye, IV47 8SL

Four adjacent hostels on a 12 acre croft on the west coast of Skye. Converted from barns by the owner, a retired mountain guide. Advice on walks & tours, free map loan, bike hire, pub 500 yds.

Bunkhouse - sleeps 14 on alpine sleeping shelves with foam mattresses, hot showers, fully equipped kitchen, washing machine, drying room & large common room with table tennis table etc

Bothy - sleeps 6 in first floor dormitory with views over crofts to Portnalong harbour. Ground floor fully equipped kitchen/living room, toilet & hot shower, drying room. A popular family unit.

Bothy Beag - sleeps 4 in a compact self-contained unit, 2 built in bunk beds in fully equipped kitchen/living room, shower and toilet.

Cabin - sleeps 2 in a bijou self-contained kitchen/living room with bunk bed, en suite toilet facilities. Fine views over crofts to the sea.

TELEPHONE/FAX CONTACT   Pete or Jean, Tel/Fax: (01478) 640254, email: skyehostel@lineone.net, Web: www.mtn.co.uk/acc

OPENING SEASON All year

OPENING HOURS No curfew

NUMBER OF BEDS Bunkhouse 14, Bothies 6, 4 and 2.

BOOKING REQUIREMENTS   Phone bookings held to 6pm. Advance payment guarantees bed (Visa/Access accepted).

PRICE PER NIGHT £6.50 per person. <u>No hidden extra charges</u>. Group bookings up to 10% discount. Camping £3 to £5.

PUBLIC TRANSPORT
Cross island Citylink coaches from mainland pass through Sligachan. Two buses daily (weekdays only) from Portree via Sligachan to Portnalong. Hostel minibus collection from Sligachan by arrangement, weekends and evenings.

DIRECTIONS
GR 348 353. From Sligachan take the A863 for 4 miles then left onto B8009 for 6 miles through Carbost and Fernilea to Portnalong. At bus stop follow signs for Croft Bunkhouse & Little Gallery, we are 500yds past the pub.

DUN FLODIGARRY HOSTEL

Flodigarry By Staffin
Isle of Skye
IV51 9HZ

The hostel is set in the beautiful Trotternish area of North Skye. The area is famous for the distinctive cliffs and rock formations of the Quiraing and enjoys spectacular views of both the Western Isles and Wester Ross. Hill walking and hiking are popular local pursuits and bicycle hire is available at the hostel. There is pony trekking and canoeing available in the area. Whilst out and about you may see otters, golden eagles, and other wildlife.

The hostel is centrally heated and fully equipped with all bedding and sheets provided. There is a hotel with bar and restaurant just 100 metres from our door. Groups are welcome and there is a camping area available. There is a public bus service from Portree to within 100 metres of our front door, at other times please phone the hostel for travel information.

We are members of Independent Backpackers Hostels Scotland.

TELEPHONE CONTACT Gavin or Myrna (01470) 552212
OPENING SEASON All year
OPENING HOURS Open all day
NUMBER OF BEDS 52 beds
BOOKING REQUIREMENTS Booking is available.
PRICE PER NIGHT £7.50 - £9.00.

PUBLIC TRANSPORT
Buses come from Portree daily, except Sunday and stop 200 metres from the hostel.

DIRECTIONS
GR 464 720. 34 kilometres north of Portree, 5 kilometres north of Staffin on the coast road. Adjacent to the Flodigarry Hotel. Landranger map 23

GERRYS ACHNASHELLACH HOSTEL
Craig, Achnashellach
Strathcarron, Wester-Ross
Scotland, IV54 8YU

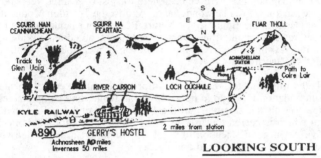

LOOKING SOUTH

Gerry's Hostel is situated in an excellent mountaineering and wilderness area on the most scenic railway in Britain. The hostel has a common room with log fire, library and stereo. Come and go as you please. No smoking inside or out.

Accommodation for none smokers.
http://www.host.co.uk/m/grl/hb/010/index.html.

TELEPHONE CONTACT Gerry (01520) 766232
OPENING SEASON All Year
OPENING HOURS Booking in times 5pm to 8.30pm
NUMBER OF BEDS 24
BOOKING REQUIREMENTS Prepay to secure bed, or phone.
PRICE PER NIGHT From £9 per person. 10% discount for large groups or long stays.

PUBLIC TRANSPORT
Achnashellach Station is 4km west of the hostel. Nearest Citylink coaches drop off at Kyle of Lochalsh.

DIRECTIONS
GR 037 493. 95 miles north of Fort William, 50 miles west of Inverness on A890.

KINLOCHEWE BUNKHOUSE
The Kinlochewe Hotel, Kinlochewe
Wester Ross, IV22 2PA

Hello, and a warm welcome from all of us here at the Kinlochewe Hotel and Bunkhouse. We've been here for just over three years now and we reckon we're in a wonderland. Amidst the Torridon Mountains and adjacent to the Beinn Eighe Nature Reserve our bunkhouse is the perfect retreat for all true lovers of the great outdoors. Walking, climbing, cycling or just laying back you'll meet people from all around the world.

Packed with character, relaxed and informal the fully centrally heated accommodation is set up to be warm in the winter and comparatively midge free in the summer. In the hotel you'll find log fires and a menu which is geared towards generous servings at affordable prices. We've got a good selection of local and imported drinks. See you soon! Gerry, Denise, David and Paula.

TELEPHONE CONTACT Gerry/Denise Thatcher, (01445)760253
OPENING SEASON All year
OPENING HOURS 24 hours
NUMBER OF BEDS 18
BOOKING REQUIREMENTS Booking essential for groups, advisable for individuals but not essential.
PRICE PER NIGHT £8 per person. Discounts are available for large groups with stays of 4 nights or more.

PUBLIC TRANSPORT
Nearest train station is in Achnasheen (10 miles away). Trains run three times a day and the postbus meets the lunchtime train and also comes to Kinlochewe. On Tuesdays, Thursdays and Fridays the 5pm Westerbus from Inverness to Gairloch stops outside the hostel around 6.45pm. The hostel will collect to or from anywhere for the cost of the fuel, eg Achnasheen station to hostel £5, Inverness to hostel £20.

DIRECTIONS
Kinlochewe is situated at the junction of the A832 Garve to Gairloch road and the A896 north from Torridon.

BADACHRO BUNKHOUSE
Badachro Village
Gairloch
Ross-shire
IV21 2AA

Situated only 100 yards from the sea this comfortable bunk house offers accommodation for individuals, families or groups. We can arrange a variety of activities which include sailing (dinghies or yachts), canoeing, sea angling, small boat hire, mountain bike hire, hill-walking, freshwater fishing, golfing, beach barbecues and visits to Inverewe Gardens or Gairloch Museum. These activities can be arranged for individuals or groups. The local pub is only a few minutes' walk and there is a sea taxi service to Gairloch from the jetty by the pub. The accommodation is in three areas, one of which can be booked as a private room (sleeping up to six). The bunkhouse has full self-catering facilities. *Groups of up to 40 can be accommodated using nearby accommodation. Brochure on accommodation and activities on request.*

TELEPHONE/FAX CONTACT Iain Thomson, Tel: (01445) 741291 advanced bookings only, (01445) 712458 immediate bookings, Fax: (01445) 741291.
OPENING SEASON All year
OPENING HOURS 24hr access. Arrive between 9am and 12 midnight. Keys collected from Badachro Inn (6 mins walk).
NUMBER OF BEDS 13 (extra available if required)
BOOKING REQUIREMENTS Booking strongly recommended
PRICE PER NIGHT £8.50 per person, duvet included. Group discounts available.

PUBLIC TRANSPORT
Westerbus from Inverness to Gairloch stops at the main road junction at Kerry Bridge (3 miles from hostel). Trains from Inverness stop at Achnasheen (28 miles from hostel). We can arrange a lift, please discuss.

DIRECTIONS
GR 778 737. The bunkhouse is signposted in Badachro village (on the B8056).

ACHTERCAIRN
HOSTEL

Gairloch Sands Hotel
Achtercairn
Gairloch
Ross-shire
IV21 2BJ

Gairloch is an ideal location for the one night visit or a longer stay in which to explore or take part in the many activities this magnificent area has to offer.

Situated in the grounds of Gairloch Sands Apartments, Achtercairn Hostel is two individual buildings. Both have fully equipped kitchens, washrooms and showers with plenty of hot water. All bedrooms are heated and furnished for two, having bunkbeds equipped with duvets and linen. There is an on site laundry room and a shop nearby.

The main building has a comfortable leisure area, pub and an excellent restaurant with take-away food.

Group meals can be catered for, ask for details.

TELEPHONE/FAX CONTACT (01445) 712131
OPENING SEASON March to November, winter dates available to groups by arrangement.
OPENING HOURS Flexible
NUMBER OF BEDS 26 + 18
BOOKING REQUIREMENTS A phone call is advised. Groups please prebook with deposit.
PRICE PER NIGHT £8 per person. Group rates on request.

PUBLIC TRANSPORT
The Wester bus will stop on request. Phone (01445 712255) for bus enquires.

DIRECTIONS
Situated at the junction in Gairloch on the main A832 close to the Gairloch Heritage Museum.

RUA REIDH
LIGHTHOUSE
Melvaig
Gairloch
IV21 2EA

Perched on the cliff tops 12 miles north of Gairloch, Rua Reidh Lighthouse must have one of the most dramatic settings of all the Scottish Hostels. The lighthouse still beams out its light over the Minch to the Outer Isles and Skye, but since its automation the adjoining house, no longer needed for keepers, has been converted into a comfortable independent hostel.

The centrally heated house has two sitting rooms with log fires, a self-catering kitchen, a drying room, three private rooms and four dorms (each sleeping four), some rooms with en-suite shower. Meals are available from the main dining room and guided walking and rock sports sessions are also offered. The area of the lighthouse is unspoiled and makes a perfect place to watch for whales, dolphins etc. For an *away from it all experience* travel to the 'edge of the world' and Rua Reidh Lighthouse. Email: ruareidh@netcomuk.co.uk

TELEPHONE CONTACT (01445) 771263
OPENING SEASON All year (except last 3 weeks in Jan)
OPENING HOURS 9am - 11pm
NUMBER OF BEDS 18
BOOKING REQUIREMENTS Pre-booking advisable.
PRICE PER NIGHT £7.50 (small dorm) to £11 (Private room)

PUBLIC TRANSPORT
Nearest train station Achnasheen (40 miles). Nearest Citylink coaches Inverness (80 miles). Westerbus (01445) 712255 run a daily connection between Inverness and Gairloch (12 miles from hostel). Pick up service from Gairloch is available by prior arrangement with hostel and costs £4 per person, each way.

DIRECTIONS
From Gairloch take the road signed Big Sands and Melvaig, follow this road for 12 miles to the lighthouse. The last 3 miles is a private road with speed limit of 20 mph.

BADRALLACH BOTHY AND CAMPING SITE

Croft No 9, Badrallach, Dundonnell
Ross-shire, IV23 2QP

On the tranquil shores of Little Loch Broom overlooking An Teallach, one of Scotland's finest mountain ranges, Badrallach Bothy and Camp Site with its welcoming traditional buildings offers a fine base for walking and climbing in the hills of Wester Ross, Caithness and Sutherland. You can fish in the rivers, hill lochs and sea, or simply watch the flora and fauna including many orchids, golden eagles, otters, porpoises, pinemartins, deer and wild goats. Guests often sit around the peat stove in the gas light (for there is no electric here) and discuss life over a dram or two. Hot showers, spotless sanitary accommodation (STB graded as 3 star very good) an unbelievable price (thanks to S.N.H), and the total peace makes our Bothy and camp site (12 tents only) one that visitors return to year after year. We also have a cottage to let (STB graded 4 star excellent) and offer B&B in July and August for even more luxury.

TELEPHONE CONTACT Mr/Mrs Stott, Tel: (01854) 633281, Email: michael.stott2@virgin.net
OPENING SEASON All year
OPENING HOURS All times
NUMBER OF BEDS 12 plus bedspaces (Alpine style platforms) We have had 20 at a squeeze - your choice.
BOOKING REQUIREMENTS Recommended as it is a long way to come if we are full.
PRICE PER NIGHT £3 per person plus £1.50 per vehicle.

PUBLIC TRANSPORT
Nearest train stations, Inverness, Dingwall and Garve (30 miles).
Nearest Citylink drop off at Braemore Junction (12 miles) on the Inverness to Ullapool route. Westerbus (01445 712255) operate a Mon/Wed/Sat service between Inverness and Gairloch which drops at the road end Dundonnell, 7 miles from the hostel.

DIRECTIONS
GR 065 915 Located on the shore of Little Loch Broom 7 miles along a single track road off the A832, one mile east of the Dundonnell Hotel.

SÀIL MHÓR CROFT

Camusnagaul
Dundonnell
Ross-shire
IV23 2QT

Sàil Mhór Croft is a small luxury hostel which is situated at Dundonnell on the shores of Little Loch Broom. The mountain range of An Teàllach, which has the reputation of being one of the finest ridge walks in Great Britain, is right on our doorstep and the area is a haven for walkers of all experience as well as for photographers. Whether you wish to climb the summits, walk along the loch side, have an afternoon up Sàil Mhór or just soak up the tranquillity of the area, you know the scenery cannot be beaten anywhere in the country.

The hostel offers accommodation for up to 16 persons in three dorms which are fitted with anti-midge screens. Guests have a choice of using our self-catering facilities or we can provide a full breakfast and evening meal if required. It is advisable to ring in advance in order to book yourself a bed, the next self-catering hostel is many miles away.

TELEPHONE CONTACT Dave or Lynda (01854) 633224
OPENING SEASON All year, except Xmas and New Year
OPENING HOURS Flexible
NUMBER OF BEDS 16
BOOKING REQUIREMENTS Always phone in advance. Groups should book as soon as possible.
PRICE PER NIGHT £8.50 per person, self-catering.

PUBLIC TRANSPORT
Unfortunately we are situated in an area of outstanding beauty which is not served well by public transport. Nearest station Inverness (30 miles). Nearest City link drop off is at Braemore Junction (15 miles). Wester Bus runs to and from Inverness on Mon, Wed and Sat only. It leaves the hostel at 9am and returns at 6.50pm (ask for the hostel).

DIRECTIONS
GR 064 893 (sheet 19) 1½ miles west of Dundonnell Hotel on A832.

CEILIDH PLACE BUNKHOUSE

West Argyle Street
Ullapool
IV26 2TY

The Ceilidh Place is a small complex consisting of a music venue/performance space, restaurant, hotel, bar, bookshop, coffee room, gallery and bunkhouse. There are regular ceilidhs and concerts (sometimes jazzy/classical) at the Ceilidh Place. We also have visits from folk musicians and small touring theatre companies. The bunkhouse does not have self-catering facilities but the coffee shop is open from 8am to late evening, 7 days a week. It serves hot food, soups, salads, great coffee and cakes and is a super place to relax, read and write cards or memoirs. The village of Ullapool is a small exciting port and fishing town, with ferries from the Outer Hebrides. The Ceilidh Place is in the centre of the village of Ullapool. It is also next to the camp site. The bunkhouse is much favoured by hill walkers and families as an ideal base for touring Wester Ross.

Phone Effie for more information today.

TELEPHONE CONTACT (01854) 612103 ask for Effie.
OPENING SEASON April to October (inclusive)
OPENING HOURS Service 8am to midnight.
NUMBER OF BEDS 30
BOOKING REQUIREMENTS Booking is advisable in summer months.
PRICE PER NIGHT £15 to £18 per person.

PUBLIC TRANSPORT
Nearest train station is Garve (33 miles). Citylink coaches from Inverness stop at Ullapool pier a short walk from the Hostel. Phone (0990 505050) for details. Also leaving from the pier are ferries to Stornoway on the Isle of Lewis.

DIRECTIONS
Turn right after the pier and first left. Check in at Ceilidh Place reception.

WEST HOUSE TOURIST HOSTEL

West House
West Argyle Street
Ullapool
Ross-shire
IV26 2TY

West House Tourist Hostel is located in the charming fishing village of Ullapool, nestling on the shores of Loch Broom. The Ullapool area offers great opportunities for walking and climbing, mountain biking, scuba diving, boating, or just chilling out and enjoying the relaxed state which is life in the Western Highlands. The village offers a range of eateries and pubs, from basic pub food to some of the best seafood restaurants in the west of Scotland.

The hostel opened in the summer of 1996. It has been refurbished to provide high quality accommodation for the discerning independent traveller, eg. some rooms en-suite. Facilities include a lounge with open fire, large dining room and a well equipped kitchen. Hostel bus available, please phone for details. Checkout our web site on www.scotpackers-hostels.co.uk

TELEPHONE CONTACT Stewart or Richard (01854) 613126.
OPENING SEASON All year
OPENING HOURS 24 hours
NUMBER OF BEDS 22
BOOKING REQUIREMENTS Not essential out of high season.
PRICE PER NIGHT £9.50 - £10.50 per person.

PUBLIC TRANSPORT
Nearest train station is Garve (33 miles). Citylink coaches from Inverness stop at Ullapool pier 400m from the Hostel. Phone (0990 505050) for details. Also leaving from the pier are ferries to Stornoway on the Isle of Lewis.

DIRECTIONS
With your back to the pier, walk to your left along West Shore Street, after 200yds turn right into West Lane, the hostel is last building on right hand side of road.

LAXDALE BUNKHOUSE
Laxdale Holiday Park
6, Laxdale Lane
Stornoway
Isle of Lewis HS2 0DR

Laxdale Bunkhouse is contained within Laxdale Holiday Park which is a small family run park set in peaceful tree lined surroundings. Located 1.5 miles away from the town of Stornoway, this is an ideal centre from which to tour the Islands of Lewis and Harris.

Built in 1998, the bunkhouse consists of four bedrooms with four bunks in each room and caters for backpackers, families or larger groups looking for convenient, low cost accommodation. A spacious fully equipped kitchen provides two cookers, fridge and microwave. There is a dining room with TV or when the weather is good picnic tables are provided. Toilets and showers are located within the building and are suitable for the disabled.

TELEPHONE CONTACT (01851) 706966 / 703234, Email: gordon@laxdaleholidaypark.force9.co.uk
OPENING SEASON All year
OPENING HOURS 8am - 11pm
NUMBER OF BEDS 16
BOOKING REQUIREMENTS July and August booking advisable one week in advance. Deposit secures.
PRICE PER NIGHT £8.50pp (high season), £7.50pp (low season). £100 sole use (high season), £80 sole use (low season).

PUBLIC TRANSPORT
Buses every ½ hour stop close to hostel. Taxi fare from town centre approximately £2.50.

DIRECTIONS
From Stornoway Ferry Terminal take the A857. Take the second turning on the left past the Hospital. Follow camping signs for one mile out of town. The Bunkhouse is located inside the holiday park. From Tarbert or Leverburgh take A859 for 40 miles to Stornoway. Turn left at the roundabout and second left after the Hospital then as above.

GALSON FARM BUNKHOUSE
Galson Farm House
South Galson
Isle of Lewis
HS2 0SH

Galson Farm Bunkhouse is situated on a croft on the west coast of Lewis overlooking the Atlantic Ocean, and is ideal for exploring the island's sandy beaches, mountains and burns, either on foot or by bicycle (cycle hire in Stornoway). The shore lies just a short walk through the croft and is ideal for fishing, bird-watching, walking and beach combing. The farm is part of a crofting village where Gaelic is the everyday language. We are twenty miles from Stornoway and eight miles from Butt of Lewis Lighthouse. The bus stops at Galson village road end.

Our newly opened bunkhouse has one dormitory with eight bunks and two shower rooms. Bedding can be supplied if required or bring your own. There is a full kitchen/dining room so that you can self-cater or you can order meals. Come and go as you please. Shop two miles away, advance booking advisable and essential for groups, Access/Visa facility.

TELEPHONE/FAX CONTACT Dorothy and John Russell (01851) 850492. Email GalsonFarm@yahoo.com
OPENING SEASON All year
OPENING HOURS All day - 24 hours
NUMBER OF BEDS 8
BOOKING REQUIREMENTS Always phone in advance. Bookings held till 6pm, deposit (Visa/Access) guarantees bed.
PRICE PER NIGHT £8 per person

PUBLIC TRANSPORT
The nearest ferry runs from Ullapool on the mainland to Stornoway which is 20 miles from the hostel. Local buses run from Mondays to Saturdays. Enquire at Stornoway Bus Station.

DIRECTIONS
GR 437 592. Follow A857 Stornoway to Ness(Nis) road for 20 miles. At Galson (Gabhsann) turn left at the telephone kiosk. Bunkhouse is ¼ mile further on.

ROCKVIEW BUNKHOUSE

Main Street
Tarbert
Isle of Harris
Western Isles
HS3 3DL

The Rockview Bunkhouse is ideally situated in the centre of Tarbert within five minutes' walk of all local amenities including the ferry terminal and craft shops. There is a good bus service to other areas of the Western Isles or if you prefer to be in the open air you can hire bikes in the town.

The Bunkhouse is centrally heated throughout and offers both single and mixed dorms with bed linen (sleeping bags, liners and towels provided on request free of charge). There is a comfortable lounge to relax in with television, board games and guitar. The self-catering kitchen is equipped with cooker, microwave, cooking utensils, washing machine and tumble dryer. Showers are also available and hot water is plentiful. The Bunkhouse is suitable for groups or individuals and we look forward to welcoming you to Rockview. No animals.

TELEPHONE CONTACT (01859) 502626 / 502211 please ask for Valerie or Mairi
OPENING SEASON All year
OPENING HOURS All day
NUMBER OF BEDS 32
BOOKING REQUIREMENTS Booking advised for groups
PRICE PER NIGHT £9 - reduced rates for groups

PUBLIC TRANSPORT
Close to Tarbert ferry from Uig on Skye. Citylink coaches provide service from mainland cities through Skye to Uig (0990 505050). Good bus service to other areas on the Western Isles, phone (01859) 502011) for details.

DIRECTIONS
In the centre of the main street of Tarbert, there is a large sign above the door.

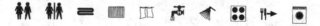

AM BOTHAN
Brae House
Ferry Road
Leverburgh
Isle of Harris
HS5 3UA

Set within half a mile of the ferry terminal this new facility overlooks the magical Sound of Harris with distant views of islands on the far western horizon as well as providing panoramic outlooks of the mountains of South Harris. It makes an ideal centre for hillwalkers, climbers, divers, canoeists, cyclists and is also perfectly suited to those simply passing through the Long Island. The Sound of Harris is rich in wildlife; here you can see otters, seals, golden eagles and other rare birds, the inevitable mink and even the wild red deer.

The building boasts a unique decor with unexpected artifacts in every corner, reflecting the industrial and historical archaeology of its surroundings. In addition to open peat fires, all rooms are centrally heated with all bedding and sheets provided and ample parking. There are a restaurant and a well stocked shop nearby.

http:/www.ambothan.com

TELEPHONE/FAX CONTACT Ruari Beaton (01859) 520251
email: ruari@ambothan.com
OPENING SEASON All year
OPENING HOURS 24 hours
NUMBER OF BEDS 12 in 4-berth cabins; 6 in dormitory; 3 futons plus settee beds for overspill.
BOOKING REQUIREMENTS Booking essential for groups, advisable for individuals but not essential.
PRICE PER NIGHT £12 all inclusive. Credit cards accepted.

PUBLIC TRANSPORT
A frequent bus service to Stornoway and Tarbert passes the door.

DIRECTIONS
The hostel is adjacent to Leverburgh/Otternish ferry, Leverburgh, South Harris.

ASSYNT FIELD CENTRE

Inchnadamph Lodge
Inchnadamph, Assynt
By Lairg, Sutherland
IV27 4HL

Situated at the heart of the dramatic Assynt mountains, Inchnadamph Lodge has been tastefully converted to provide luxury hostel accommodation at a budget price. Twin, family and dormitory (4-8 people) rooms are available and a continental-style breakfast is included. There are a self-catering kitchen, lounge and dining room (with real fires), study facilities and games room. Packed lunches are available on request and bar meals are served at the Inchnadamph Hotel. At the foot of Ben More Assynt, and overlooking Loch Assynt, you are free to explore one of the wildest areas in the Highlands. Mountains can be climbed from our door! Within walking distance are two National Nature Reserves which are home to a wide diversity of birds, plants and animals. Interesting rock formations provide excitement for geologists. Nearby lochs are popular for fly fishing.

Email us on assynt@dial.pipex.com.
Details and photos on our website www.assynt.co.uk

TELEPHONE CONTACT Chris/Issie 01571 822218 fax 822232
OPENING SEASON All year
OPENING HOURS 24 hours
NUMBER OF BEDS 34 (dormitory) 14 (twin/double rooms)
BOOKING REQUIREMENTS Advised, required Nov-March.
PRICE PER NIGHT £8.95 - £10 (dormitory) £14 - £16 (twin room) inc continental breakfast and linen. Group discounts.

PUBLIC TRANSPORT
Transport is available to our door from Inverness 6 days a week, either by train to Lairg and then postbus, or by coach to Ullapool and minibus to Inchnadamph. Times vary - please call us for details.

DIRECTIONS
Inchnadamph is 25 miles north of Ullapool on the Lochinver/Durness road. The lodge is the big white building across the river from the hotel.

ROGART RAILWAY CARRIAGES
Rogart Station
Sutherland
IV28 3XA

Stay on a first class train in Rogart in the heart of the Highlands halfway between Inverness and John O'Groats. The two railway carriages have been tastefully converted, with many original features. Each sleeps 8, with two beds per room, and has a kitchen, dining room, sitting room and two showers and toilets. They are heated and non-smoking. All bedding is included and breakfast is available.

Three trains per day in each direction serve this small crofting community which has a shop, post office and pub with restaurant. Glenmorangie and Clynelish distilleries, Dunrobin Castle and Helmsdale's Heritage Centre are easy to reach by train or car. See the silver salmon leap at Lairg and the seabirds and seals in Loch Fleet. Or just enjoy the peace of Rogart. The climate is good and the midges are less prevalent than in the west! Families welcome. Free use of bikes for guests.

www.users.globalnet.co.uk/~rograil/hostel.htm

TELEPHONE/FAX CONTACT Kate/Frank, Tel/Fax: (01408) 641343
Pager: 04325 549292, E-mail rograil@globalnet.co.uk
OPENING SEASON All year
OPENING HOURS 24 hours
NUMBER OF BEDS 20
BOOKING REQUIREMENTS Booking is not essential.
PRICE PER NIGHT £8.50 per person, (10% discount for rail users and cyclists).

PUBLIC TRANSPORT
Wick to Inverness trains stop at the door.

DIRECTIONS
We are at the railway station, 4 miles from the A9 trunk road, 54 miles north of Inverness.

SANDRA'S BACKPACKER'S HOSTEL

24-26 Princes Street
Thurso, Caithness
KW14 7BQ

This newly opened family-run hostel is situated in the centre of the most northerly mainland town in Scotland. It is ideal for those touring Caithness and the north coast or departing/returning from Orkney. Caithness is a land of hills rather than mountains, of heather moors, lochs, rivers, burns and lush pasture, and offers relaxation and a sense of freedom rarely found elsewhere in Britain. Nearby are fantastic cliff and shore hikes with spectacular views and interesting flora.

The hostel sleeps 16 in four bunkrooms. All are centrally heated with ensuite facilities including cooking and plenty of HOT water. Other facilities include payphone, drying room, secure storage for bicycles and motorbikes, and laundry. A snack bar/take-away is situated on the ground floor, and shops, pubs and hotels are all to be found within metres of the hostel. Price includes showers, sheets, free tea and coffee and a free breakfast pack for each backpacker.

TELEPHONE CONTACT George or Sandra, (01847) 894575 or (01847) 890111
OPENING SEASON All year
OPENING HOURS Reception open 0700 - 2400 hrs. No curfew - access possible with own keys.
NUMBER OF BEDS 16
BOOKING REQUIREMENTS Booking is advisable in summer.
PRICE PER NIGHT £8.50 per person. 10% discount for groups of over 6 people.

PUBLIC TRANSPORT
Thurso railway station is 200m from hostel. Citylink buses call at Thurso. P&O ferries for the Orkneys dock at Scrabster 2 miles from Thurso.

DIRECTIONS
From railway station the hostel is 200m down Princes Street. From bus stop at Skinandi's nightclub head to the north of the Town Square - hostel is 20m on the right.

THURSO YOUTH CLUB HOSTEL
Old Mill, Millbank Rd
Thurso, KW14 8PS

Thurso Youth Club Hostel occupies part of a converted 200 year-old water mill which is ideally located in a quiet area overlooking the river and the park. The railway station, bus station, tourist information office and shops are all within a few minutes' walk. Our hostel is the ideal base for exploring the surrounding countryside. There are many sites of archaeological and historic interest along with museums and visitor centres. Fly fishing, surfing, walking, horse riding, sea angling, cycling and golf are available nearby. The ferry to the Orkney Islands sails from Scrabster, which is 2 miles away. We provide clean and comfortable accommodation in a friendly environment. We have a large well-equipped kitchen, dining area, games room, TV/video lounge, parking and ample hot water. Price includes showers, bed linen and continental breakfast (served 5am to 9am). Email t.y.c.hostel@btinternet.com

TELEPHONE CONTACT Allan Hourston (01847) 892964
OPENING SEASON July and August (all year for groups)
OPENING HOURS All day, no curfew
NUMBER OF BEDS 22
BOOKING REQUIREMENTS Booking essential for large groups.
PRICE PER NIGHT £8 (including continental breakfast and bed linen). 10% discount for groups of 10+

PUBLIC TRANSPORT
Thurso train station and Citylink stops are both within 10 minutes' walk from the hostel as are local coach connections for Wick, John O'Groats, Scrabster, Tongue and Durness. Coach for ferry connection to Orkney Islands leaves from the train station.

DIRECTIONS
By foot:- From Tourist Information Centre, follow the river past road traffic bridge to the foot bridge, cross the river and the hostel is in front of you. From railway station, turn right down Lovers Lane, at the bottom turn left, walk 25m, turn right, cross the foot bridge. Hostel is the large stone building with white windows. **By car:-** Millbank Road is at east end of road bridge, turn down where theatre is signposted.

THURSO HOSTEL
Ormlie Lodge, Ormlie Road
Thurso, Caithness
KW14 7DP

Thurso Hostel is a family run hostel just a few minutes' walk from the railway and bus stations. Accommodation consists of single, family and dormitory rooms. Sleeping bags /duvets are not supplied but can be hired. Self-catering facilities are available, also laundry and drying rooms, shower/bath with ample hot water, TV and video lounge and a public phone. There are several pubs, hotels and restaurants near the hostel. Cars can be safely parked within the grounds (bicycles can be kept inside). There are several places of interest within the Caithness area, Caithness Glass Factory, Pulteney Distillery, Castle of Mey, John O'Groats, Camster Cairns, Clan Gunn Museum, Thurso Castle, to name just a few. The area is also well known for fishing, shooting, golf, surfing and walking. A year round ferry service operates between Scrabster and the Orkney Isles with up to three sailings daily between March and October, and trips can be booked at the hostel with Go-Orkney. Scrabster is approximately 2 miles from the hostel and transport to the ferry can be arranged.

TELEPHONE CONTACT George Dunnett (01847) 896888
OPENING SEASON All year
OPENING HOURS 24 hour access, service between 11.00am and 10.00pm.
NUMBER OF BEDS 40
BOOKING REQUIREMENTS Booking not essential but advisable if family or single rooms are required.
PRICE PER NIGHT Millennium year special rates: Dorm bed £5, Single room £8, Double room £7 per person.

PUBLIC TRANSPORT
Thurso has a train station which is also the Citylink coach stop. Ferries travel from Scrabster (2 miles from hostel) to the Orkney Islands. Transport to the ferry can be arranged.

DIRECTIONS
Thurso Hostel sits in its own grounds at the top end of Princes Street, Thurso, on the corner junction of Castlegreen Road and Ormlie Road. Opposite the railway station.

        1m

ORKNEY ISLANDS
Summer passenger Ferry from
JOHN O'GROATS

MV Pentland Venture Every Day 1 May to 30 September 2000.

Every Day	Dep John O'Groats				Dep Burwick (Orkney)			
1 May-31 May	9am			6pm	9.45am			7.00pm
1 June-10 Sept	9am	10.30am	4pm	6pm	9.45am	11.30am	5.15pm	7.00pm
11 Sept-30 Sept	9am			4.30pm	9.45am			5.30pm

Special off peak return to Kirkwall.

£24

Depart John O'Groats any afternoon.
Return from Orkney any morning.
(Free bus for ferry meets afternoon train
approx 2.30pm at Thurso Rail Station every day).

OR, Travel to & from Orkney direct from
INVERNESS
on
The Orkney Bus
Special return fare £39

Every Day	Dep Inverness (Northbound)	Arrive Kirkwall	Depart Kirkwall (Southbound)	Arrive Inverness
1 May-31 May	2.20pm	7.30pm	9.00am	1.45pm
1 June-10 Sept	7.30am *	12.05pm	9.00am	1.45pm
	2.20pm	7.30pm	4.15pm*	9.00pm

JOHN O'GROATS FERRIES, Ferry Office
John O'Groats, Caithness, KW1 4YR.
Tel (01955) 611353 FAX (01955) 611301
www.jogferry.co.uk ALPHADIAL 07000 ORKNEY
* Telephone (01955) 611 353 to book 7.30am from Inverness and 4.15pm from Kirkwall

BROWNS HOSTEL
Victoria Street
Stromness
Orkney
KW16 3BS

This family run hostel is ideally situated in the centre of a small fishing town, **Stromness**. It makes an excellent base for the tourist - a few minutes' walk from the ferry terminal and bus stops. There is a bus service to Kirkwall every few hours Monday to Saturday. Bus tours also run every day and cycles are available for hire to visit the various sites of interest - **Skara Brae, Maeshowe, Standing Stones** etc. Ferries run to the smaller islands daily.

In summer there is daylight all evening and one can stroll through our peaceful town and along the shore to watch the seals. Our kitchen/common room looks onto the street and coming back from a pleasant walk to chat to the other hostellers over a cup of tea seems to be a popular way of relaxing before going to bed. There are 2,3 or 4 beds per dorm and there is **no curfew**. There is a provisions shop and bakehouse across the street that opens at 7.30am selling new bread and rolls for your breakfast.

TELEPHONE CONTACT Mrs Brown (01856) 850661
OPENING SEASON All year
OPENING HOURS All day
NUMBER OF BEDS 14
BOOKING REQUIREMENTS Booking advisable during March to October.
PRICE PER NIGHT £8 per person (inc linen).

PUBLIC TRANSPORT
Train or bus to Thurso, bus 2 miles to Scrabster then boat to Stromness. Alternatively from John O'Groats by boat to Burwick then bus to Stromness via Kirkwall. The evening John O'Groats ferry has no bus connection.

DIRECTIONS
Hostel near to harbour in Stromness.

EVIEDALE BOTHY AND CAMPSITE
Evie, Orkney, KW17 2PJ

Eviedale Bothy is a small, stone walled, one room cottage. It has been renovated to provide basic accommodation for the budget traveller. The attached annex has a toilet and a kitchen with calor gas stove, cooking/eating utensils and a sink with hot and cold water. Showers may be taken across the road at the camp site. The living area has a solid fuel stove which can also be used for cooking, four bunks, dining table and easy chairs. Bedding is not provided so please bring your sleeping bag. Electricity is by coin meter but gas is free. There is a provisions shop, post office and pub 200yds from the hostel. The Bothy is 10 minutes' walk from Aikerness Sands and 1½miles from the Broch of Gurness. Eviedale also has a small campsite with pitches for about 12 tents and hard standing for two camper vans. The campsite is ideal for those people who wish to avoid larger sites and who enjoy a rural setting. We offer simple safe camping on an uncrowded site with clean toilets, showers, washing up station, rubbish removal and a few picnic tables.

www.orknet.co.uk/eviedale

TELEPHONE CONTACT Mr Heaton, (01856) 751270 or Mr and Mrs Richardson, (01856) 751254, Email: colin.richardson@orkney.com
OPENING SEASON May to September (inclusive).
OPENING HOURS Flexible
NUMBER OF BEDS 4
BOOKING REQUIREMENTS Bookings accepted with payment.
PRICE PER NIGHT £5 per person. Exclusive use of the bothy is available for £20 per night or £100 per week. Camping £1 per adult plus £3 (small tent), £4 (large tent) or £3 camper-van.

PUBLIC TRANSPORT
Ferry from Thurso to Stromness. Regular bus service from Stromness to Kirkwall, get off in Finstown (8 miles from hostel). There may be a few buses from Finstown to Evie, but it would be best to hitch hike.

DIRECTIONS
Take the A966 in Finstown (on the Kirkwall to Stromness road) for 8 miles. Enquiries at Dale Farm. Bothy in Evie village next to camp site.

1m

STRONSAY FISH MART

Whitehall Village
Stronsay, Orkney
KW17 ZAR

For many years Stronsay was a very important and extremely busy herring fishing port, with as many as three hundred 'drifters' setting off for the fishing grounds from the shelter of the Stronsay harbour. At the centre stood the Stronsay Fish Mart where each morning the fishermen would arrive with a sample of the previous nights' catch to be examined for quality. At the end of the nineteen thirties the herring fishing went into decline, and the Fish Mart ceased to operate.

Happily, the Fish Mart is once again being put to good use, having recently been completely re-furbished and opened as an Interpretation Centre. The hostel is within the building with bunk beds to sleep ten people (bring your own sleeping bag) a fully equipped kitchen for self-catering and shower and washing facilities, all at a very reasonable price. Between the hostel and the Interpretation Centre is a very comfortable, brand new cafe, where drinks and snacks can be enjoyed whilst admiring the beautiful views over the Stronsay harbour. So why not spend a few days getting to know all about Stronsay from the comfort of the Fish Mart, where the accommodation is inexpensive, and the centre is open for all to enjoy. **No smoking in hostel please**.

TELEPHONE CONTACT Alan, (01857) 616213
OPENING SEASON All year
OPENING HOURS As required - 24 hour access.
NUMBER OF BEDS 10
BOOKING REQUIREMENTS Best to telephone - July and August bookings essential. 10% deposit for block/group bookings.
PRICE PER NIGHT £8.00 per person, £50 pp per week, £45 per pp per week for group bookings.

PUBLIC TRANSPORT
Ferry operates daily.

DIRECTIONS
At the Pier head of the roll-on/off Ferry Terminal opposite the Stronsay Hotel.

IRELAND

Irish Republic. All phone numbers are given with the national code required to phone from anywhere in the Irish Republic. To phone from overseas (including Northern Ireland and the UK) remove the first 0 and add 353.

Northern Ireland. All phone numbers are given with the national code required to phone from anywhere in the UK. To phone from overseas and the Irish Republic remove the first 0 and add 44.

North Ireland

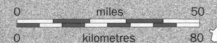

Choose a place of interest and
then refer to page number/s
shown in italics (*12–19*) for
hostels in that area

0   miles   50

0   kilometres   80

Donegal
313

307–309

Sligo
306

Charlestown

Carrick
-on-Shannon   *305*

304
Westport

Longford

Roscommon

Athlone

Galway

314

315

317

316 **Coleraine**

Londonderry

Strabane

312

Ballymena
Larne

311
Omagh

Cookstown

318 **Belfast**

Enniskillen

Armagh

Craigavon

Downpatrick

310
Belturbet

Cavan

Newry

319
Newcastle

Dundalk

Drogheda

Navan

Mullingar

Dublin
Dun Laoghaira

Kildare

Mullingar

Athlone
301

302

Dublin
250–262
Dun Laoghaira

Kildare

Portlaoise

Carlow

Arklow
264

Kilkenny

265

Tipperary

266

Clonmel

268

Waterford

Wexford

269

267

0   miles   50

0   kilometres   80

Choose a place of interest and
then refer to page number/s
shown in italics (*12–19*) for
hostels in that area

South Ireland

BELGRAVE HALL
34 Belgrave Square
Monkstown
Dublin

Treat yourself to Belgrave Hall when you visit Dublin and experience the ambience and style. It is situated south of the City Centre between Blackrock and Monkstown on the coast with spectacular views of Dublin Bay. There is a plenitude of pubs, restaurants and nightclubs. The Irish Cultural Institute is next door, which is HQ of the Irish Traditional Musicians, and you can experience evenings of live traditional Irish music, song and dance.

The house has been renovated and furnished to the highest standards. It now incorporates the beauty of the past with all the modern conveniences such as underfloor heating, all en-suite and polished timber floors. You will find a perfect mix of peace, comfort and elegance in the mellow ambience of this gracious house. Above all you will be welcomed as personal guests and enjoy genuine Irish hospitality in an atmosphere of informality and friendliness.

TELEPHONE CONTACT (01) 284 2106 Dan Casey
OPENING SEASON All year
OPENING HOURS All day
NUMBER OF BEDS 50
BOOKING REQUIREMENTS Not required
PRICE PER NIGHT (1999 RATES) From £9 per night

PUBLIC TRANSPORT
From Stena Ferry take Dart train in front of ferry terminal towards City Centre, to Seapoint Station - 2 stops.

DIRECTIONS Take the M50 City Ring Road South. Turn left onto N.81 and follow "Stena Ferry" signs. In Blackrock take N31 (Seapoint Avenue). Take right turn into Belgrave Road (just after Alma Road). Turn first left into Belgrave Square.

MOUNT ECCLES COURT

Budget Accommodation Centre
42 North Great Georges Street
Dublin 1

Mount Eccles Court is located right in the heart of the city on one of Dublin's finest Georgian streets, just a few doors up from the James Joyce Centre. We are only a short walk from Dublin's most popular tourist attractions including the GPO, museums and galleries.

Experience your stay in our beautifully renovated Georgian town house featuring its large airy rooms, fine ceilings and fireplaces with the inclusion of central heating and all modern creature comforts. After a long day sightseeing you might want to relax in our cosy lounges or cook-up a meal in our self-catering kitchen diner. For the more energetic we are close to Dublin's most popular restaurants, theatres and nightlife. Accommodation ranges from twin and double en-suite rooms to small and large dormitory rooms. Mount Eccles Court combines comfort, style and a friendly atmosphere with our convenient city location, making us the ideal choice for your Dublin excursion.

TELEPHONE CONTACT Sharon Clerkin, Tel: (01) 8730826, Fax: (01) 8746472, Email: reservations@eccleshostel.com
OPENING SEASON All year
OPENING HOURS 24 hours
NUMBER OF BEDS 115
BOOKING REQUIREMENTS Advanced booking advised. Bookings can be held by credit card or deposit of first night's fee.
PRICE PER NIGHT From IR£8.50 in large multi-bed dorm. Including light breakfast.

PUBLIC TRANSPORT
From Dublin airport take bus 41 and ask for Mount Joy Square. Walk down hill to the main traffic lights and turn right onto Parnell Street. From Ferry take a bus to city centre and get out on O'Connell Street.

DIRECTIONS
From the Parnell monument at the top of O'Connell Street, turn right up Parnell Street and first left up North Great Georges Street. Hostel is on the left half way up the Street.

INDEPENDENT HOSTELS IN IRELAND 1999

Free list of:-

·144 Hostels Nationwide·
91 hostels in Scotland, England and Wales
·Open all day·
No Membership Card required
·All Ages Welcome·

**Information Office, Dooey Hostel,
Glencolmcille, Donegal, Ireland.
Phone (073) 30130 Fax (073) 30339
http://www.eroicapub.com.ihi**

GLOBETROTTERS
46 Lower Gardiner Street
Dublin 1

Globetrotters is a unique place for you to stay offering real value and is highly regarded by all the major tourist guides. "more relaxed and welcoming... this is a clean, modern place with good security. The breakfast in a pleasant dining room overlooking a small garden, is well worth the few extra pounds" Lonely Planet.

Located in the city centre close to bus, rail and airport services Globetrotters offers dormitories and private rooms. All dormitories come with free en-suite showers; full Irish breakfast is served from 7am to 10am. There is no curfew.

Registered with the Irish Tourist Board.

TELEPHONE CONTACT (01) 8735893
OPENING SEASON All year
OPENING HOURS 24 hours
NUMBER OF BEDS 168
BOOKING REQUIREMENTS Booking is advised. VISA, AMEX, Master, Access accepted. Identity required on check-in.
PRICE PER NIGHT   Dorms IR£10-15 per person, 3 night special IR£30-35. Private rooms IR£25 - IR£52.50 per person per night. All prices inclusive of full Irish breakfast.

PUBLIC TRANSPORT
Airport bus terminal is just outside the hostel front door.

DIRECTIONS In centre of Dublin. From central bus station leave by main door, turn right and cross the road to Keatings pub on the corner of Frenchmans Lane. Walk to the end of Frenchmans Lane, Globetrotters is across the road beside the Townhouse. 3 minutes' walk total.

ISAACS HOSTEL
2-5 Frenchmans Lane
Dublin 1

Isaacs Hostel is Dublin's first independent holiday hostel. Situated in the city centre, five minutes from O'Connell Street Bridge, the hostel is adjacent to the City's central bus and train station. Originally a warehouse, the hostel still retains many of its original features and unique character.

Accommodation is offered in large and small dormitories, triple, twin/double and single rooms with prices starting from £7.50 per person per night. For the budget conscious traveller, Isaacs Hostel is definitely the perfect choice in Dublin. Meals are served all day in the friendly restaurant which offers good value meals. A fully equipped kitchen is also available for those who wish to cater for themselves. For Internet users our Cybercafe is open all day. Facilities include Bureau de Change, free bed linen, free hot showers, bicycle storage, free left luggage facilities and security lockers. Live music is on offer during the summer months. A visit to Dublin would not be complete without a visit to Isaacs.

TELEPHONE CONTACT (01) 8556215
OPENING SEASON All year
OPENING HOURS 24 hours
NUMBER OF BEDS 263
BOOKING REQUIREMENTS Recommended especially in high season and at weekends. Group bookings need a deposit.
PRICE PER NIGHT IR£7.50 (low season), IR£8.50 (high season) per person for bunk in large dorm.

PUBLIC TRANSPORT
From Dublin Airport: take the airlink bus to BusAras (central bus station). **From Dun Laoghaire Ferryport:** take the DART into Connolly Station.

DIRECTIONS
Isaacs Hostel is one minutes' walk from central bus station. From Connolly Station walk down Talbot Street take third on left for Isaacs Hostel.

JACOBS INN
21 - 28 Talbot Place
Dublin 1

Definitely the crème de la crème in budget accommodation. Jacobs Inn is situated in Dublin city centre just minutes by foot from the main bus and train stations, the shopping centre and the main visitor attractions.

All rooms are en-suite with shower. Accommodation is offered in twin, triple, family and multi-bedded rooms. Facilities include self-catering kitchen, restaurant (open all day), lift, Bureau de Change, TV Lounge, left luggage facilities, Internet access and key card access to all rooms.

Linen is provided in all rooms and towels are provided in twin, triple and family rooms. Towel hire is also available.

TELEPHONE CONTACT Therese (01) 8555660
OPENING SEASON Closed 23rd to 27th December
OPENING HOURS 24 hours
NUMBER OF BEDS 212
BOOKING REQUIREMENTS Recommended in high season and at weekends. Deposit required for group reservations and private rooms. Credit cards accepted.
PRICE PER NIGHT IR£9.25 (low season), IR£11.25 (high season) per person, for multi-bed accommodation.

PUBLIC TRANSPORT
From Dublin Airport: take the airlink bus to BusAras (central bus station). **From Dun Laoghaire Ferryport:** take the DART into Connolly Station

DIRECTIONS
Jacobs Inn is adjacent to the police station opposite to bus station. From Connolly station walk down Talbot Street and take first road on the left.

TEMPLE BAR HOUSE
19 Temple Lane
Temple Bar
Dublin 2

Temple Bar House is located right in the centre of Temple Bar, home to a super mix of pubs, clubs, and restaurants, a "Buzzing" music scene and numerous cultural centres with theatres, galleries, shops and cafes lining the narrow cobbled streets. Just minutes from Trinity College, St. Stephen's Green, Grafton Street and O'Connell Bridge and a short walk from Dublin Castle, Olympia Theatre and St Patrick's Cathedral.

Our centre offers 2,4,6 and multi-bedded rooms, all en-suite; Bureau de Change, self-catering facilities, left luggage, shop, free light breakfast, free hot showers and bed linen, laundry/drying service, international payphones and lots of information on local events and activities. We accept credit cards and groups are always welcome. It's high standards at low prices so for comfort and value with a friendly welcome, there's no excuse!, it's got to be Temple Bar House.

TELEPHONE/FAX CONTACT tel: (01) 6716277 fax: (01) 6716591
OPENING SEASON All year
OPENING HOURS 24 hours
NUMBER OF BEDS 78
BOOKING REQUIREMENTS Booking is strongly advised.
PRICE PER NIGHT From IR£9.50 in dorm; IR£15 in twin/double room.

PUBLIC TRANSPORT
From Dublin airport: Take airport link to BusAras. Cross the River and turn right along the Quays. **From Dun Laoghaire Ferryport:** Take the Dart to Tara Street Station, walk along by the River to Merchants Arch and then left into Temple Bar.

DIRECTIONS
Hostel is situated in Temple Bar.

KINLAY HOUSE
CHRISTCHURCH
2-12 Lord Edward Street
Christchurch
Dublin 2

Kinlay House Christchurch was built in the late 19th century and is a restored red brick Victorian building located in the heart of Temple Bar. It is the ideal base to discover the many visitor attractions Dublin City has to offer, including Trinity College, Dublin Castle, St Patrick's Cathedral and much much more!

We offer single, twin, 4/6 bedded and multi-bedded rooms, some with en-suite facilities. Our prices also include bed linen, hand towels & soap, and a continental breakfast. There are large meeting rooms, self-catering kitchens and a TV lounge for the evenings, and we offer laundry facilities for the traveller.

Email: kindub@usit.ie

TELEPHONE CONTACT (01) 679 6644
OPENING SEASON All year
OPENING HOURS All day
NUMBER OF BEDS 149
BOOKING REQUIREMENTS Groups are advised to book
PRICE PER NIGHT (1999 RATES) From IR£9.00 (low season) IR£10.50 (high season) per person in dormitory. Additional costs for 2 bedded, en-suite and single rooms. Reduction for groups of 20 plus.

PUBLIC TRANSPORT
Buses 47, 50, 54, 65 and 77 pass our door. The central bus station (BusArus) is in walking distance for connections to and from the airport and ferry port.

DIRECTIONS
Kinlay House is situated on Lord Edward Street between Dublin Castle and Christchurch Cathedral.

MOREHAMPTON HOUSE TOURIST HOSTEL

78 Morehampton Road
Donnybrook, Dublin

Morehampton House Tourist Hostel is a fine Victorian house ideally situated in the fashionable Dublin 4 area. The hostel is near to the Lansdowne Rugby Stadium, R.D.S, University College of Dublin and good restaurants and excellent pubs.

The hostel consists of comfortable twin/double/triple rooms and small/large dormitories. Several of the rooms have their own en-suite facilities. We offer a self-catering kitchen, TV room, 24 hour reception, luggage store, private car parking. Bike rack facilities on the premises.

Rates include FREE bed linen and hot showers. Morehampton House provides quality budget accommodation in a secure and relaxed atmosphere.

TELEPHONE/FAX CONTACT tel; (01) 6688866 fax; (01) 6688794 Email morehamp@indigo.ie
OPENING SEASON All year
OPENING HOURS 24 hours
NUMBER OF BEDS 69
BOOKING REQUIREMENTS Booking advised.
PRICE PER NIGHT IR£7 (large dorm), IR£10 (small dorm), IR£12.50 per person in double room. Group rates negotiable.

PUBLIC TRANSPORT
Buses 10, 46a, 46b from city centre pass our door. From Dun Laoghaire take the 46a bus or the DART to Lansdowne Station.

DIRECTIONS
We are on the N11 between Dublin and Dun Laoghaire - signed for Ballsbridge.

260

THE OLIVER ST JOHN GOGARTY

18-21 Anglesea Street
Temple Bar
Dublin 2

The Oliver St John Gogarty is located in Dublin's most prosperous region, Temple Bar, Dublin's Bohemian Quarter. This area is a home to a wealth of artists and musicians of many styles and degrees of talent and hosts an array of galleries, restaurants, pubs and nightclubs. Distinguished buildings such as Trinity College, Dublin Castle and Christ Church surround the hostel. There are exclusive shopping areas such as Grafton Street and St Stephen's Green.

The Oliver St John Gogarty offers private rooms or multi-bedded rooms which are all en-suite. The hostel is fully heated and provides hot showers, self-catering facilities, common areas, tourist information and secure parking. Everybody is made welcome from individuals and families to small and large groups. Gogarty's offers you top quality accommodation at unbeatable prices!

TELEPHONE CONTACT (01) 6711822
OPENING SEASON All year
OPENING HOURS All day
NUMBER OF BEDS 134
BOOKING REQUIREMENTS Advanced bookings advisable
PRICE PER NIGHT From IR£14 in dorms/IR£17 in Twin

PUBLIC TRANSPORT
From airport a bus operates every half hour to BusAras Central. From ferry terminal, North Wall, catch the city express to BusAras. From Dun Laoghaire take the Dart to Tara Street Station and walk along river to Bedford Row.

DIRECTIONS
From Tara Street Station walk along river to Bedford Row.

HARPUR HOUSE
HOSTEL
William Street
Drogheda
Co Louth

Harpur House is a large old period house with high ceilings and marble fireplaces, and is conveniently situated in the centre of Drogheda Town.

Drogheda is the ideal location for visiting the Tumulus of Newgrange, Knowth and Dowth as well as the ruins of Mellifont and Monasterboice Abbeys. The Church of St. Peter on Drogheda's West Street has a shrine to St. Oliver Plunket which contains his head. Around the corner from Harpur House is the medieval barbican St. Laurences Gate. There is also the Old Abbey, Magdalene Tower and Millmount with its museum, restaurant and craft shops. Drogheda is a lively town at night with lots of good restaurants, pubs and nightclubs.

TELEPHONE CONTACT Eric Boyle (041) 9832736
OPENING SEASON All year
OPENING HOURS 24 hours
NUMBER OF BEDS 23
BOOKING REQUIREMENTS Not necessary but advisable in busy season July and August
PRICE PER NIGHT (1999 RATES) IR£8.00 (dorm) IR£12.00 (private room) IR£1.00 per person discount on group bookings over 10 people.

PUBLIC TRANSPORT
For transport details contact Bus Eireann (01) 836 6111

DIRECTIONS
Follow directions to town centre. Go along Shop Street and Peter Street. Turn right onto William Street. We are the last house on the right hand side.

CREEKLODGE AT TOSS BYRNES

Inch
Gorey
Co Wexford

Creeklodge at Toss Byrnes offers something new and different in holiday accommodation in the Sunny Southeast. There is something for everyone in the area with beautiful long sandy beaches, places of historic interest, golf courses, scenic walks, drives and lively towns all within easy reach. The lodge is perfect for touring the many attractions of County Wexford and County Wicklow.

You will find the best value and service for your money with twin, double and family size rooms available. All rooms are en-suite with TV's. We also cater for people with disabilities. For the comfort of our guests we provide a TV room and a self-catering kitchen. Creeklodge is attached to Toss Byrnes Lounge, Bar and Restaurant - popular with holidaymakers and locals for years. A full menu is served all day and there is live entertainment every weekend.

TELEPHONE CONTACT (0402) 37188
OPENING SEASON All year
OPENING HOURS 10.00 am - 12 midnight
NUMBER OF BEDS 22
BOOKING REQUIREMENTS Booking is recommended in the summer.
PRICE PER NIGHT From IR£18.50 per person, including full breakfast.

PUBLIC TRANSPORT
Hostel is on main Dublin-Rosslare bus route.

DIRECTIONS
On the N11 halfway between Gorey and Arklow (the N11 is the main route between Dublin and Wexford).

PLATFORM 1 ACCOMMODATION COMPLEX
Railway Square
Enniscorthy
Co. Wexford

Enniscorthy is a pretty hillside town divided by the meandering River Slaney, in the heart of the Sunny South East. Perfectly situated for walking in the Blackstairs Mountains, cycling along quiet country lanes or visiting the numerous historic sites and beautiful coastline of Co Wexford, unhindered by mass tourism. Platform 1 has clean, modern facilities including games room, comfortable spacious lounge with multi-channel TV, fully equipped self-catering kitchen, large secluded BBQ patio and a secure bicycle store. All our guests receive discounts for the local attractions including golf, swimming pool, nightclubs, 1798 Visitor Centre and National County Museum in the 13th century Castle. Other hostels in the group, all with individual character, are located throughout Ireland in beautiful scenic areas such as counties Kerry, Cork and Kilkenny and near Rosslare Europort. Phone for more information or Email.

CLEAN BEDS AND HOT POWER SHOWERS A PRIORITY!!

TELEPHONE/FAX CONTACT Liam/Kati, Tel: (054) 37766, Fax: (054) 37769, Email: plat@indigo.ie
OPENING SEASON All year
OPENING HOURS All day
NUMBER OF BEDS 56
BOOKING REQUIREMENTS Pre-booking advisable with deposit
PRICE PER NIGHT From IR£9.00(Dorm),IR£15 Twin,IR£11 Family

PUBLIC TRANSPORT
Platform 1 is next door to train station and 2 minutes' walk from bus stop, both on Dublin to Rosslare route. Rosslare Europort 23 miles.

DIRECTIONS
Car: cross over the Old Bridge, take left, 2nd left at small crossroads. Turn in at end of road under arch. Bus stop: walk back towards Old Bridge turn right, 150m and take 2nd Left, hostel on left end of road.

MAC MURROUGH FARM HOSTEL

Mac Murrough
New Ross
Co Wexford

Mac Murrough Farm Hostel is the perfect base for touring the South East of Ireland - an undiscovered area of rivers, hills and beaches, rich in history and natural beauty.

The warm comfortable cottage hostel is on a sheep and tillage farm on route to and from Rosslare. We offer full hostel self-catering facilities with 18 beds available in dormitories and a private room, or a cottage which may be rented separately. Free hot showers are provided and farm produce is available in season. Under 16s must be supervised by an adult.

We look forward to welcoming you to our farm and our county.

E.Mail: machostel@eircom.net

TELEPHONE CONTACT (051) 421383 Brian or Jenny
OPENING SEASON All year
OPENING HOURS All day
NUMBER OF BEDS 18
BOOKING REQUIREMENTS Booking advisable - Visa accepted
PRICE PER NIGHT From IR£7.00

PUBLIC TRANSPORT
Buses from Dublin, Wexford, Waterford and Kilkenny. For details contact Bus Eireann (01) 836 6111. Ferries operate from Rosslare.

DIRECTIONS
Signposted from N30 and N25, 1 mile north of New Ross or please telephone for directions.

KILTURK
HOSTEL
Kilmore Quay
Co Wexford

Kilturk Hostel is a hostel with a difference, we seem to be more concerned with your wellbeing than your money, though we are working hard to reverse this as our survival is at stake. Sometimes we even go out of our way to entertain you, though most times we don't. If you can find an old bike that works you can cycle down to the village for a pint of Guinness or stroll along the beach. We also have a boat "The Banana Boat" as it's called, and if you pay us £10 (up front of course) we can take you to see the Great Saltee Islands, to have a picnic or simply sit under a palm tree and watch the ships go by, dream of pirates, treasure and mermaids. Dream, Kilturk is a bit of a dream, plenty of space, space of plenty, peaceful garden café, wine bar, dandelion tea, tunnel of love, roller coaster of fun - but beware! checking in at Kilturk could have a profound effect on your life.

TELEPHONE CONTACT (053) 29883
OPENING SEASON 1st May to 30th Sept
OPENING HOURS 24 hours
NUMBER OF BEDS 25
BOOKING REQUIREMENTS   Booking recommended but not essential.
PRICE PER NIGHT Dorm IR£7; private/family room IR£9.

PUBLIC TRANSPORT
For transport details contact Bus Eireann (01) 836 6111

DIRECTIONS
Turn off main Rosslare-Wexford road direction of Kilmore Quay. Continue for 6 miles, go through Kilmore village, Kilturk Hostel is halfway between Kilmore village and Kilmore Quay on left, distance 1½ miles.

VIKING HOUSE
Coffee House Lane
Greyfriars, The Quay
Waterford City

Barnacles's Viking House is located right in the heart of bustling Waterford City. The City offers a unique mix of modern shopping complexes, craft/design centres, traditional pubs and gourmet restaurants. It is the gateway to the entire southern region and provides the perfect base for people travelling down along the East coast from Dublin or visitors arriving into Rosslare Ferryport.

We have 2,4 and multi-bedded rooms, many en-suite. You can enjoy guided walks along the ancient walls, a heritage centre displaying artifacts from the City's Viking past or visit the world famous Waterford Crystal factory. We offer a free breakfast and there is an excellently equipped self-catering kitchen available. Our services and facilities include 24 hour reception, Bureau de Change, laundry/drying service, international payphones, free hot showers, left luggage/bike storage and spacious lounge with TV and open fire. Make Barnacle's Viking House your No.1 choice in Waterford City.

TELEPHONE/FAX CONTACT tel: (051) 853827 fax: (051) 871730
OPENING SEASON All year
OPENING HOURS 24 hours
NUMBER OF BEDS 100
BOOKING REQUIREMENTS Booking is strongly advised.
PRICE PER NIGHT From IR£7.50 in dorm; IR£13 in twin room.

PUBLIC TRANSPORT
For transport details contact Bus Eireann (01) 836 6111

DIRECTIONS
From Bus/Train Station. Cross the river, turn left along the Quays past the Tourist Office onto Custom House Parade and then right onto Greyfriars.

THE GUEST HOUSE
Mount Melleray
Cappoquin
Co. Waterford

Nestling in the Knockmealdown Mountains, The Guest House is situated beside Mount Melleray Abbey which belongs to the Cistercian Monks.

The area is renowned for its spectacular scenery and there are many beautiful walks nearby including the Glensheelane River Walk. You can trek in the mountains and a visit to the Vee (scenic drive) is a must. The Blackwater river at Cappoquin is famous for salmon fishing.

A short drive away is the heritage town of Lismore with its magnificent castle, the gardens of which are open to the public. The Guest House is a good base to travel to the seaside towns of Youghal and Ardmore.

There is a shop at the Guest House and the pub is just a short distance down the road. Accommodation is available in single, twin and family rooms. In addition, a full Bed and Breakfast service is available. A warm welcome awaits you.

TELEPHONE CONTACT John, (058) 54373
OPENING SEASON April - November
OPENING HOURS All day
NUMBER OF BEDS 20
BOOKING REQUIREMENTS Booking not essential but advisable.
PRICE PER NIGHT (1999 RATES) IR£8 - IR£10 per person

PUBLIC TRANSPORT
For transport details contact Bus Eireann (01) 836 6111

DIRECTIONS
From the main Rosslare to Cork road at Dungarvan, take the turn for Cappoquin. Mt. Melleray is signposted in Cappoquin.

BEECHMOUNT
TOURIST HOTEL
Cobh
Co. Cork

Beechmount Tourist Hostel sits high above the seaside town of Cobh, with spectacular views of Cork Harbour. Situated on Great Island, Cobh is a great centre for fishing, sailing, bird-watching, cycling and walking. The town is of architectural and historical interest, especially rich in maritime history, with links to the Titanic and the Lusitania which can be explored in the Queenstown Story Heritage Centre.

The hostel is only five minutes' walk from the town centre, a great spot for strolling and trying out the variety of restaurants to suit all pockets, and the many lively pubs with plenty of live music available. No curfew! Accommodation comprises an annexe with two bunk rooms (en-suite) with kitchen, and a twin room in the family house. One bunk room is wheelchair friendly.

On parle français. Wir sprechen Deutsch. Se habla español.

TELEPHONE CONTACT Sue (021) 812177
Email: skids@indigo.ie
OPENING SEASON January 2nd - December 20th
OPENING HOURS Flexible - no curfew
NUMBER OF BEDS 12 (hopefully 20 for 2000 season)
BOOKING REQUIREMENTS Recommended. No deposit required
PRICE PER NIGHT IR£8 per person

PUBLIC TRANSPORT
Mainline trains and Expressway buses to Cork City. Cobh trains every hour from Cork City - 25 minute journey - 10 minutes' walk to hostel from station. From Cork (Ringaskiddy) Ferryport, 4 miles to Cobh via cross river ferry.

DIRECTIONS
From wherever you arrive in Cobh - head for the Cathedral (can't miss it). Second right above Cathedral, Hostel 100m ahead (five minutes' walk from town centre).

ISAACS HOSTEL
48 MacCurtain Street
Cork

In the heart of Cork city, just minutes by foot from the train and bus station, the shopping district and many tourist attractions, Isaacs Hostel is famous in Cork for being the friendliest and best equipped hostel in Cork city centre. Located in a beautiful Victorian building, accommodation is offered in small and large dormitories. Facilities include: restaurant opened for breakfast, self-catering kitchen, free left luggage facilities, bike storage, Bureau de Change and TV lounge. Guests also have the opportunity of checking their E-mail while staying at our hostel.

The building houses two of the best restaurants in Cork along with Hotel Isaacs and Isaacs Apartments. Outside the hostel, a beautiful courtyard with it's own waterfall cascading down a red rock face gives the image of being in the country rather than the city centre. Well worth a visit.

TELEPHONE CONTACT (021) 508388
OPENING SEASON Closed 23rd to 26th December
OPENING HOURS 24 hours
NUMBER OF BEDS 85
BOOKING REQUIREMENTS Recommended in high season and at weekends. Deposit required for group reservations. Credit cards accepted.
PRICE PER NIGHT IR£6.95 (low season), IR£7.95 (high season) per person in large dorm. IR£8.25 (low season), IR£9.25 (high season) per person in small dorm.

PUBLIC TRANSPORT
For transport details contact Bus Eireann (01) 836 6111

DIRECTIONS
From train station: walk towards city centre. Isaacs Hostel is on the right, 500 yards down. **From city centre:** Go down Patrick Street towards Patrick Street Bridge. Cross bridge. Follow the road to the right. Isaacs Hostel is on the left.

KINLAY HOUSE
SHANDON
Shandon
Cork

Kinlay House Shandon is situated in the centre of Cork City, right beside St Anne's Church and under the famous *Bells of Shandon*.

The historic buildings that surround Kinlay House Shandon were completely refurbished in 1991 to the highest standards of comfort and safety and comply with all authority fire, health and safety regulations. The accommodation comprises of single, twin and multi-bedded rooms, all bed linen, hand towels and soap. There are meeting rooms to relax with your fellow guests or you can watch television in the TV lounge. Full cooking facilities are available as well as free continental breakfast.

Email: kincork@usit.ie

TELEPHONE CONTACT (021) 508966
OPENING SEASON All year
OPENING HOURS All day
NUMBER OF BEDS 118
BOOKING REQUIREMENTS Groups are advised to book
PRICE PER NIGHT (1999 RATES) From IR£7.00 (low season) to IR£8.00 (high season) pp in dormitories. Additional cost for 2 bedded rooms. Reduction for groups of 20 plus.

PUBLIC TRANSPORT
For transport details contact Bus Eireann (01) 836 6111

DIRECTIONS Kinlay House is located five minutes' walk from the bus station and fifteen minutes from the railway station. Located beside the most famous landmark in Cork, *Bells of Shandon* Kinlay house is easy to find - even for the first time visitor.

RUSSAGH MILL HOSTEL AND ADVENTURE CENTRE
Skibbereen
West Cork

Russagh Mill is directly in the heart of West Cork and is an ideal base to explore the mountains, coast and numerous archaeological sites in the area. Activities are available for all so why not try canoeing, abseiling, or some of the local rambles.

The beautiful stone building of the Mill, which was originally built to produce corn, has been delightfully restored with all modern facilities. There is a separate area for school groups or scout groups and catering is available. We especially welcome family groups.

TELEPHONE/FAX CONTACT Mick, Tel: (028) 22451, Fax: (028) 22988
OPENING SEASON 15th March - 31st October
OPENING HOURS All day
NUMBER OF BEDS 63
BOOKING REQUIREMENTS IR£8 pp in dorm. IR£11 pp in private room. IR£30 for family rooms.
PRICE PER NIGHT Booking recommended in high season.

PUBLIC TRANSPORT
Three buses a day from Cork City, last bus 6pm. Buses also run from Killarney. For details contact Bus Eireann (01) 836 6111

DIRECTIONS
One mile outside Skibbereen on the Castletownshend Road.

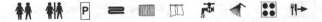

CLEIRE LASMUIGH
CAPE CLEAR ADVENTURE
CENTRE AND HOSTEL

Cape Clear Island
Skibbereen
Co. Cork

The Hostel is stunningly located on the beachfront on Cape Clear Island, Ireland's most southerly and Gaeltacht Island. A range of activities are available for you to try out including sea kayaking, snorkelling, diving, as well as lovely cliff walks, and places to visit like the famous Ornithological Observatory and a boat trip to Fastnet Rock Lighthouse nearby. Some of the activities you can take part in to get the feel of this unique area - or just relax and soak it up! Whatever you decide you can be sure that you will find a warm, friendly, comfortable hostel to make things easier while you think!

The centre is a Bord Failte and West Cork Tourism member as well as being approved by the Association for Adventure Sport. Private camping is available on the grounds and as we cycle tour ourselves there are plenty of spanners and helping hands around if your bike needs it! Families are especially welcome.

TELEPHONE/FAX CONTACT Paula or Sam (028) 39198, Fax: (028) 39144, Email: lasmuigh@eircom.net
OPENING SEASON 1st March to 31st October
OPENING HOURS 24 hours
NUMBER OF BEDS 32
BOOKING REQUIREMENTS Booking strongly recommended at least 24 hrs in advance - saves lost journey. Essential for Groups.
PRICE PER NIGHT IR£8.00 Jun,Jul,Aug,Sept - IR£7.00 other

PUBLIC TRANSPORT
Trains from Dublin or Limerick to Cork then 11.00 am Bus Greann connects with 2.15 pm ferry at Baltimore/Schull. 45 minute boat journey to Island.

DIRECTIONS
5 min walk from ferry berth, just keep left! Car park near piers in Baltimore (year round) or Schull (summer only).

SHIPLAKE
MOUNTAIN
HOSTEL
Shiplake
Dunmanway
Co Cork

Stay in a traditional homely stonebuilt farmhouse with all hostel comforts like self-catering kitchen, hot showers, cosy common room with a stove, spacious dormitories. Spend your night privately in one of the romantic gypsy barrel-top caravans or pitch your tent in the big garden. Nestle with us in this superb setting on the side of a hill viewing onto the foothills of the Sheehy Mountains. Enjoy the friendly and welcoming atmosphere, delicious vegetarian cooking, homemade products, organic vegetables. There are excellent walks, cycles and swims in this unspoilt rural and mountainous area. We are situated in the centre of West Cork and there is a big variety of sites of interest. Castles, stone circles, nature reserve, nice beaches, all in easy reach. We offer a peaceful and relaxing haven for singles, couples and families alike.

TELEPHONE/FAX CONTACT Uli (023) 45750
OPENING SEASON 1st Mar to 31st Dec, all year for groups and anybody who makes a reservation.
OPENING HOURS All day and night
NUMBER OF BEDS 20
BOOKING REQUIREMENTS Booking is essential in high season, especially for private rooms. 20% deposit .
PRICE PER NIGHT From:- IR£7.50 (dorm), IR£8.50 (private room), IR£6.50 (group booking), IR£4 (camping). Further reductions for children, families and weekly stays.

PUBLIC TRANSPORT
Bus Eireann run to Dunmanway. Hostel may provide a courtesy pickup/drop off to hostel. Or phone for a Local taxi (087) 211167.

DIRECTIONS
From Dunmanway, take Castle Road next to 'Market Diner House'. Follow road for 5km/3miles out of town in the direction of Coolkelure. Look for hostel sign on right.

COTTAGE BAR
AND RESTAURANT
Cottage Bar and Restaurant
Glengarriff
Co Cork

The Cottage Bar and Restaurant is a newly built holiday complex comprising of eight cottages, a bar and restaurant. Situated in the beautiful village of Glengarriff the Cottage Bar is central to all facilities including music nightly during the high season.

The Cottage Bar and Restaurant provides comfortable, centrally heated accommodation with bed linen and all rooms en-suite. The rooms are mostly family and double size so you can have some privacy. Kitchen facilities are provided and meals are available if required. We are fifty metres from bus stop and two minutes' walk from the sea. Activities in the local area include; horse riding, hill walking, fishing, boating and cycling (bike hire available). Groups are welcome to visit for hill walking and mountain climbing supervised by a qualified instructor. The local golf club, overlooking the harbour, also welcomes visitors. No bookings required. Taxi service available. No DHSS. Over 16s only.

TELEPHONE/FAX CONTACT tel; (027) 63226 or 63331
fax; (027) 63532
OPENING SEASON All year
OPENING HOURS No curfew, access with key.
NUMBER OF BEDS 20
BOOKING REQUIREMENTS To be sure of accommodation send deposit with booking.
PRICE PER NIGHT IR£7.50 per person

PUBLIC TRANSPORT
For transport details contact Bus Eireann (01) 836 6111

DIRECTIONS
Leaving the village of Glengarrif on the road to Bantry, the hostel is on the left.

MURPHY'S VILLAGE HOSTEL
The Village
Glengarriff
Co. Cork

Glengarriff is located in Ireland's beautiful Southwest. It is home to Garinish Island and some of West Cork's most spectacular scenery; combining the best of sea and mountains. There is also a nature reserve one mile from the hostel with some of Ireland's oldest oak forest. Glengarriff is the gateway to the Beara Peninsula, offering easy access to the Beara Way and the Sheep's Head Way, both long distance walking routes. You can hike in the Caha Mountains to Barley Lake and beyond, or discover the legend of 12 Cow Lake. We have maps to borrow, and we will share our favourite spots with you.

Murphy's Village Hostel is newly built (1997), and sleeps 33 in your choice of dormitories or private rooms. Our powerful showers will revitalise the weariest traveller. Cook in our well equipped kitchen and enjoy the south facing veranda, or you can eat in the café downstairs. We do our own baking using organic eggs and flour. The banana and chocolate chip muffins are particularly popular.

TELEPHONE/FAX CONTACT tel/fax: (027) 63555 Tony and Susan Murphy
OPENING SEASON All year
OPENING HOURS All day
NUMBER OF BEDS 33
BOOKING REQUIREMENTS Booking advised during high season and for families. Groups must pre-book with first night deposit.
PRICE PER NIGHT Dorms from IR£8 per person. Private rooms IR£11 per person. Group rates negotiable.

PUBLIC TRANSPORT
Bus service to and from Cork city stops at our door, three times daily, year round. There is also a Tralee/Killarney bus service which runs in the summer only.

DIRECTIONS
Located in the village of Glengarriff next to the bus stop. There is a café on the ground floor called the Village Kitchen.

GARRANES FARMHOUSE HOSTEL

Cahermore, Beara
West Cork

No one who visits Garranes comes away unmarked by its dramatic beauty. From the majestic setting on cliffs high above the Atlantic Ocean, views unfold across the shimmering surface of Bantry Bay, and along one of Europe's last unspoiled stretches of coastline. Here is nature at her most untamed, raw and magical. The hostel is an old farmhouse providing a cosy atmosphere, comfortable accommodation and excellent facilities.

Garranes is an ideal base for walking, cycling, and for visits to Dursey Island, Allihies, Dunboy Castle and Bere Island. The hostel is next to Dzogchen Beara, an internationally renowned Tibetan Buddhist Retreat Centre where introductory meditation classes, courses and retreats, take place throughout the year. There are also self-catering cottages available to let. Limited provisions are available at Cahermore post office (2½miles). Plenty of shops in Castletownbere. A warm and friendly welcome awaits you.

TELEPHONE CONTACT Andrew Warr (027) 73147
OPENING SEASON All year
OPENING HOURS All day
NUMBER OF BEDS 20
BOOKING REQUIREMENTS For family room & high season.
PRICE PER NIGHT IR£7 (dorm) IR£9 (double room) per person. IR£12 (single room) off season only.

PUBLIC TRANSPORT
Private bus service to Castletownbere from Cork, Bantry and Glengarriff and summer bus from Killarney / Kenmare to Castletownbere (phone hostel for details).

DIRECTIONS
Five miles west of Castletownbere on the R572 to Allihies, there is a track signposted to hostel and Retreat Centre, follow for ½ mile to end.

FÁILTE HOSTEL

Shelbourne St
Kenmare
Co Kerry

Opposite the Kenmare Post Office you will find the warm and welcoming Fáilte Hostel. Our wonderfully clean and well run hostel is an ideal base from which to explore the 'Ring of Béara' and 'Ring of Kerry'.

This home from home has kitchen facilities including an Aga Cooker and hot water. Those not wanting to cook will find meals available locally.

The hostel is centrally heated including the common room and also has free hot showers and drying facilities. The beds are to be found in small dormitories and private rooms, with sheets and duvets provided. To ensure a good night's sleep a 1am curfew is observed.

TELEPHONE CONTACT (064) 42333
OPENING SEASON 1st March to 31st October (2000)
OPENING HOURS All day, 1am curfew
NUMBER OF BEDS 39
BOOKING REQUIREMENTS Please book in writing with 33% booking fee.
PRICE PER NIGHT IR£8 (dorm) IR£10.50 pp (double room).

PUBLIC TRANSPORT
Bus to Killarney daily. Bus to Sneem, Cork and Castletownbere during the summer season. For details contact Bus Eireann (01) 836 6111.

DIRECTIONS
The hostel is opposite the post office in Kenmare town.

KERRY WAY HOSTEL
Darrynane Beg
Caherdaniel
Co. Kerry

Kerry Way is situated one mile west of Caherdaniel village and about a quarter of a mile off the Ring of Kerry road. If you enjoy walking the 'Kerry Way' is less than 200m and there are many more walks to enjoy. The Atlantic beaches and Darrynane National Park are within easy walking distance (10 minutes) and there are many other activities to experience which include: boat trips to Skellig Rock, scuba diving, horse riding and fishing. There is a choice of restaurants/pubs selling a variety of food to suit everyone's taste and pocket.

All accommodation at the hostel is in private rooms, mostly suiting travelling couples. Cyclists/walkers and bona fide travellers are especially welcome. The hostel has heated common room, hot showers and cooking facilities where only vegetarian and wholemeal cooking is permitted. Absolutely No smoking in the hostel please.

More comprehensive and detailed information can be provided by either calling, faxing or email.

TELEPHONE/FAX CONTACT Pat (066) 9475148
Email: kerrywayhostel@ireland.com
OPENING SEASON 1 May to 30 September (or by arrangement). Hostel fully booked 27th July till 21st August.
OPENING HOURS 8am to midnight
NUMBER OF BEDS 8 beds in 4 private rooms
BOOKING REQUIREMENTS Advance booking only.
PRICE PER NIGHT IR£12 per person (includes light breakfast)

PUBLIC TRANSPORT
Nearest Railway Station Killarney. From station take Ring of Kerry Bus and ask driver to stop at Darrynane Beg junction. Cross road and walk ¼ mile to hostel.

DIRECTIONS
After about 1 mile travelling West on Ring of Kerry (N70) Road, from Caherdaniel Village (towards Waterville) turn left at junction. Hostel is quarter of a mile down road on left. Crossed Irish Flags at entrance.

THE RING LYNE

Chapeltown
Valentia Island
Co Kerry

The Ring Lyne hostel is a former guest house located in an old village at the heart of Valentia Island. We offer quality accommodation and en-suite B&B, all in well furnished bedrooms with h/c in all rooms. We have a modern kitchen and food is served all day (steaks and seafood a speciality) in our chef managed bar.

Valentia, although an island in its sense of remoteness and the character of its people, is accessible from the Ring of Kerry by road bridge and car ferry. The island has a rich history with prehistoric standing stones (Ogham Stones), wedge tombs and beehive huts. At Glanleam Gardens tropical plants have run riot in the island's mild climate and now provide a profusion of colour and perfume. You can swim at Glanleam beach and shore angling offers over 30 species, there is also a scenic walk organised on the island. Take a boat trip to Skellig Michael and visit an example of early Christian architecture with 1,400 year-old stone built cells, oratories, terraces and stairways.

TELEPHONE/FAX CONTACT Frances/Sean, Tel: (066) 94 76103. Fax: (066) 94 76174
OPENING SEASON All year
OPENING HOURS All day
NUMBER OF BEDS 22
BOOKING REQUIREMENTS Booking is not essential but could be useful. Please book a week in advance (20% deposit).
PRICE PER NIGHT IR£9 per person, group rate negotiable. B&B en-suite also available.

PUBLIC TRANSPORT
Nearest train station is in Killarney. Nearest bus depot is Cahirciveen.

DIRECTIONS
The hostel is in the centre of Chapeltown which is 2 miles from the road bridge on to the island of Valentia and 3 miles from the Knightstown car ferry(summer only).

ROYAL PIER
HOSTEL AND BAR
Knightstown, Valentia Island
Co Kerry

Valentia Island is a sub-tropical island situated off the Kerry coast and is reached by bridge from Portmagee on the mainland or by a car ferry which runs every 10 minutes. Once on the island you can find abundant places to explore such as the rugged cliffs of Fogher, Foilhameron, and Bray Head. The famous Blasket Islands, Beginish with its beautiful silver sands, Skelligs Rocks and Church Island can be reached by motor boats which operate daily. The Skelligs Rocks were inhabited by monks in the fifth and sixth centuries and the beehive dwellings still remain preserved.

The smallest is the second largest Gannet sanctuary in the world. Staying at the Royal you will be ideally placed to enjoy one of the best deep sea fishing grounds in Ireland, and the hostel can arrange tackle and boats for guests. Freshwater angling is available within a radius of seven miles. For the swimmer there are numerous sandy beaches within a couple of miles of the hostel, and there is also first class boating, diving, water-skiing, yachting and golfing. Pony trekking is available just seven miles from the hostel.

TELEPHONE/FAX CONTACT Tel: (066) 9476144, Fax: (066) 9476186
OPENING SEASON All year
OPENING HOURS 8am till 12 midnight
NUMBER OF BEDS 60
BOOKING REQUIREMENTS Booking is essential 7 days ahead and a deposit of 20% secures a bed.
PRICE PER NIGHT From IR£8.50 to IR£10.50 pp. B&B IR£20 pp. Camping with use of hostel kitchen and facilites IR£5 pp.

PUBLIC TRANSPORT
For transport details contact Bus Eireann (01) 836 6111.

DIRECTIONS
In Knightstown (Valentia Island) by the ferry, at the top of the pier. Portmagee bridge is 5 miles away.

MORTIMER'S RING OF KERRY HOSTEL
Town Centre
Cahirciveen
Co. Kerry

So you love the great outdoors! Your boots are waxed and ready for the mountains. Your bike is oiled and geared up to go. Whether you are interested in photography or painting, history or archaeology, fishing or pony trekking, swimming or sailing, or simply slowly strolling the lane ways looking at wild flowers, Cahirciveen is the place to be. You may intend to stay for just a night but you are likely to be here for a week or more! Situated in the centre of a small market town on the magnificent Ring of Kerry Coast, Mortimer's offers immaculately clean, cosy accommodation. There is a large south-facing dining room and self-catering kitchen and the sitting room has an open fire for the cooler evenings. The atmosphere is relaxed, informal and friendly. I look forward to meeting you at Mortimer's Ring of Kerry Hostel. Activity groups especially welcome.

Mortimer's Hostel is on the new Ring of Kerry cycle route. Please phone or write to the hostel for a free leaflet showing the route on detailed maps.

TELEPHONE CONTACT (066) 9472806
OPENING SEASON Open 1st May to 30th September. Can open at other times of the year by arrangement.
OPENING HOURS All day
NUMBER OF BEDS 18
BOOKING REQUIREMENTS Essential for groups and out of season. Deposit at time of booking.
PRICE PER NIGHT IR£7 per person in dorms (maximum of 4 beds). IR£8 pp private rooms. Block bookings IR£6 pp.

PUBLIC TRANSPORT
Busses run from Tralee and Killarney and the Ring of Kerry bus operates between mid-June and mid-September.

DIRECTIONS
In town centre, opposite The Old Oratory Craft Centre and Tourist Information Office.

CLIMBERS INN
Glencar, Killarney
The Highlands of Kerry
Co Kerry

Climbers Inn, in the heart of Ireland's highest mountain range, is now run by the family's 4th generation. This is a Pub/Hostel where you will find the locals and travellers sitting around a turf fire enjoying the Guinness, song and dance. The hostel has beds for 25 people all en-suite rooms, full central heating with a drying/laundry room. There are a shop/post office, Bureau de Change and tourist information services on site. In addition we provide full B&B service, free camping (no services). You can enjoy a highland lamb stew and something sweet for £5.95 in the bar, as well as great vegetarian dishes, packed lunches and full dinners. The Climbers Inn is situated on the famous Kerry Way long distance walk and it is 2km from the summit of Ireland's highest mountain. Salmon and trout fishing (licences at the post office) and bikes can be hired. Ask about our Into the Wilderness Tour run daily in the summer season. Come and visit the real hidden Ireland.

Web site http://www.climbersinn.com

TELEPHONE/FAX CONTACT Tel: (066) 9760101, Fax: (066) 9760104, Email Climbers@Iol.ie
OPENING SEASON All year except Christmas (weekends only from Nov 1 - 10th March)
OPENING HOURS Service from 8.30am to 12 midnight
NUMBER OF BEDS 25
BOOKING REQUIREMENTS None
PRICE PER NIGHT (1999 RATES) IR£10 (continental breakfast).

PUBLIC TRANSPORT
For transport details contact Bus Eireann (01) 836 6111

DIRECTIONS
GR 841 724. OS map 78. Buses from Killarney (10 miles) to Killorglin, then 9 miles to Glencar the highlands.

KILLARNEY
RAILWAY HOSTEL
Killarney Town Centre
Killarney
Co. Kerry

Killarney Railway Hostel is conveniently located opposite the train and bus stations in the beautiful town of Killarney. There are lots of activities to participate in including wilderness rafting in the Killarney National Park, Cabin Waterbus Tours, windsurfing and loads of fishing. Guided pony trekking tours are also available through the National Park or relax and see the lakes on a horse-drawn jaunting car.

The hostel offers a combination of dormitory budget accommodation, ensuite dormitories or ensuite private rooms. Prices range from a basic £8.50 per person to £12.50 for a twin ensuite - all including showers, linen and towels - open all day with cooking facilities always available. The hostel is redecorated and upgraded every year without fail, showers are always hot and linen always changed. We are dedicated to ensuring that your stay in the Hostel and in Killarney is most enjoyable and that you will return to stay with us again in the near future.

Conveniently located opposite the train and bus stations.

TELEPHONE CONTACT Daniel (064) 35299
OPENING SEASON All year
OPENING HOURS 7.00 am - 4.00 am
NUMBER OF BEDS 79
BOOKING REQUIREMENTS Booking required peak season, recommended at all times.
PRICE PER NIGHT Dorm £8.50 pp. Ensuite double £12.50 pp

PUBLIC TRANSPORT
Killarney train and bus stations are opposite to hostel.

DIRECTIONS
Located in the town centre opposite the bus station, go up Laneway beside the Friary Church.

WESTWARD COURT
Mary Street
Tralee
Co. Kerry

Westward Court is situated in the very heart of Tralee, the capital town of Kerry and gateway to this beautiful, friendly county. The town offers the family and budget traveller an absolute plethora of activities and amenities - all within walking distance of Westward Court. Visitor attractions include a modern museum, medieval exhibition centre, steam railway and a plenitude of pubs offering a variety of entertainment from traditional Irish music to jazz and blues. There are many excellent restaurants offering a delightful array of fine food and wines for you to enjoy.

Westward Court is a newly established, purpose built, budget accommodation facility. It offers exceptional value and service. We can accommodate 100 guests with a variety of comfortable en-suite rooms catering for large or small groups, families and individuals. Its pleasant atmosphere makes it the ideal location where you can relax, enjoy yourself and experience the warmth and hospitality that has made Kerry the most popular holiday destination in Ireland.

TELEPHONE/FAX CONTACT Matt O'Connell, Tel: (066) 71 80081, Fax: (066) 71 80082
OPENING SEASON All year.
OPENING HOURS 8am to 4am the following morning
NUMBER OF BEDS 100
BOOKING REQUIREMENTS Recommended during August, Bank Holiday and Festivals. Group booking essential.
PRICE PER NIGHT(1999 RATES) IR£15 pp twin, IR£17.50 pp single, IR£10 pp four bedded, IR£9 pp six bedded

PUBLIC TRANSPORT
For transport details contact Bus Eireann (01) 836 6111

DIRECTIONS
Mary Street is situated behind the Cinema on Denny Street off Day Place near the centre of town.

BILLERAGH HOUSE HOSTEL
Billeragh
Listowel
Co Kerry

Billeragh House Hostel is situated near Listowel, a renowned market town designated as a Heritage Town and home of the literary geniuses Dr JB Keane and Dr B McMahon. J.B.K's pub has its own *pub-theatre* where you can enjoy a pint and a laugh. At St Johns Arts centre there are plays, comedy sketches and music. Activities in the area include fishing, horse riding, golf and wonderful walks along roads, railways and the banks of the river Feale. Fifteen miles drive away in Tralee you can visit Aqua World, Blennervile Windmill and the Medieval Experience.

Billeragh House is a period Georgian house, dating from the mid-eighteen century. Set in mature woodland area the house is an ideal base for families and groups. The accommodation is all en-suite with 3-8 bunk beds per room. Private rooms and dorms are available on request. The hostel has an excellent, fully equipped self-catering kitchen, TV room, laundry and drying facilities. Breakfast can be provided on request. Camping available.

TELEPHONE CONTACT Liam (068) 40322, (068) 40321 and (086) 2111037
OPENING SEASON All year
OPENING HOURS 8am to 11.30pm
NUMBER OF BEDS 28
BOOKING REQUIREMENTS Recommended for groups.
PRICE PER NIGHT IR£8 per person

PUBLIC TRANSPORT
Please provide details of any buses/trains/ferries that hostellers might find useful. **FREE** pick up from Listowel.

DIRECTIONS
Hostel is situated on the main Listowel to Tralee Road (N69). Hostel is 3km from Listowel on the right. Look out for hostel signs at entrance.

LYNCHS CASTLEGREGORY HOSTEL

Opposite the Church
Castlegregory Village
Co Kerry

This friendly hostel is situated directly across the street from Castlegregory village church. The village has seven pubs, which provide Irish music and songs. The family run hostel is **always** attended by the husband and wife and all visitors are made to feel at home by the proprietors who chat and drink coffee with them.

There are no extra charges for electricity, heating or showers. Self-catering facilities are provided again at no extra charge. There is no night-time curfew and hostellers are welcome to arrive at any time of day. Blankets/duvets and pillows are provided and towels and sheets can be hired for a minimal fee. The hostel is very warm, cosy and comfortable.

Mountain bikes are available for hire and the hostel also supplies a taxi service.

TELEPHONE CONTACT Mr and Mrs Lynch (066) 7139128
OPENING SEASON All year
OPENING HOURS 24 hr service
NUMBER OF BEDS 18
BOOKING REQUIREMENTS Booking not required.
PRICE PER NIGHT IR£8 per person (dorm), IR£10 per person (private room). Group rates available for six or more people, please enquire.

PUBLIC TRANSPORT
Buses from Tralee to Dingle pass through the village. The hostel also supplies a taxi service.

DIRECTIONS
Castlegregory is on the R560 between Tralee and Dingle. The hostel is directly across the street from the village church.

LOVETT'S HOSTEL
Cooleen
Dingle
Co. Kerry

Lovett's Hostel is a small family run hostel in one of the most beautiful parts of Ireland and is close to all the local amenities. During the day you can visit the beaches which are close by and in the evening why not relax at one of the pubs and enjoy some real Irish hospitality.

This home from home hostel offers 12 beds in dormitories or private rooms, and is fully heated with hot water and showers. If you do not feel like going out to eat why not use the cooking facilities provided.

TELEPHONE CONTACT (066) 9151903 Helen
OPENING SEASON All year
OPENING HOURS All day
NUMBER OF BEDS 12
BOOKING REQUIREMENTS Booking advisable to be sure of a bed.
PRICE PER NIGHT Low Season: dorm IR£6.50, private room IR£8.50. High Season: dorm IR£7-£7.50, private room IR£9.50.

PUBLIC TRANSPORT
For transport details contact Bus Eireann (01) 836 6111

DIRECTIONS
Two minutes from the bus stop.   Opposite the Esso Garage.

KILREE LODGE
Clare Street
Dublin Road
Limerick City

Kilree Lodge is a warm and friendly-run hostel five minutes' walk from the city centre and ten minutes' walk from bus and train stations. It has all the amenities for the modern traveller. There is a full laundry service, secure bicycle store and car parking. The hostel has self-catering facilities and a TV room with video and cable TV. Our bedrooms are en-suite and cleaned daily. We have facilities for the disabled, public phones and 24 hour customer service.

Close to the Hostel are Limerick's historical sights, pubs, restaurants, sport/leisure facilities and city centre shopping. Limerick City is magnificently sited on one of Europe's finest rivers, the lordly Shannon. To walk through Limerick is to follow in the footsteps of time through the echoes of bygone generations that gave shape to our ancient city rich in heritage.

TELEPHONE CONTACT Bernadette (061) 401288
OPENING SEASON All year
OPENING HOURS 24 hours
NUMBER OF BEDS 92
BOOKING REQUIREMENTS Not essential
PRICE PER NIGHT From IR£9

PUBLIC TRANSPORT
For transport details contact Bus Eireann (01) 836 6111

DIRECTIONS
We are 500m below Barringtons Bridge, situated on the right hand side, on the main Dublin Road.

BARRINGTONS LODGE
Georges Quay
Dublin Road
Limerick

Barringtons Lodge is situated in Limerick City, the centre of the mid west. The Lodge welcomes individuals, groups and families to Limerick's best appointed, conveniently located, and longest established budget accommodation centre. Only ten minutes' walk from the train/bus station beside the main Dublin Road, overlooking the Abbey river.

We can accommodate up to 88 people in a flexible range of accommodation from private, double, twin and four-bedded standard and en-suite rooms. Facilities include 24 hour staffing, wash basins in each room, free hot showers, left luggage facilities, secure bike storage, bike hire, private car park, launderette, pay phone, meeting rooms, TV lounge, tourist information and an onward booking service. There is also a restaurant and a self-catering kitchen and dining area. Local attractions within five minutes' walk include King John's Castle, the Hunt Museum, fishing facilities, the Civic Buildings, St.Mary's Cathedral, Limerick Museum and Limerick City Gallery of Art. There are Traditional Music Pubs and restaurants a few minutes 'crawl' away. Email: info@barringtons.ie Web: www.barringtons.ie

TELEPHONE/FAX CONTACT (061) 415222 fax (061) 416611
OPENING SEASON All year
OPENING HOURS 24 hours
NUMBER OF BEDS 88
BOOKING REQUIREMENTS Recommended in high season. Credit cards accepted.
PRICE PER NIGHT IR£7 per person

PUBLIC TRANSPORT
For transport details contact Bus Eireann (01) 836 6111

DIRECTIONS
Beside St. Mary's Cathedral at Georges Quay overlooking the Abbey River off the main Dublin Road.

SUMMERVILLE AND WESTBOURNE HOLIDAY HOSTEL

Dock Road
Limerick

Summerville and Westbourne Holiday Hostel is in Limerick which is by far the best located city to reach the entire western seaboard of Ireland. The city centre with its historical streets is dominated by the magnificent King John's castle. Around this ancient core there is now a bustling commercial centre with a great array of shopping and entertainment venues. The many traditional pubs feature great Irish music and the city boasts a superb range of restaurants, cinemas and theatres. Ballyhoura country, which is fast becoming a mecca for hillwalkers, is close by.

The hostel provides modern facilities that are definitely the best value budget accommodation in the Shannon region. *Limerick at the right price* as we like to say ourselves. We offer comfortable single, twin and dormitory bedrooms serviced with clean modern toilet and shower room. All our prices include a light breakfast and the use of our kitchens and common rooms. There is a well equipped laundry plus a well maintained tennis court. Our best asset is our friendly and helpful staff.

TELEPHONE/FAX CONTACT Karen Ryan, Tel: (061) 302500, Fax: (061) 302539, Email: info@summer-west.ie
OPENING SEASON All year
OPENING HOURS 9.00 am - 10.30 pm
NUMBER OF BEDS 189
BOOKING REQUIREMENTS Booking required the day before
PRICE PER NIGHT Single IR£13, Twin IR£11pp, Dorm IR£8pp (discount for groups).

PUBLIC TRANSPORT
Limerick has train and bus stations. 15 minute walk to hostel from stations or £2.50 taxi fare, call 313131 or 415566 for taxis.

DIRECTIONS
Go straight down the dock road and turn left after the Shell petrol station.

BOGHILL CENTRE
Boghill
Kilfenora
Co Clare

The Boghill Centre is situated at the edge of the Burren, just two miles from Lisdoonvarna and three and half miles from Kilfenora where regular music sessions are held. Set in 50 acres of protected bogland it is secluded, private and offers quiet walks both on its own grounds and down country lanes.

The centre is owned and run by musicians. We conduct traditional music workshops thoughout the summer, Christmas and during the New Year. We are open all year to accommodate groups and individuals. Diverse activities can be arranged by us to suit you. The area is ideal for cycling, walking and horse riding. Bikes can be hired locally and there are several riding stables nearby. Groups are welcome to use all the facilities of the centre and to organise their own events. Comfortable accommodation and delicious food create a relaxing atmosphere.

TELEPHONE CONTACT Sonja O'Brien (065) 74644
OPENING SEASON All year
OPENING HOURS 24 hours
NUMBER OF BEDS 28
BOOKING REQUIREMENTS Booking is essential for group bookings.
PRICE PER NIGHT IR£7 per person

PUBLIC TRANSPORT
For transport details contact Bus Eireann (01) 836 6111

DIRECTIONS
From Lisdoonvarna take the main road to Kilfenora. Take the second turning to the right - about 1½ miles and on a bad bend. Then take the first turning to the left - about 60 yds. Boghill centre will be the first building on the road.

THE BRIDGE HOSTEL

Fanore
The Burren
Co Clare

The Bridge Hostel is a converted country Police station (a listed historic building), beside the Caher River, facing the sea, at the foot of Blackhead and Slieve Elva Mountains in the *Burren* region of North Clare. Graham and Frances are always available with advice, maps and information to help you explore the Burren's unique limestone landscape, with its profusion of wild flowers and archaeological sites.

The Hostel is five minutes' walk from the beach and ideally placed for the most important rock climbing and caving areas. We provide dormitory, family room and private (double bed) accommodation with hot showers, self-catering kitchen and common/dining room with cosy turf fire. The hostel is fully centrally heated. Home made bread, soups and meals available. Garden eating areas for sunny days.

A visit to the Burren is an experience that's hard to beat.

TELEPHONE CONTACT Graham (065) 7076134
OPENING SEASON 1st March to 31st October
OPENING HOURS Open all day
NUMBER OF BEDS 22
BOOKING REQUIREMENTS Groups should book ahead.
PRICE PER NIGHT IR£7 (dorm), IR£9 (private room), IR£4 camping per person. Special rates for groups of 10+.

PUBLIC TRANSPORT
Trains and buses to Galway from all over Ireland. Bus leaves Galway at 6pm for Fanore, runs Mon to Sat from 23rd May to 18th September and Tue and Thur only in winter. Bus from Galway to Ballyvaughan runs daily, with a pick up from hostel by arrangement.

DIRECTIONS
Fanore is on the coast road, midway between Ballyvaughan and Lisdoonvarna, one mile south of Blackhead Lighthouse. Hostel is beside the river, in front of church and 50yds off coast road.

CLARE'S ROCK HOSTEL
Carron
(The Heart of the Burren)
Co Clare

Clare's Rock Hostel is a beautiful, stone faced building, situated in the heart of the Burren region of North Clare/South Galway. From the front of the hostel can be seen a breathtaking view of the largest Turlough (disappearing lake) in Western Europe. At the rear is a unique cliff-face, giving a profile of limestone rock, which is the main feature of the Burren. Carron is ideally suited to outdoor enthusiasts, providing numerous walks and sites of historical interest (Poulnabrone Dolman, castles, stone forts, churches). Visit the oldest family run Perfumery in Ireland which also gives the visitor a free slide show, detailing the wonderful flora of our region. We are situated 100 metres from an old style pub/restaurant (established 1830). Bike hire available. Come to interpret the Burren for yourself, and be prepared to take your time! Web site www.claresrock.com

TELEPHONE/FAX CONTACT Pat Cassidy tel: (065) 7089129, fax: (065) 7089228, Email claresrockhostel@tinet.ie
OPENING SEASON 1 May- 30 Sept (bookings only, after this)
OPENING HOURS All day (booking until 10.30 pm)
NUMBER OF BEDS 40
BOOKING REQUIREMENTS Booking preferred, not essential.
PRICE PER NIGHT IR£8pp dorm, IR£8-11 private. Group rates.

PUBLIC TRANSPORT
From Galway CIE station, take Ballyvaughan/lisdoonvarna bus and request stop at Bellharbour Pub (6 miles from hostel). Also try Neachtain Coaches (091 553188). From Limerick or Ennis. Barratt summer service has a request stop just past Leminagh Castle (3 miles from hostel), phone to arrange (061 384700). CIE (065 6824177) and post bus (enquire Ennis post office 065 6821054) run services to Leminagh Castle (5 miles) via Corofin. Pickup can be arranged from Bellharbour and Leminagh Castle. All travel times are on our web site.

DIRECTIONS
From Ennis - N85 for 1 mile, turn right through Corofin and on to Leminagh Castle, turn right. Follow signs for Carron (5m). From Galway - Coast road to Kinvara, 2 miles after Kinvara turn left for 8m.

WOODQUAY HOSTEL
23/24 Woodquay
Galway
Co Galway

Woodquay Hostel is located in the heart of Galway City, on the west coast of Ireland. We offer comfortable accommodation in a friendly atmosphere, at a budget price. The hostel has a bureau de change, tourist information, laundry service, international pay phone and tickets to the Aran Islands!

The hostel is in a safe and central location near the train and bus stations, and a stone's throw from the main shopping and cultural sites of Galway City.

Galway is a fast growing city, where the modern meets the traditional on almost every street corner. It is an ideal spot to begin a trip further west along the coast of Connemara; to head across the sea to the Aran Islands; or to go further inland.

TELEPHONE CONTACT Tel or fax 091 562618, Bridie
OPENING SEASON All year
OPENING HOURS 24 hours
NUMBER OF BEDS 84
BOOKING REQUIREMENTS Booking strongly advised, especially in high season. Groups must pay cost of first night's stay as deposit, balance on arrival.
PRICE PER NIGHT IR£8 per person in dorm; IR£10 per person in twin or four bedded en-suite. Group rate, please enquire.

PUBLIC TRANSPORT
For transport details contact Bus Eireann (01) 836 6111

DIRECTIONS From train and bus station, walk into Eyre Square, then onto Eyre Street and Woodquay, 5 minutes' walk.

QUAY STREET HOUSE
10 Quay Street
Galway

Situated in the heart of Galway's "Latin Quarter", Barnacle's Quay Street House is recognised by leading travel guides as Galway's best-located hostel. Galway is Europe's fastest growing city and has a wonderful cosmopolitan atmosphere. Surrounded by the liveliest pubs, clubs, restaurants etc., our centre provides the perfect base from which to explore the City's Theatres and Galleries or visit the famous Spanish Arch, The Claddagh, Connemara or the Aran Islands.

Our hostel offers two, four and multi-bedded rooms, all with en-suite facilities. We are open 24 hours, provide free hot showers and linen, super fully equipped self-catering facilities, laundry/drying service, shop, bike/luggage storage, bureau de change and lots of information on local events/activities. We accept credit cards. It's high standards and friendly comfortable surroundings at low prices. So! For scenery and relaxation or "Buzzing" nightlife and entertainment, come and stay with us in the Burning Hot Centre of everything!.

TELEPHONE/FAX CONTACT tel/fax (091) 568644
OPENING SEASON All year
OPENING HOURS 24 hours
NUMBER OF BEDS 112
BOOKING REQUIREMENTS Booking is strongly advised.
PRICE PER NIGHT From IR£8 in dorm; IR£13 twin/double room.
Groups should ask about reduced rates.

PUBLIC TRANSPORT
For transport details contact Bus Eireann (01) 836 6111

DIRECTIONS
Just 5 mins' walk from bus/rail station. Walk across Eyre Square, straight down town onto Quay Street and we are directly opposite "The Quays" bar.

CORRIB VILLA HOSTEL
No.4 Waterside
Woodquay
Galway

The Corrib Villa Hostel, situated in a quiet area beside the Corrib River, is less than five minutes from the city centre and bus/train station. Ideally situated for sightseeing, shopping, pubbing and clubing.

This small hostel is known for its friendly atmosphere and offers dormitory accommodation with bed linen provided. Other facilities include self-catering kitchen which is well equipped, TV lounge with VCR, hot showers and laundry facilities. A new addition to the hostel is a hotmail Kiosk. A secluded enclosed courtyard ensures privacy and security for guests. There is ample parking available at the front of the hostel as well as a bicycle storage area.

TELEPHONE CONTACT Gerry/Alan, (091) 562892
OPENING SEASON All year
OPENING HOURS 24 hours
NUMBER OF BEDS 50
BOOKING REQUIREMENTS No advanced booking
PRICE PER NIGHT IR£8.50 - reducing to IR£8 for bookings of 10 or more.

PUBLIC TRANSPORT
Bus/Train Station in the Galway city centre, 5 minutes' walk from hostel.

DIRECTIONS
Five minutes from bus/train station. Turn onto Williamsgate Street from Eyre Square. Then turn right onto Eglington Street. Straight to end of street, past the Town Hall Theatre. The hostel is located on left hand side of street past the theatre.

KINLAY HOUSE
EYRE SQUARE
Merchants Road
Eyre Square
Galway

Located on Eyre Square, the heart of historic Galway, Kinlay House is surrounded by the best shops and restaurants in Galway. The City is noted for its traditional Irish music and pubs and is the ideal base for touring Connemara and the Aran Islands. Galway offers a host of attractions including Lynch's Castle and the Spanish Arch.

Kinlay House, Eyre Square, offers good quality budget accommodation comprising of single, twin and 4/6 bedded rooms some with en-suite and all with bed linen, hand towel and soap. Cooking facilities are available if required but we do provide a continental breakfast in the price of the room. The hostel is fully heated and hot showers are provided to revive the weary traveller. There are meeting rooms, TV lounge and laundry facilities.

Email: kingal@usit.ie

TELEPHONE CONTACT (091) 565244
OPENING SEASON All year
OPENING HOURS All day
NUMBER OF BEDS 150
BOOKING REQUIREMENTS Groups are advised to book
PRICE PER NIGHT (1999 RATES) From IR£8.00 (low season) IR£9.00 (high season) pp in Dormitory. Additional cost for 2 bedded, en-suite and single rooms. Reduction for groups of 20 plus.

PUBLIC TRANSPORT
For transport details contact Bus Eireann (01) 836 6111

DIRECTIONS
Kinlay House is located on Eyre Square in the heart of historic Galway. Five minutes walking distance from the bus and rail stations. Near the tourist information point.

GREAT WESTERN HOUSE
Frenchville Lane
Eyre Square
Galway
Co Galway

The Great Western House is the best appointed and most conveniently located budget accommodation centre in the west of Ireland. The hostel has Bureau de Change, tourist information, bike hire, sauna, laundry service, restaurant, international pay phones and wheelchair facilities. It is situated directly opposite the train and bus station in the heart of Galway City, which is now recognised as one of the most cosmopolitan cities in Europe.

From the Great Western House there is easy access to a wide range of scenery and cultures. To the west of the city lies Connemara, which is mountainous and for the most part Gaelic speaking. To the south of Galway Bay is the limestone district of the Burren. Located off the coast are the Aran Islands, just a short affordable sea voyage away, where the way of life and even the language are of an older, slower and more courteous era.

TELEPHONE CONTACT (091) 561139 or freephone 1800 425929 (credit card bookings)
OPENING SEASON All year
OPENING HOURS 24 hrs
NUMBER OF BEDS 191
BOOKING REQUIREMENTS Booking is strongly advised. Groups should book with cost of first night, balance on arrival.
PRICE PER NIGHT IR£10 (dorm) IR£16 (sharing twin or double en-suite room). Groups should enquire for reduced rates.

PUBLIC TRANSPORT
For transport details contact Bus Eireann (01) 836 6111

DIRECTIONS
Great Western House is opposite the train and bus stations in Galway City centre.

HYNES
HOSTEL
Aughrim
Ballinasloe
Co Galway

This is a family run Hostel with an Old World bar attached where visitors can relax over a drink by the open turf fire, and enjoy a chat with locals. We have a piano sing-a-long most nights and travelling musicians are always welcome to "come in and give us a tune" and there is live music at the weekends. The bar is full of old Irish memorabilia hanging from the walls and ceiling including artifacts from the Battle of Aughrim. Guests can cook their own meals in the Hynes family kitchen or you can enjoy a filling home cooked meal.

The hostel is situated 25 yards from the superb Battle of Aughrim Centre which commemorates the famous 1691 Battle of Aughrim. Also nearby is Clonmacnoise Abbey which is a popular choice with visitors. On August bank holiday weekend the Aughrim Music Festival takes place and the famous Ballinasloe Horse Fair is in the first week of October. Fishing, horse riding and golf can all be enjoyed locally. We are known as the Friendly Hostel in a Unique Location, and only 30 miles from Galway City.

TELEPHONE CONTACT (0905) 73734 Freddie or Moira. Email: fishing@iol.ie
OPENING SEASON All year
OPENING HOURS 24 hours
NUMBER OF BEDS 20
BOOKING REQUIREMENTS Pre booking is essential for groups a few days in advance.
PRICE PER NIGHT IR£7, private room IR£9 per person.

PUBLIC TRANSPORT
Buses from Dublin-Galway and Galway-Dublin call at the village every hour on the hour. Ballinasloe train station is 3 miles away and has three trains a day.

DIRECTIONS
The hostel is in the village of Aughrim 3½ miles from Ballinasloe on the Dublin Galway road.

CRANK HOUSE
HOLIDAY HOSTEL
Main Street
Banagher
Co. Offaly

Crank House Hostel is situated in the heart of Ireland in Banagher on the Shannon with its excellent traditional pubs and restaurants and great literary connections including Charlotte Bronte and Anthony Trollope. As well as offering excellent fishing - central to the River Shannon, Canal and Brosna it is a perfect area for botany, archaeology and environmental students. Other local attractions include St. Brendan's Cathedral Clonfert, Clonmacnoise Monastic site, Birr Castle with its world famous telescope, Cloghan Castle, plus many more.

The family run hostel offers a quality and cosy place to stay and welcomes people of all ages. Recommended by the Rough Guide to Ireland and Lonely Planet, facilities include bed linen, hot showers, laundry, wash basins in every room, TV/Lounge area, self-catering kitchen, bike hire, tourist information, coffee shop.

TELEPHONE CONTACT Ann or Brian (0509) 51458 / (0509) 51003, e.mail: abguinan@tinet.ie
OPENING SEASON All year
OPENING HOURS Booking in time 5pm-10pm. No Curfew
NUMBER OF BEDS 40 (twin, double, four & six bedded)
BOOKING REQUIREMENTS 2 weeks in advance in high season and 1 week in advance for low season.
PRICE PER NIGHT £8.00 - Group discounts available

PUBLIC TRANSPORT
Kearns Buses (0509 20124) operate daily to Dublin and Galway. Bus Eireann goes through Birr, 7 miles from Banagher. Taxi fare is £1.00 per mile. Nearest train station is Tullamore, 18 miles from Banagher.

DIRECTIONS
Once in Banagher, hostel is at the lower end of Main Street on left hand side if coming down the town. From Birr Castle it is straight to Banagher. From Clonmacnoise Monastic site, go back into Shannonbridge, road to village of Shannon Harbour, through village to crossroads, take right to Banagher.

 # OLD MONASTERY

Letterfrack
Connemara
Co. Galway

The Old Monastery is situated in Letterfrack which is located at the crossroads of the Connemara National Park and despite its three pubs, popularity with musicians and of course its legendary hostel it hasn't quite reached town status. Its just a short spin to reach the sea and beautiful beaches of Renuyle, Killary Harbour and the Island of Inisbofin.

Uphill from the intersection the hostel is one of Ireland's finest, beautifully decorated and furnished with the philosophy of camaraderie. Sturdy pine bunks, desks and couches fit the spacious high-ceilinged rooms. A peat fire burns in the lounge and framed photos of jazz greats hang in the cosy basement cafe and Steve, the owner, cooks mostly organic vegetarian buffet dinners and fresh scones for breakfast (breakfast is included in the price). Other facilities include bike hire, laundry and Internet access. Good pub grub, groceries, pints and 'locals' are all available at Veldon's which fills at 10.30am. and empties late, sometimes after a traditional session.

TELEPHONE CONTACT Steve (095) 41132
OPENING SEASON All year
OPENING HOURS 24 hours
NUMBER OF BEDS 50
BOOKING REQUIREMENTS Price of one night's stay is required in advance.
PRICE PER NIGHT IR£8.00

PUBLIC TRANSPORT
For transport details contact Bus Eireann (01) 836 6111

DIRECTIONS
Letterfrack is on the Mail Road, 9 miles north of Clifton. The hostel is beside the church.

OLD MILL
HOLIDAY HOSTEL
Barrack Yard
James Street
Westport
Co Mayo

Built around 1780, the Old Mill building was used as part of a brewery which has now long since closed down. It is located just off one of the many side alleys of James Street and was part of an old network of warehouses that were known as the "Shambles" in the last century.

The Old Mill Hostel is owned and run by the Carr family who try their best to offer every visitor a warm and friendly welcome. Westport is an ideal base for your holiday as it is situated in the shadow of Croagh Patrick and by the shores of Clew Bay. The town is very attractive with a small tidy street plan which has the Carrowbeg river flowing through its tree lined Mall. As the base for your holiday, the wonders of the West of Ireland, with its wild and dramatic scenery, are only a few short miles away from the heart of Westport, where you can spend many safe and happy evenings.

TELEPHONE/FAX CONTACT tel: (098) 27045, fax: (098) 28640
OPENING SEASON All year
OPENING HOURS 8am to 11pm
NUMBER OF BEDS 52
BOOKING REQUIREMENTS Booking for groups is desirable with deposit.
PRICE PER NIGHT Low season: IR£7 per person. High season: IR£8 per person.

PUBLIC TRANSPORT
Westport has train and bus services from Dublin.

DIRECTIONS
Situated down an alley off James Street in the town centre. The hostel is on the left halfway down the street, from the Monument.

TOWN CLOCK HOSTEL

Main Street
Carrick-on-Shannon
Co Leitrim

Carrick-on-Shannon is Ireland's loveliest inland resort, with landscaped river banks, busy marina, canoeing and watersports. On the Kingfisher Cycle Trail and adjacent to hill walking in lovely Leitrim and Roscommon. There are 41 lakes within 6 miles and 14 pubs (some with music) within five minutes' walk. Other amenities are, in season, heated outdoor swimming pool, sports complex, horse riding, 9 hole golf course, cinema, launderette, good restaurants and take away foods.

The Town Clock Hostel is a 7+ bed hostel in a picturesque courtyard with patio tables. The hostel has parking for cars and bikes. The fully equipped small kitchen has a dining bar. The accommodation is provided in one en-suite double room (with an extra bed), and 1 en-suite 4 bed dorm which can be booked alternatively as a twin or three bed room. Linen is provided for twin and double. Sheet bags and towels can be hired for 50p each per night.

TELEPHONE/FAX CONTACT Breda (078) 20068
OPENING SEASON 1st June-30th Sept. All year if pre-booked.
OPENING HOURS No curfew. Hostellers leaving, please do so by 11am. Hostel closed for cleaning 11.30am to 1.30pm.
NUMBER OF BEDS 7+
BOOKING REQUIREMENTS Phone call advised. 50% deposit.
PRICE PER NIGHT Double and twin £10, 3 in 4 bed room £8.50, 4 in 4 bed room £7.50. All prices per person per night.

PUBLIC TRANSPORT
Trains and buses run direct to Carrick-on-Shannon on Sligo routes from Dublin (Connelly station, Amiens street and BusAras bus station).

DIRECTIONS
Carrick-on-Shannon is on the N4 Dublin-Sligo Road. The hostel is on the junction of Main Street and Bridge Street, under the arch by the town clock (on pedestal), opposite Flynn's corner pub.

1m

TRISKEL FLOWER FARM
Cloonagh, Beltra
West Sligo

Triskel Flower Farm is a pretty, private, small organic farm with dormitory accommodation for 6 in a restored stable block (en-suite), a sleeping loft in a separate building sleeps 4 (en-suite) and camping. The farm overlooks the Atlantic and is surrounded by woodland with direct access onto Ox Mountain's nature wilderness "Ladies Brae". There are panoramic views of sandy beaches and Knocknarea and Ben Bulben mountains. Boats are available at Aughris Head for sea angling and Innishmurray Island trips - viewing seal banks, sharks and dolphins. Beltra is an ideal base for touring the wild west. The grassy boreens (roads) are perfect for cycling and walking or exploring the local heritage, with its castles, ring forts, celtic ruins and folklore. Woodland's riding centre ((071) 84207) preserves native Irish breeds for trekking over the mountains. The farm cottage with wood stoves and solar heating, has a session room for artists, musicians and dancers. This is the only hostel on the "Sligo Way" hill walk. Web site:- www.goireland.com/sligo/horses/triskel

TELEPHONE/FAX CONTACT Joseph tel: (071) 66714, fax: (071) 66967, Email: touristhostel@yahoo
OPENING SEASON All year
OPENING HOURS Phone for details.
NUMBER OF BEDS 8
BOOKING REQUIREMENTS Pre-phone. Book in July and Aug.
PRICE PER NIGHT IR£7, Camping IR£3 per person.

PUBLIC TRANSPORT
Local Bus Eireann from Sligo to Ballina on the N59. Hostel is 23km from Ballina. Hostel can collect from Sligo Airport and Station.

DIRECTIONS
From Ballina (N59) turn right at Fiddlers Elbow pub, take next right turn, 2km up to T junction at ridge (Ross Rd), turn left, then through 1st green gate on right at sign. **From (N4) and Sligo** look for Ballysodare on N59 (Ballina Rd) go west to Beltra PO (5km). Turn left at PO and up Ross Rd for 2km past high stone walls & Crofton's Castle iron gates, after 3 houses on left see the Triskel sign on tree at top of hill. Phone for a lift if you are lost or tired.

EDEN HILL
HOLIDAY
HOSTEL
Pearse Road
(Marymount)
Sligo

Eden Hill is a comfortable Victorian period house only 10 minutes'
walk from the tourist office and city centre. The hostel has full self-
catering facilities, spacious common room, dining room/study, 5
dorms, 2 private rooms, hot showers, central heating, laundry and
drying facilities. No curfews, no registration card needed. Described
by the poet W.B Yeats as *'The Land of Hearts Desire'*, Sligo is an
ideal base to tour the beautiful countryside of Donegal, Leitrim and
North Mayo. Sligo city has a museum, art gallery, theatre and
woodland sculpture trail. In the surrounding country are abbeys, old
houses and many Megalithic sites to visit.

TELEPHONE/FAX CONTACT (071) 43204, tel (071) 44113
OPENING SEASON All year
OPENING HOURS 24 hour access, staffed 8am to midnight.
NUMBER OF BEDS 32
BOOKING REQUIREMENTS Booking is essential in July and
August (10% non-refundable deposit required).
PRICE PER NIGHT IR£7.50 pp, 10% reduction for Groups 20+.

PUBLIC TRANSPORT
Sligo has a train station on the railway line from Dublin. Bus/Coach
travel to all parts of Ireland is available from Sligo. Buses stop by
request on Pearse Road.

DIRECTIONS
Coming by bus or car from Dublin, Mayo or Galway turn left into
Marymount (estate) opposite the Innisfree 'Esso' service station.
Coming from the north by car follow signs to Dublin N4 out of the
town centre and look for the 'Esso' station on your left. From bus or
rail station follow signs to Tourist Office on Temple St. Walk (10
mins) up Mail Coach Rd to the junction with Pearse Rd. We are on
the right, opposite Christies supermarket. Entrance via
Marymount/Ashbrook Estates

SLIGO INTERNATIONAL TOURIST HOSTEL

Harbour House
Finisklin Road
Sligo

Built in the early 1800s for the City's Harbour Master, this house has been converted into clean comfortable accommodation. With most of the rooms en-suite, from spacious dorms to family and twin rooms, custom made pine bunks and mattresses will add to the comfort of your stay. If you don't want to use our modern kitchen facilities you may have breakfast served to you in our dining room. Evening meals are also available to groups. Other facilities available to our guests include bicycle hire, laundry facilities, car and coach parking. For groups, Harbour House can also arrange walking tours, golfing holidays and coarse and sea angling trips, all with the benefit of local guides. Lets Go Ireland described Harbour House as "The Taj Mahal of Irish hostelling.. with more showers than an Irish afternoon".

Web page: http:>>homepage.eircom.ie>~HarbourHouse

TELEPHONE CONTACT (071) 71547 Email: Harbourhouse@eircom.ie
OPENING SEASON All year
OPENING HOURS Reception till 11pm.
NUMBER OF BEDS 50
BOOKING REQUIREMENTS Essential for groups and twin rooms.
PRICE PER NIGHT IR£8 pp (dorm) IR£10 pp (twin)

PUBLIC TRANSPORT
Sligo has 3 trains a day from Dublin. There are also bus services from Dublin (4 a day), Belfast (3 a day), Derry (5 a day), Galway (6 a day). Hostel is 9 mins' walk from bus and train stations.

DIRECTIONS
From the Bus/Train station turn left onto Lord Edward St, then left at the traffic lights onto Union St. and left again at TDs pub. Follow Finisklin Road to the junction of Ballast Quay. From Donegal and Northern Ireland (N15), turn right at the end of Hughes Bridge and follow Ballast Quay to the junction of Finisklin Road.

YEATS
COUNTY
HOSTEL

12 Lord Edward Street
Sligo
Co Sligo

Yeats County Hostel is located in the centre of Sligo town, and directly opposite Sligo rail and bus station. Each party is given their own keys, so their rooms are always secure, and a residential manager is on duty from 8.00a.m. until 12 midnight, seven days a week. Our free facilities include car parking, secure bicycle storage, duvets, sheets changed daily, hot showers and clean toilets, cleaning facilities for camping equipment, well equipped kitchen, free tea and coffee, common room and heating throughout. We also provide information on local amenities and tourist activities. Museum, theatre, shops, pubs, restaurants, sports complex within minutes' walk. Blue flag beaches, Megalithic Tombs, Lisadell, Innisfree, tourist and nature trails within a 5 mile radius. The hostel is now under new family owned management and has been fully refurbished in 1996.

Sorry no youth or school groups.

TELEPHONE CONTACT Liam on (071) 46876
OPENING SEASON All year
OPENING HOURS 8.00am-12.00 midnight
NUMBER OF BEDS 29
BOOKING REQUIREMENTS Confirmed bookings on receipt of payment in full, including key deposit. No refunds.
PRICE PER NIGHT IR£6.50 per person.

PUBLIC TRANSPORT
For transport details contact Bus Eireann (01) 836 6111

DIRECTIONS
Directly opposite rail and bus station.

SANDVILLE HOUSE HOSTEL
Ballyconnell
Co Cavan

Loads of space ! Acres of garden ! You won't feel like a sardine - even if you bring the family !

We also offer peaceful and private space for groups and retreats, with easy bus access from Dublin.

A base for the many unspoilt lakes of Cavan and the gorgeous, empty hills of Leitrim and Fermanagh. Why go where everyone else is?

Double rooms at no extra charge to first comers. Camp if you prefer. Borrow a bike to head for the local bar, or just relax by the fire. You'll like the place. Well; *Let's Go, Rough Guide, Le Routard, Cadogan, Lonely Planet* and *Ireland per Rad* did - and they can't all be wrong.

Web page: http://homepage.tinet.ie/~sandville

TELEPHONE CONTACT (049) 9526297
OPENING SEASON All year
OPENING HOURS 24 hours
NUMBER OF BEDS 30
BOOKING REQUIREMENTS Booking is essentail between 1/10/00 and 30/4/01
PRICE PER NIGHT IR£8 per person. Private hire of whole hostel IR£120.

PUBLIC TRANSPORT
Dublin-Enniskillen-Donegal bus stops in Ballyconnell town.

DIRECTIONS
Signed off main Dublin road 2 miles from Ballyconnell.

        3m

OMAGH INDEPENDENT HOSTEL
Glenhordial
9a Waterworks Road
Omagh, Co Tyrone, BT79 7JS

We are a small family run hostel, nestling at the edge of the Sperrin Mountains. Billy and Marella Fyffe with their children and sundry dogs etc, look forward to having you to stay. This new hostel, has 28 beds, the rooms are of varying sizes sleeping from 1 to 7 people. We have all the usual facilities (check out the symbol chart below), we also have a large conservatory area for relaxing in, an outdoor play area where children can play in safety, and an unbelievable panoramic view of the Northern Irish countryside!

We positively encourage families, disabled people, dog owners and any other minority group, as well as the usual mainstream folk. The hostel is convenient to the Ulster American Folk Park (4 miles), the Ulster History Park (5 miles) and we are 2 miles from the Ulster Way. Megalithic sites abound in this area.

Web site: www.bmp.de/atc/IHH/Omagh/omaghentry.html

TELEPHONE/FAX CONTACT Marella and Billy UK, Tel: (02882) 241973, Email: mfyffe@netcomuk.co.uk
OPENING SEASON 1/2/00 to 30/11/00
OPENING HOURS All day, please arrive before 10pm.
NUMBER OF BEDS 28
BOOKING REQUIREMENTS Pre-booking essential for groups one month in advance, deposit required.
PRICE PER NIGHT £7 per adult, £6 if under 18 years.

PUBLIC TRANSPORT
Free pickup from Omagh bus station by arrangement.

DIRECTIONS
From Omagh take B48 towards Gortin. Turn right onto Killybrack Road before The Spar Shop. Keep on road and follow signs to hostel.

GORTIN OUTDOOR CENTRE

Glenpark Road
Gortin, Omagh
Co Tyrone

Gortin Outdoor Centre is an old school which has been converted to a self-catering hostel. There are three bedrooms each with 6 bunks, and the open plan kitchen/living/dining area allows ample room for an evening chat around the fire. There is also a drying room and showers with hot water.

Gortin village is on your doorstep and has a wide variety of pubs and shops. It is a picturesque village set in the heart of the extremely attractive Sperrin Mountains, within walking distance of the Ulster Way. A bus can take you to the Ulster History Park and the Ulster American Folk Park is also in the vicinity. This is an ideal area for walking and cycling and you can hire our bikes to explore. Fishing, canoeing, pony riding and nature trails are also near at hand.

Email: Lucinda.BH@dial.pipex.com

TELEPHONE/FAX CONTACT tel: UK (02881) 648083 and UK (02890) 480285, fax: (02881) 648599
OPENING SEASON Open all year for groups and individuals.
OPENING HOURS 9am to 10.30pm
NUMBER OF BEDS 18
BOOKING REQUIREMENTS Booking required (£50 deposit required for group bookings.)
PRICE PER NIGHT £6 per person. Phone for group rates.

PUBLIC TRANSPORT
Bus stop 50 metres from the hostel. Regular buses from Omagh.

DIRECTIONS
The hostel is 50 metres from the cross roads in Gortin Village. Gortin is 10 miles north west of Omagh.

BLUE MOON HOSTEL
Main Street
Dunkineely
Co Donegal

Blue Moon Hostel is situated in the centre of Dunkineely village, besides St John's point. County Donegal is well known for its beautiful rugged scenery and friendly atmosphere. Dunkineely is ideally situated for visiting West Donegal.

Blue Moon Hostel provides accommodation for individuals, families and groups in family rooms of six bunks and double rooms. Bedding and linen are provided free of charge at the hostel and 2 self-catering kitchens are available for guests' use. The hostel is heated throughout and has a drying room and provisions shop. The hostel also has a camp site.

The hostel and camp site are well situated for Scuba diving and fishing in rivers, seas and lakes. The area is also ideal for hill walking, sightseeing, cycling, swimming and touring the north west coast of County Donegal.

TELEPHONE CONTACT Dominic or Mary, Tel: (073) 37264, Mobile: 087 297 2896, Email: bluemoonhostel@eircom.net
OPENING SEASON All year
OPENING HOURS 24hr access
NUMBER OF BEDS 23
BOOKING REQUIREMENTS You are advised to book for the holiday season and at weekends. Deposit required.
PRICE PER NIGHT IR£6 (adult) IR£1 (child). IR£3(camping) per person.

PUBLIC TRANSPORT
There are CIE and Independent buses from Dublin to Donegal town. Local connections from Donegal to hostel.

DIRECTIONS
The hostel is in the centre of Dunkineely village on the N56 between Donegal town and Killybegs, 12 miles from Donegal.

SANDROCK HOLIDAY HOSTEL

Port Ronan Pier, Malin Head
Inishowen Peninsula
Co Donegal

Malin Head is Ireland's most northerly point and is unspoilt and unhurried. The hostel is situated on the seafront above Port Ronan Pier in a bay just 2kms south of Malin Head. It overlooks the sea and headlands of Inishowen and Fanad. The views from the hostel are spectacular especially at sunset or during a stormy sea. This new hostel has been built to strict environmental and tourist board guidelines and contains facilities for persons with limited mobility. Local attractions include walking, cycling (bike hire available at the hostel), fishing, bird watching (Corncrakes put in seasonal appearances), photography, swimming and golfing. There is a shop, restaurant, petrol, three bars (licenced to 1am) and post office available 1 mile away. *Let's Go* recommends.

see us on *www.inishowen.com* and *www.hostels-ireland.com*

TELEPHONE CONTACT Margaret or Rodney (077) 70289, Email sandrockhostel@eircom.net
OPENING SEASON All year
OPENING HOURS All day
NUMBER OF BEDS 20
BOOKING REQUIREMENTS Advised. Essential for large groups
PRICE PER NIGHT IR£6.50 per person.

PUBLIC TRANSPORT
Buses leave Dublin (Parnell Square) 6pm daily for Carndonagh then free pick up available. 'North West' and 'Lough Swilly' buses also service Malin Head, phone hostel for details.

DIRECTIONS
Once on the Inishowen Peninsula follow signs for Malin Head. At the Crossroads Inn (3km from Malin Head) turn left. Continue past the radio station on your right. At next minor cross road follow signs to Port Ronan. The hostel is above the pier on the seafront.

MOVILLE HOLIDAY HOSTEL
Malin Road
Moville
Inishowen Peninsula
Co Donegal

This is a family owned and managed hostel. Re-constructed in 1993 from old stone buildings beside the family period house in mature grounds. The stone building character is retained with all modern facilities including central heating, power showers, duvets, organic shop, payphone, common room, fully equipped kitchen and information office. We also have a large meeting/seminar/activity room for groups. Bicycle hire is available. Within 5 minutes are a variety of services and entertainments; traditional Irish music, restaurants, banks, post office, pubs, water activities, fishing; and many fascinating archaeological and historic sites. Charley, the Warden will tell many stories of local folklore. Moville is a seaside town and fishing village. Inishowen has tremendous natural and unspoilt beauty with much to discover. We are Irish Tourist Board approved, an Independent Holiday Hostel of Ireland, and an Inishowen Tourism Member.

Email scanavas@iol.ie

TELEPHONE CONTACT Anne or Charley (077) 82378
OPENING SEASON All year
OPENING HOURS All day
NUMBER OF BEDS 33
BOOKING REQUIREMENTS Booking required with 25% deposit.
PRICE PER NIGHT IR£7.50 in dorms; IR£12 in private room

PUBLIC TRANSPORT
Regular bus connections to Moville from Derry and Letterkenny with North West Busways (077 82619/82722) and Lough Swilly Bus Company (074 22863). Direct buses to and from Dublin (074 35201 or 077 82619/82722).

DIRECTIONS
In Moville look for hostel signs. Hostel is 450 metres west from the central square, then travel 50 metres left down wooded lane.

CAUSEWAY COAST HOSTEL

4 Victoria Terrace
Atlantic Circle
Portstewart
Co Derry

Causeway Coast Hostel is a cosy, people-friendly place for individuals, families and groups. It is set in Portstewart, a small seaside town on the north coast of Ireland, with a harbour at one end and two miles of sandy beach at the other.

The hostel is 50 yards from the ocean and close to shops and pubs, although with an open fire and music in the common room it can prove a struggle to drag yourself out at night. It is definitely worth struggling out to see the unique Giant's Causeway, Dunluce Castle, Bushmills Whiskey Distillery and (for those with a head for heights) Carrick-A-Rede rope bridge. The hostel can arrange or provide information about :- spectacular coastal walks, cycle tours, scuba diving, horse riding, golf, bird watching, boat hire and fishing.

TELEPHONE CONTACT Rick UK (01265) 833789
OPENING SEASON All year
OPENING HOURS All day access, no night-time curfew
NUMBER OF BEDS 28
BOOKING REQUIREMENTS Not essential but recommended during high season. Phone/postal bookings, normally no deposit.
PRICE PER NIGHT £7 (dorm), £8.50 (private) per person

PUBLIC TRANSPORT
Direct buses from Belfast/Dublin/Derry and Coleraine go to the Atlantic Circle bus stop 100yds from hostel (phone 01265 43334 for bus enquiries). Trains from Derry/Belfast to Coleraine Station (5km from hostel).

DIRECTIONS
GR 816 387. The hostel is 100yds from the A2 road on the eastern edge of town. Take turning opposite public toilets.

SHEEP ISLAND VIEW HOSTEL

42a Main Street
Ballintoy
Ballycastle
Co Antrim
BT54 6LX

Sheep Island View Hostel is ideally located for exploring the Causeway Coast and Glens of Antrim. Local attractions include the famous Giant's Causeway and the Carrick-A-Rede rope bridge. Experts in the local area provide guided walks and bike hire is available for exploring. There are plenty of pubs and restaurants near by for the evenings. The hostel is a new building and has scenic views of Rathlin and the Western Isles of Scotland. All the rooms are en-suite and family rooms are available. The building is wheelchair friendly. The hostel will accept group bookings and has a room available for group meetings. The hostel provides meals on request and there is a shop on site for those using the self-catering facilities. There are laundry facilities. Camping is available.

Web http://sheepisland.hypermart.net

TELEPHONE CONTACT Aileen/Seamus UK (028207) 69391 or 62470
OPENING SEASON All year
OPENING HOURS Flexible
NUMBER OF BEDS 50
BOOKING REQUIREMENTS Essential in summer and for groups.
PRICE PER NIGHT £10 high season, £9 low season.

PUBLIC TRANSPORT
Public bus stops at hostel entrance. Free pickup can be arranged from the nearest town, please phone hostel to enquire.

DIRECTIONS
On the B15 Coast Road between Bushmills and Ballycastle. 10 minutes' walk from the rope bridge.

THE LINEN HOUSE
BACKPACKERS HOSTEL
18 Kent Street
Belfast, BT1 2JA

The Linen House is Belfast's newest and largest Independent Holiday Hostel. It's located in the Cathedral Quarter and is just around the corner from Tourist Information and the main shopping district of Royal Ave and Donegal Street/City Hall. The hostel is within easy walking distance of the Laganside Bus Terminal, Europa Bus/Rail Centre and Central Train Station. It is also the closest hostel to the Ferry and Airport terminals.

The Linen House is a restored old building and has cobblestone, tile and wood floors. There is a roomy self-catering kitchen with microwaves, fridges, stoves and lots of counter space. The common room is lovely and large. There are plenty of tables and chairs where you can eat and read the pamphlets provided about what's going on in Belfast. Private tours of Belfast sights (including Shankill, Falls and Murals) are available nearby as are black taxis. The Central Library, which is next door, has the most economical prices to use the Internet at only £2 per hour.

TELEPHONE/FAX CONTACT Tel: (028) 90586400 Tel/Fax: (028) 90586444
OPENING SEASON All year
OPENING HOURS 24 hours
NUMBER OF BEDS 130
BOOKING REQUIREMENTS Recommended at weekends and in high season. Deposits required for group bookings.
PRICE PER NIGHT (1999 RATES) £6.50 to £8.50 per person (dorms) all year. £10.50 to £14.00 per person (twin/doubles) all year.

PUBLIC TRANSPORT
For transport details contact Bus Eireann (01) 836 6111

DIRECTIONS
From central railway station take free bus to city centre. From North Street in city centre, take right after the Tourist Information Centre and then turn left into Kent Street.

TÁIN HOLIDAY VILLAGE
Ballyoonan
Omeath
Co Louth

Táin Holiday Village is one of the most extensive holiday complexes in Ireland and is exactly what a family seeking non-stop entertainment might want. The touring park is within a 10 acre holiday village nestling at the foot of the Cooley Mountains and overlooking Carlingford Lough with views towards the Mourne Mountains. Included in the accommodation charges is the use of the 40,000 square feet of indoor leisure facilities. These include a heated swimming pool with slides, an indoor play area, laser quest, games room, jacuzzi and steam room. Outdoor facilities include two adventure playgrounds, tennis courts and pleasant grounds with neat flowerbeds. Táin Adventure Centre offers canoeing, kayaking, hill walking, orienteering, archery and banana ski.

On site we have B&B accommodation with a communal kitchen for self-catering and hostel accommodation with a large hostel kitchen. There are also 87 pitches with hard standing and electrical hookups, plus 10 pitches for tents. The licensed restaurant offers varied menus and there is a lounge and bar.

TELEPHONE CONTACT (042) 9375385.
OPENING SEASON March to October.
OPENING HOURS Flexible.
NUMBER OF BEDS 52
BOOKING REQUIREMENTS Pre-booking is essential. Two weeks in advance.
PRICE PER NIGHT IR£10 per person per night; IR£9 per night for groups of 20+; IR£8 per night for groups of 50+.

PUBLIC TRANSPORT
For transport details contact Bus Eireann (01) 836 6111

DIRECTIONS
From Newry take B79/R173 road signed Omeath. Site is 1.6km south of Omeath village, on the left.

CONTACTS BRITAIN AND EUROPE

Mountaineering Council of Scotland. National representative body for Scottish hill walking and climbing clubs. Individual membership is available; 4a St Catherine's Road, Perth, PH1 5SE, UK. (01738) tel 638227, fax 442095. www.theMCofS.org.uk See page 244 for details.

IBHS Independent Backpackers Hostels of Scotland, Contact Pete Thomas, Croft Bunkhouse, Portnalong, Isle of Skye, IV47 8SL for a free leaflet to approximately 100 hostels in Scotland. See page 179.

CTC Britain biggest cycling organisation, representing on and off road cyclists throughout the UK. Membership from £15 per year. CTC Cotterell House , 69 Meadrow, Godalming, Surrey GU7 3HS. Tel (01483) 417217.

Ramblers's Association, The Ramblers yearbook is indispensable for walkers in Britain. In addition to details of accommodation it also tells you your rights in the countryside, bus enquiry lines, details of long distance paths, walking holidays in Britain and contact lists for Ramblers Association groups, countryside organisations, European walking organisations and equipment shops. For more information contact:- The Ramblers Association, 1-5 Wandsworth Road, London, SW8 2XX, Tel: 020 7339 8500, Fax: 020 7339 8501, Web: www.ramblers.org.uk, Email:ramblers@london.ramblers.org.uk

LDWA, Long Distance Walkers Association: For those who enjoy long distance walking, membership includes group events/challenge walks and excellent informative journals 3 times a year. In addition the LDWA handbook details over 500 long distance paths in the UK and has 288 pages. The handbook is edited by Brian Smith and is available from all good booksellers, ISBN 071364835X, price £11.99. For details of membership contact:- LDWA, 10 Temple Park Close, Leeds, LS15 0JJ. For the handbook contact, Merchandising Officer, 2 Sandy Lane, Beeston, Nottingham, NG9 3GS.

Highland Hostels For a brochure contact Gavin tel (01397) 712900 Aite Cruinnichidh, 1 Achluachrach, Roy Bridge, PH31 4AW. See page 186.

Accommodation for Groups. A guide to good value, group accommodation in UK and Ireland. Ideal for schools, outdoor activity groups and anyone who likes to holiday with friends. See page 335.

Backpackers Club, UK based club for the light weight camper. Pitch directories, weekend meets, quarterly magazine, advice and information on camping in the UK and abroad. For details contact:- P Maguire, 29 Lynton Drive, High Lane, Stockport, Cheshire, SK68JE.

National Association of Field Studies Officers (NAFSO). This association represents 300 members working in 200 centres in England, Wales and Northern Ireland. The organisation aims to promote quality field studies in centres and at schools. It produces a variety of publications including an annual journal. For more details contact NAFSO, Stibbington Environmental Education Centre, Great North Road, Stibbington, Peterborough, PE8 6LP

IHO, Independent Hostel Owners of Ireland. Contact Information Office, Dooey Hostel, Glencolmcille, Co Donegal, Tel: +353 73 30130 Fax: +353 73 30339 http://www.eroicapub.com/ihi See page 252 for details.

Ireland all the Hostels Leaflet on Irish hostels from all associations. See page 335 for details.

IHH, Independent Holiday Hostels of Ireland. 57 Lower Gardiner Street, Dublin1. See page 256 for details.

CONTACTS WORLDWIDE

The Internet Guide to Hostelling, Great site, features all the IHG hostels and thousands more around the world. See page 323 for details or surf the web to http://www.hostels.com

New Zealand, BBH Backpackers Accommodation Guide listing 270+ hostels with BPP % customer satisfaction ratings. Available free and post free from BBHNZ, 99 Titiraupenga Street, TAUPO, NZ, tel/fax +64 7 377 1568. Internet http://www.backpack.co.nz Email ihginfo@backpack.co.nz

VIP Backpackers. For a guide to 130 VIP hostels in Australia (costs $AUD5) write to:- :- VIP Resorts, PO Box 600, Cannon Hill, QLD 4170, Tel: (61-7) 3268 5733, Fax: (61-7) 3268 4066. Email backpack@backpackers.com.au http://www.backpackers.com.au

NOMADS International, is a young and feel good group of hostels around OZ and NZ. Their £13 membership card (Nomads Adventure Card) offers the traveller discounts on accommodation, travel, tours, adventure activities, phone calls and many more things Backpackers are known to enjoy. Excellent Start Here packages are available from £54 into all capital cities of OZ and NZ - organise yourself a fun, safe and easy arrival! Web: www.nomadsbackpackers.com, Email: info@nomads-backpackers.com, Fax: +61 8 8224 0972, Tel: +61 8 8224 0919

Backpackers Hostels Canada. A list of over 200 hostels, send US$5 and a SAE to, Backpackers Hostels Canada, RR13 (10-1) Thunder Bay, Ontario, Canada, P7B 5E4. Fax (807) 983 2914; Tel (807) 983 2042; Web site http://www.backpackers.ca

The Hostel Handbook for the USA and Canada. This is a listing of almost 800 hostels in the USA and Canada. It includes HI, Backpackers and other independent hostels. The handbook is updated each year to assure you of the most up-to-date information. The Handbook is also online at www.hostelhandbook.com. For information contact The Hostels Handbook, 722 Saint Nicolas Avenue, New York, NY 10031, Tel: (212) 926 7030, Fax (212) 283 0108, Email editor@hostelhandbook.com

Jim's Backpackers Guide to USA and Canada. Details over 1000 places to stay for $20 or less. Send an international money order for $9 to:- PO Box 5650, Santa Monica, CA 90409, USA. Tel: USA (310) 399 4018. Fax: USA (310) 399 4216

Big World Magazine. The magazine for Independent World Explorers. Published in USA for travellers the world over. Send $25 for 1 year's subscription. There are four issues each year. Write to:- Big World Magazine, PO Box 8743, Lancaster, PA 17604, USA. Email: bigworld@bigworld.com, Web site http://www.bigworld.com

Transitions Abroad. For details of these publications contact:- PO Box 1300, Amherst, MA 01004-1300, USA, Tel: 413 256 3414, Fax: 413 256 0373, Email: editor@TransitionsAbroad.com

A MILLENNIUM PROJECT
SUPPORTED BY FUNDS
FROM THE NATIONAL LOTTERY

The
National
Cycle Network

NATIONAL
cycle network

in the year 2000

The National Cycle Network will provide 5000 miles of
safe, signed, attractive routes designed to provide a
pleasureable cycling experience away from heavy motor traffic.

•

Half the Network will be on quiet lanes and
traffic-calmed roads. The rest will be on traffic-free
paths, providing a major amenity for walkers and
people in wheelchairs as well as cyclists.

•

Linking the centres of towns and cities and
connecting urban centres to the countryside, the
National Cycle Network provides the ideal way to
travel whether for utility or leisure.

•

All routes will be clearly mapped in a unique format
that has already won awards.

For more information about Sustrans and the
National Cycle Network and for a free catalogue of
maps and guides please call the
Sustrans Information Service on 0117 929 0888,
www. sustrans. org.uk or *e.mail to info@sustrans.org.uk*

Sustrans
ROUTES FOR PEOPLE

9,000 miles

— 5,000 miles open June 2000

— 4,000 miles forecast for completion by 2005

Shetland Islands — Lerwick

Orkney Islands — Kirkwall

John o' Groats

John o' Groats

Inverness

Edinburgh

Glasgow

Coleraine
Londonderry

Carlisle

Newcastle
Sunderland
Middlesbrough

Omagh

Belfast
Whitehaven

Enniskillen

Lancaster

York

Hull

Dublin

Liverpool

Barnsley

Holyhead

Derby

Norwich

Birmingham

Peterborough

Fishguard

Stratford

Milton Keynes

Harwich
Chelmsford

Swansea

Oxford

LONDON

Canterbury

Cardiff

Bristol

Dover

Barnstaple

Winchester

Taunton

Exeter

Portsmouth

Eastbourne

Penzance

Plymouth

INDEX BY COUNTRY/COUNTY

INDEX BY COUNTRY/COUNTY

INDEX BY HOSTEL NAME

HOSTEL NAME	PAGE

HOSTEL NAME	PAGE

HOSTEL NAME	PAGE

Accommodation for Groups

Produced by the Backpackers Press and edited by Sam
Dalley, this handy 128 page guide gives detailed information
on over a hundred group accommodation centres in the UK
and Ireland. The centres range from simple self-contained
bunkhouses to full board outdoor education centres. Each
page gives details of the centre's facilities and suggestions for
activities in the surrounding area. Ideal for schools, youth
groups and outdoor sports clubs; this is an essential guide for
anyone who likes to holiday with friends.

Accommodation for Groups is available by mail order (see
overleaf) or can be ordered from your local bookshop ISBN
0-9523381-6-5.

BACKPACKERS PRESS PUBLICATIONS
BY MAIL ORDER.

The Backpackers Press
2 Rockview Cottages
Temple Walk
Matlock Bath
Derbyshire, DE4 3PG
Tel/Fax (01629) 580427

Book	Price	. No	Total cost
The Independent Hostel Guide, 2000	£4.95		
The Independent Hostel Guide 2001 (available Jan 2001)	£4.95		
Accommodation for Groups (see pg 335)	£2.95		
Postage and Packing	UK. £1 first book + 50p for each extra book		
	Overseas. £2 first book +£1 for each extra book		
Total			

Please send the above order to :

I enclose a UK cheque or Eurocheque for:- £
(in Sterling, payable to the Backpackers Press)

OR

Please charge my Mastercard/Visa account (we do not accept AMEX or Switch) the sum of :- £

The credit card statement address is the same as that given above and the credit card number is :-

Expiry date _____ Name on card _____

Signature _____ Date _____